D1216850

Sweden and Visions of Norway

Sweden and Visions of Norway

Politics and Culture, 1814–1905

H. Arnold Barton

Southern Illinois University Press

Carbondale and Edwardsville

Copyright ©2003 by the Board of Trustees,

Southern Illinois University

All rights reserved

Printed in the United States of America

06 05 04 03 4 3 2 1

Library of Congress Cataloging-in-Publication Data

Barton, H. Arnold (Hildor Arnold), 1929–
     Sweden and visions of Norway : politics and culture, 1814–1905
/ H. Arnold Barton.
          p. cm.
     Includes bibliographical references and index.
          1. Sweden—History—1814–1905. 2. Norway—History—
     1814–1905. 3. Sweden—Relations—Norway. 4. Norway—
     Relations—Sweden. 5. Nationalism—Norway. I. Title.
DL805 .B37 2002
948.1'03—dc21
ISBN 0-8093-2441-5 (alk. paper)   2002024663

Publication partially funded by subvention grants from the Kungl. Patriotiska
Sällskapet and the Letterstedska Förenignen, Stockholm, Sweden.

Printed on recycled paper. ♻

The paper used in this publication meets the minimum requirements
of American National Standard for Information Sciences—Permanence
of Paper for Printed Library Materials, ANSI Z39.48-1992.⊚

In Norway I learned all the better to understand
Sweden, and all of the North.

—Fredrika Bremer, 1847

Let us therefore work toward national independence, an
independence that does not depend upon appropriating
for ourselves the sagas of Norwegian kings or Iceland's
Eddas, not upon boasting over the misdeeds of the past,
but upon being ourselves—like [Ibsen's] Peer Gynt!

—August Strindberg, 1883

My boundless love for Norway is at once my greatest
joy and my greatest sorrow.

—Ann-Margret Holmgren, 1899

Contents

List of Illustrations   *ix*

Preface   *xi*

Part One. Politics

1. The Road to Union   3
2. The Civic Vision   19
3. High Noon and Decline of the Union   58

Part Two. Culture

4. The Cultural Vision   87
5. Norway and the Swedish Self-Image   118

Epilogue and Conclusions   159

Notes   183
Select Bibliography   211
Index   219

Illustrations

Following page 83

Carl XIV Johan, by Emil Mascré

Oscar I, by K. T. Staaf

Carl XV, by A. J. G. Virgin

Oscar II, by Edvard Perséus

Lorenz Dietrichson, by Fritz von Dardel

Bjørnstjerne Bjørnson, by Erik Werenskiold

Henrik Ibsen, by Erik Werenskiold

August Strindberg, by Carl Larsson

Verner von Heidenstam, by Oscar Björck

Vossevangsdalen, by M. G. Anckarsvärd

From Hjelle in Valdres, by Johan Christian Dahl

Peasant Wedding at Hardanger, by Adolf Tidemand and Hans Frederik Gude

Sunday Morning in Blekinge, by Bengt Nordenberg

The Emigrants, by S. V. Helander

Norwegian Landscape from Valdres

Norwegian Fjord in Moonlight, by Marcus Larson

Thor's Battle with the Giants, by Mårten Eskil Winge

Borgund stave church, by Johan Christian Dahl

"Storstugan II," the Curman summer home in Lysekil

The Military Society Masquerade Ball in Stockholm

From Telemark, by Erik Werenskiold

Our Daily Bread, by Anders Zorn

The Water Spirit, by Ernst Josephson

Summer Night, by Eilif Peterssen

Early Spring at Ballingsta, by Prince Eugen

Nordic Summer Evening, by Richard Bergh

Midsummer Dance, by Anders Zorn

Autumn, by Helmer Osslund

The Victors' Ships Return from Svolder, by Erik Werenskiold

Frognerseteren Restaurant, by Holm Munthe

Gustaf III Receives the Antique Statues from Italy, by Carl Larsson

A private villa in Gävle

The Stockholm Law Courts Building, by Carl Westman

Preface

S O OFTEN, it is the recollections and impressions from our early years that in time lead to scholarly research as well as to literary or artistic creation. So it was with me. My father, Sven Hildor Barton, who was born in Oregon, was deeply proud of his purely Swedish origins. (His own father, who left Sweden as a child in 1867, was originally named Svensson.)

Growing up in California, I absorbed from my father much of the ancestral cultural heritage well before either of us ever visited his parents' old homeland. In time, I became aware that much of what he passed on to me was in fact *Scandinavian* — most particularly Norwegian — rather than Swedish as such. The Viking tales he told dealt mainly with Norwegian kings and jarls (as related by Snorri Sturlason and other medieval Icelandic skalds), his picturesque details of archaic folklife in the North often evoked Norwegian fjelds and fjords, and he loved and was more familiar with the music of Edvard Grieg and Christian Sinding than with the compositions of their Swedish contemporaries.

As a thoughtful and well-read man with a good knowledge of the Scandinavian languages, my father recognized what was Norwegian. But he regarded such things as unquestionably the common birthright of *all* the Scandinavian peoples. At the same time, he would proudly point out significant aspects of Sweden's history and culture for which Norway, during its long centuries of Danish domination, could offer no equivalents. Deep down, he wanted it both ways.

These attitudes, I eventually came to realize, were ones that had been prevalent in cultivated Swedish circles during the 1870s and 1880s when his mother was growing up in Uppsala and Stockholm, before she departed for America. The reflections they have often aroused since then underlie the present study of relations between Sweden and Norway during the period when they were joined together in dynastic union.

Following centuries of being essentially a part of the Danish kingdom and having been ruled since the 1660s by Europe's theoretically most absolute monarch, Norway was wrested from the Danish crown as a result of the Napoleonic wars. In 1814, it became once again a separate kingdom with its own government, albeit as a domain of the king of Sweden. The Swedish-Norwegian union was created under highly ambivalent circumstances, thanks to which two markedly different societies, governed under strongly contrasting constitutions, proved in the long run unable to coexist under the same royal house without mounting conflict, which ultimately brought about its end in 1905.

The union has thus been seen, on the whole, as a failure in both Sweden and Norway by the general public and by scholars alike. The voluminous historical literature on both sides devoted to the union has above all concerned itself with its controversial origins and with opposing views of the juridical relationship between the two kingdoms, the numerous disputes and crises that arose, and the union's final demise. Much of this literature has been sharply polemical from both sides. Out of national pride, neither Swedish nor Norwegian historians have been much inclined to see in the union any deeper or lasting significance for the internal histories of their own countries.

Yet, it stands to reason that lasting as it did for close to a century, the union must have had considerable impact upon developments in both kingdoms, quite aside from the controversies it engendered. A promising beginning in examining its concrete effects on both sides was first attempted as recently as 1987 with a series of conferences sponsored by the Royal Norwegian Embassy in Stockholm over the following three years. Here, a number of leading Norwegian and Swedish scholars examined aspects of the relationship, both during and after the union. Since that time, interest in detailed research in this area has been growing, not least in anticipation of the one hundredth anniversary of Norway's full independence in 2005.

The present study can make no claim to survey all the many aspects of the mutual impact of the Swedish-Norwegian union. Much will have to be done by the Scandinavian scholars who individually and collectively are presently engaged in detailed research. My contribution may thus be best considered an extended essay and a preliminary exploration of certain basic questions. Because the union has received the greatest scholarly attention in Norway, I have chosen to focus on the Norwegian impact on Sweden, above all in the closely intertwined areas of politics and culture. It is my contention that although Norway before 1814 lacked the political, administrative, and cultural institutions essential for an independent nation that Sweden had long possessed, paradoxically, it came to exercise a greater influence upon Sweden during the union than Sweden did upon Norway.

The Norwegian constitution of 1814, the most democratic of its time, became the guiding star of Swedish liberals and radicals striving to reform their antique system of parliamentary representation, while by the same token it became the bugbear of Swedish conservatives. Norway's great burst of creative energy in the cultural field by midcentury had an immense impact upon literature, art, architecture, and music in Sweden between around 1850 and the late 1880s, during a period there of relative cultural stagnation. Thereafter, there was a growing reaction against an exaggerated "norvegomania" in Sweden. This reaction I see as a fundamental impetus to the highly creative Swedish national romanticism of the 1890s and the early twentieth century. In both politics and culture, Norway provided a vital catalyst for the crystallizing of Sweden's own national distinctiveness during the period of the union. Although it is not my primary focus, I also devote some attention to Swedish political and cultural impulses in Norway.

The complex question of national or ethnic identity is one that I found particularly challenging and rewarding when undertaking my previous study, *A Folk Divided: Homeland Swedes and Swedish Americans, 1840–1940*. Many of the insights I gained through that research have informed my understanding of Sweden's relationship with Norway during the union. And although in many ways the Swedish-Norwegian relationship during the nineteenth century was unique to its time and place, it offers thought-provoking parallels and contrasts to similar relationships between other nationalities in Europe and beyond.

A few words on translation and orthography are in order. All the translations are my own, except where noted. Since the end of the union in 1905, considerable changes have been made in orthography and capitalization in the Scandinavian languages, especially Norwegian. I have thus sought to achieve a balance between old and new. Place names and occasional words or phrases are generally given in their present spellings, except in direct quotations. The names of royal persons are given in the forms most familiar at the time; for example, *Carl* rather than *Karl*; *Gustaf* instead of *Gustav*; *Oscar* in place of *Oskar*. It should be noted in this regard that Norway's medieval capital, Oslo, was renamed Christiania after the Danish king Christian IV in 1624. This was officially respelled Kristiania in 1877, although many continued to use the older spelling, as I have done here. In 1924, the Norwegian capital would reassume its old name, Oslo.

In writing this book, I have incurred many debts, which I gratefully acknowledge. I am deeply indebted to Kungliga Biblioteket in Stockholm and to the Morris Library of Southern Illinois University Carbondale and to their staffs. I also wish to thank the institutions in Scandinavia that have provided illustrations. The late Franklin D. Scott, Sten Carlsson, Peter A. Munch, Raymond E. Lindgren, and Lennart Seth all gave inspiration and valuable insights into the subject of the study. Others to whom I am especially beholden in recent years include Stig Ekman, Eva Eriksson, Bo Grandien, Bo O. Nilsson, Göran B. Nilsson, Elisabet Stavenow-Hidemark and Ove Hidemark, Eva Tedenmyr, and Jarl Torbacke in Sweden; Ruth Hemstad, Anne-Lise Seip, and Øystein Sørensen in Norway; and Michelle Facos, Anita Olson Gustafson, Clarence Burton Sheffield Jr., and Rochelle Wright in the United States. My thanks go to John Wilson for his expert editing of my manuscript. Again, I am deeply grateful to my Swedish wife, Aina, for her unfailing support throughout the course of another extended excursion into the past.

This book is dedicated to the memory of Raymond E. Lindgren, historian and friend.

H. A. B.

Part One

Politics

1

The Road to Union

SWEDES AND NORWEGIANS are the closest of neighbors and cousins through geography, kinship, physical appearance, basic culture, language, religion, and character. They share between them the long Scandinavian peninsula, extending from around 71 degrees north latitude, well above the Arctic Circle at the North Cape, to about 55 degrees north at the southern tip of Sweden, with the crest of a mountain range, the "Keel" (*Kölen* or *Kjølen*), forming Europe's longest land frontier between them.

Still, there are notable contrasts in topography and landscape. The western side of the peninsula rises steeply from the North Sea, and most of Norway is mountainous, with an average altitude almost twice that of Europe as a whole. Much of the interior, both in the southern massif and along the lengthy northern frontier, is wild and uninhabited, while the population is concentrated on the coasts, along the numerous fjords, some of which penetrate far inland, and in often isolated mountain valleys. Its most densely inhabited areas lie around Oslo Fjord in the southeast and Trondheim Fjord to the northwest.

The Keel slopes off more gradually on its eastern side, and while it includes much rugged, broken terrain, most of Sweden lies fairly close to sea level. If the Norwegian landscape is on the whole more spectacular, the Swedish is considerably more varied, ranging from the broad and fertile ploughlands and deciduous or mixed forests in the south, to the innumerable lakes and scattered offshore skerries in the south-central region, to the vast coniferous forests and rushing rivers of the north, to the semiarctic tundra, high mountains, and glaciers of Lapland. From north to south, the climate is essentially the same, with long, hard, dark winters and short, intense, light summers.

The resources and economies of the two countries are largely similar, although fishing and seafaring have played a more prominent part in Norway while forest products and iron production have been dominant in Sweden. During the nineteenth century, both countries began to industrialize. Here, Norway initially led the way but was overtaken by Sweden by the 1890s.[1]

Swedes and Norwegians share common genetic traits. Local folk culture and dialects extend in a gradual continuum from the western capes of Norway across Sweden to the Swedish-speaking coastal districts in Finland as well as across the Sound in Denmark. The official languages of both countries are mutually understandable to a degree practically unparalleled in Europe. The state church in both countries is Lutheran. The social elites share the same cosmopolitan European culture and social conventions.

By the beginning of the Swedish-Norwegian union in 1814, wide differences in social structure and outlook had nonetheless developed in the two lands based on their divergent histories since the Middle Ages. Around A.D. 1000, during the Viking age, the numerous petty kingdoms and jarldoms in Scandinavia began to coalesce into distinct Norwegian, Swedish, and Danish kingdoms. Down to the thirteenth century, Norway and Denmark alternated as the leading powers in the region, while Sweden played a less prominent role. A large part of what is now western Sweden was Norwegian territory, while much of present-day southern Sweden, east of the Kattegat, was Danish, down to the mid-seventeenth century. Sweden meanwhile Christianized and incorporated Finland, across the Baltic, into its domain beginning in the thirteenth century.

By the fourteenth century, Scandinavia was overtaken by mounting problems of overpopulation and crop failures and then devastated by the Black Death at midcentury. Norway in particular was disastrously affected. In their weakened state, the Scandinavian lands fell prey to exploitation by German merchants of the Hanseatic League and to the incursions of powerful and ambitious north German lords.

Faced with this threat from the south and through a complex combination of circumstances, the three Scandinavian kingdoms individually accepted Margaret, Danish princess and dowager queen of Norway, as their ruler under various titles in 1387–88. Meeting at Kalmar in Sweden, the aristocratic councils of Denmark, Norway, and Sweden entered into a dynastic union in 1397, recognizing Margaret's young grandnephew, Erik of Pomerania, as their sovereign.

A good deal of mystery surrounds the terms of the Kalmar Union. Margaret remained regent until her death in 1412 and is remembered as one of Scandinavia's greatest medieval rulers. It became evident, however, during her rule and even more after the beginning of Eric of Pomerania's regime that there were fundamental differences between the councils of the three kingdoms, which envisioned self-rule under their leadership, and the sovereigns, who strove to centralize authority. Already by the 1430s, Engelbrekt Engelbrektsson led a widespread revolt against King Erik in Sweden, and this was followed throughout the rest of the century and beyond by periods in which Sweden, with Finland, was able to establish its virtual autonomy.

The centralizing and antiaristocratic policies of King Christian II (1481–1559) led by 1521 to insurrection throughout the Scandinavian lands. Under the leadership of Gustaf Vasa, who in 1523 was acclaimed king, Sweden, including Finland, broke out permanently from the union. Christian was deposed in Denmark the next year. Following a period of civil war in Denmark and Norway, Christian III succeeded by 1536 in consolidating his reign in both kingdoms, thus preserving a union that would continue for nearly another three hundred years down to 1814. In 1536, moreover, the Danish council declared, in a secret rescript, that Norway was henceforward to be regarded as an integral part of the Danish kingdom. In fact—if not entirely in theory—Norway ceased to exist as a separate national entity.

Political traditions developed along differing lines in the Swedish and Danish monarchies. During the fourteenth century, a diet, or *riksdag*, evolved in Sweden, consisting of the four estates, namely the nobility, the clergy, the burghers, and—almost uniquely in Europe—the freehold peasantry, which by the sixteenth century came to play a politically powerful role. More rudimentary diets thereafter developed in Denmark and in Norway, although they remained far less active than in Sweden until they disappeared altogether during the late seventeenth century. Sweden's political history from the sixteenth through the eighteenth centuries saw constant conflict, often violent, between ambitious monarchs seeking to extend their authority and the nobility, both in the Riksdag and on the royal council, striving to limit the powers of the crown. Throughout, the Swedish estates upheld their place in the political order and their proud traditions of law-bound freedom.[2]

In the Danish monarchy, the high aristocracy, acting through the royal council and the high offices of state, largely dominated the regime until King Frederik III, capitalizing on military disasters in the mid-seventeenth century widely attributed to their misgovernment, was able to establish a complete royal absolutism under the *Lex Regia* of 1665.

In Norway, the old nobility had died out or had been absorbed into the Danish (or in some cases the Swedish) aristocracy by the sixteenth century, although to this day there are peasant families that proudly claim descent from medieval kings and noblemen. While there remained some measure of local autonomy within the parishes, Norway was thereafter administered by Danish nobles or, from the 1660s on, bureaucrats. The social structure came to consist of a vast peasant majority, a narrow stratum of town merchants and artisans, many of Danish, German, or other foreign derivation, and a small governing and clerical bureaucracy. The Old Norse literary language fell out of use. The peasantry spoke a variety of local dialects, which differed widely due to the isolation of many rural settlements. Meanwhile, the language of the administration, courts, church, and upper classes became—and long remained—literary Danish, although generally pronounced in a distinctively Norwegian manner.

Following Sweden's break with the Kalmar Union in 1521, there followed a long series of wars between the two neighboring monarchies, making hereditary enemies of Swedes and Finns on the one side, Danes and Norwegians on the other. The situation became further embittered as both kingdoms allied themselves with each other's rivals. Most notably, Denmark, fearful of Norway's vulnerability to Swedish attack, allied itself with Russia throughout the eighteenth century, exposing Sweden and Finland to the constant threat of war on two fronts.

By the seventeenth century, Sweden came to eclipse Denmark as the dominant Scandinavian power, conquering territories in the Baltic provinces and on the north German coast while establishing an enduring tradition of Swedish martial prowess. It was thus in the nature of things that Swedish monarchs, from this "Era of Greatness" on, should seek to acquire Norway to protect their long western border. In 1645, Sweden conquered the Norwegian provinces of Jämtland and Härjedalen on the north-central frontier together with Danish Halland on the Kattegat and the Baltic island of Gotland; the Swedes even briefly laid claim to a long stretch of the north-central Norwegian coast (Trondheim *Stift*, or province) until driven out by the local population. In 1658, Sweden forced Denmark to cede the southern Norwegian province of Bohuslän to Sweden along with Danish Skåne and Blekinge, thus at last incorporating the whole southernmost part of the peninsula. The newly acquired lands were amalgamated administratively and culturally into the Swedish realm.

Before his untimely death in 1660 while laying siege to Copenhagen, the Swedish king Carl X Gustaf had plans of acquiring the whole of Norway. His grandson, Carl XII, attempted during the Great Northern War to conquer Norway, where he died while besieging Fredriksten fortress in 1718. During the latter part of the eighteenth century and the first years of the nineteenth, Gustaf III and Gustaf IV Adolf constantly sought their chance to seize Norway from Denmark.

The eighteenth century saw important developments throughout Scandinavia.[3] After its final burst of glory under Carl XII during the Great Northern War, Sweden went down in defeat by 1721, losing its Baltic provinces and retaining only Finland and western Pomerania. The remainder of the century was relatively peaceful, although Sweden was at war with Russia during 1741–43 and 1788–90, the latter case involving Denmark as Russia's reluctant ally in a brief attack on Sweden from Norway in 1788.

During the eighteenth century, the economies of the Scandinavian monarchies developed steadily. In Norway, fish and sawn timber were highly profitable exports, while Sweden sent abroad large quantities of bar iron and naval stores—the masts, spars, hemp, and tar indispensable to seafaring. The great European wars of the period offered lucrative opportunities for neutral maritime trade. The merchant oligarchies of Copenhagen, Stockholm, Christiania (now Oslo), Bergen, and other maritime towns amassed sizable fortunes. Population increased throughout the century. Norway's indeed grew more rapidly than that of Denmark proper, reaching 883,353 by 1801, at which point it was only 5 percent smaller than Denmark's.[4]

While Norway was administratively a part of the Danish realm, it possessed its own law code. Most importantly, the status of the peasantry differed markedly in the two lands. Denmark was well endowed with broad ploughlands suited for the European manorial system. Since the late Middle Ages, most of the Danish peasants had become manorial tenants; by the mid-eighteenth century, only some 3 percent of them remained freeholders.[5] From the fourteenth century on, those on the larger islands were reduced to serfdom. In 1733, a modified servitude (the *stavnsbånd*) was extended to virtually the entire peasantry, until it was abolished in 1788.

The Norwegian peasantry, meanwhile, always remained juridically free and was relatively lightly taxed by the crown in return for militia service in defending Norway against Sweden. While some were tenant farmers, occupying widely scattered farms, they seldom owed any labor service to their landlords and often held hereditary leases. Most were freeholders. On the whole, Norwegian peasants were a good deal more prosperous than their Danish brethren. Freeholding increased in Norway throughout the eighteenth century at the same time that it decreased in Denmark, at least down to the 1760s. The Norwegian peasants were proverbially loyal to the king in Copenhagen, regarding him as their protector against bureaucratic abuse and not infrequently sending their own delegations directly to him with their grievances.

The Swedish and Finnish peasants occupied a socioeconomic position somewhere between the Danish and the Norwegian. They were legally free, and the freehold peasants had, as has been noted, their own estate in the

Riksdag. Nonetheless, around a third of them were manorial tenants under varying obligations. In addition, they were more heavily taxed than in Norway and bore more pressing military obligations. By the end of the century, however, agrarian reforms in both Denmark and Sweden began to even out the differences between landholding peasants in the three Scandinavian lands. With increasing population, meanwhile, there was everywhere a growing rural underclass of cotters—*torpare* in Sweden, *husmænd* or *husmenn* in Denmark and Norway—and landless laborers.[6]

It was during the eighteenth century that Scandinavia became a creative part of the world of European higher culture. Before then, the arts had been mainly imported luxuries or were left to sojourning foreigners. Now, native Scandinavians entered the field, creating in the international styles of the time, and some of them attained international repute. Stockholm and Copenhagen became cultural capitals in the full European sense with the construction of new royal palaces and summer residences, monumental squares and public buildings, opera houses and theaters, and with the founding of royal academies of science, belles lettres, art, and music.

As an outlying domain, Norway possessed none of these amenities. It had no royal court, palaces, administrative bureaus, or central bank, no university, opera, or theater, and no academies of its own. Bergen—then its largest town—Christiania, Christiansand, and Trondheim were no more than the administrative centers of provinces *(stifter)*, although Christiania enjoyed a certain precedence. Ambitious Norwegians had to seek their opportunities in Denmark, the best known being the Bergen-born dramatist and polyhistor Ludvig Holberg (1684–1754). During the century, as Norway's merchant class became ever more prosperous, there arose a growing demand for specifically Norwegian institutions, in particular for a university—at a time when virtually the whole bureaucracy and clergy was educated at the University of Copenhagen—as well as for a central bank.

These demands reflect a notable revival of Norwegian national feeling in a cultural, even if not yet political, sense.[7] A Trondheim Scientific Society was founded in 1760, at about the same time that there was a renewed interest in Norway's proud medieval past. An important landmark was the establishment of the Norwegian Literary Society in 1771 by young Norwegian intellectuals in—characteristically—Copenhagen, the monarchy's cultural metropolis. Accusations of Danish exploitation by Norwegian pamphleteers could at times be sharp during the late eighteenth century, but typically, they were combined with earnest protestations of loyalty to the crown.

Another intellectual trend of the period would likewise be of significance for the future: the growing sense of a wider Scandinavian community transcending the traditional enmities of the past. During the brief hostilities in 1788, it was apparent that Swedes, Danes, and Norwegians had come to regard such a conflict between them as fratricidal and unnatural. In an address entitled "The Importance of the Union of the Three Nordic Kingdoms" in 1792, the Dane Henrik Sneedorf proclaimed to a group in London calling itself the Scandinavian Society that "we united Swedes, Norwegians, and Danes consider ourselves as belonging to only one fatherland—Scandinavia." A Scandinavian Literary Society was established in Copenhagen in 1796. Its members were characterized by their enthusiasm for radical social and political ideals and by their belief in Scandinavian brotherhood as a step toward the higher goal of world citizenship.[8]

As elsewhere in the Western world, the revolutions in America and France had a profound impact in the Nordic lands. News of America's independence and of the fall of the Bastille evoked emotional condemnations of royal despots and aristocrats. Such sentiments were, however, by no means new in Scandinavia, for the ground had already been well prepared both by serious social and political conflicts and by enlightened reforms in both the Swedish and Danish monarchies since the 1760s. That most of the basic reforms that led to violence and bloodshed during the French Revolution had already been carried out in a peaceful and orderly fashion under royal auspices in the Nordic lands affected, moreover, the nature of the Scandinavian response.[9]

There were, nonetheless, telling differences in reactions to the French Revolution on either side of the Sound and the Keel. In Sweden, there had been growing conflict between the nobility, who upheld the tradition of constitutional and parliamentary liberty, and King Gustaf III, who showed ever more autocratic ambitions. Thus, initially, it was the Swedish and Finnish aristocracy that most enthusiastically hailed the revolution in France, seeing in it above all the overthrow of royal despotism. In 1792, Gustaf III was assassinated by a group of noble conspirators who saw their act as high-minded tyrannicide.[10]

In the Danish realm, the crown, in the person of the reforming regent, Crown Prince Frederik (after 1808, Frederik VI), enjoyed wide popularity. Discontent was focused primarily on the landowning aristocracy. In Norway, where a native nobility was almost nonexistent, there was, nonetheless, suspicion and resentment of lingering aristocratic power and influence in the monarchy as a whole. Foreign travelers noted the enthusiasm they encountered in Norway for France and for its revolutionary ideals. Still, such enthusiasm remained firmly linked to loyalty to the Danish crown. The

Copenhagen publicist Knud Rahbek could well describe himself only half-jokingly as "a Jacobin in France but a royalist in Denmark." It is evident in retrospect that this characteristically democratic royalism in the Danish monarchy was based increasingly upon a fundamentally revolutionary principle: a tacit social contract by which the monarch justified his power as long as it benefited the majority of his subjects. The king and his bureaucracy had come to be regarded as the bulwark of the nation against selfish corporate interests.[11]

The turn of the century brought new and threatening developments for the Nordic lands.[12] Since the beginning of the French revolutionary wars in 1792, they had once again profited from neutral maritime trade, but this had led increasingly to the seizure and confiscation of ships and cargoes by the belligerent powers. In 1800, Denmark, Sweden, Russia, and Prussia formed a League of Armed Neutrality aimed especially at Great Britain. To counter this challenge to their command of the seas, the British sent a fleet under Admiral Horatio Nelson to attack Copenhagen in April 1801, compelling Denmark, after a valiant resistance, to abandon the league, which collapsed altogether after the death of Tsar Paul that same month. The Battle of Copenhagen Roads was a portent of what would soon follow.

In the spring of 1805, Scandinavian neutrality was breached when Sweden under Gustaf IV Adolf brought Sweden into the Third Coalition against Napoleon, together with Britain, Austria, and Russia. The allies suffered a disastrous defeat at Austerlitz in December, compelling Austria to make peace and the Russians to retreat into Poland. Gustaf IV Adolf staunchly stood by his remaining allies, and his small Swedish force was driven out of Swedish Pomerania by the fall of 1807.

In the meantime, Tsar Alexander I not only made peace with Napoleon but entered into an alliance with him at Tilsit in July 1807. The previous fall, Napoleon had imposed his Continental blockade to drive Britain out of the war by destroying its commerce. France and all of Europe controlled by or allied with France were closed to the import of British products. At Tilsit, Russia too entered into Napoleon's Continental System. The greatest remaining gaps were now neutral Denmark and Britain's obdurate ally, Sweden.

The British quickly anticipated that both Nordic kingdoms would be pressured into joining the Continental System. In particular, they feared—and through false reports were led to believe—that Denmark was on the verge of acceding and adding its fleet to the combined naval forces of their foes. To forestall this seeming threat, a British expeditionary force under the Marquis of Wellesley (later the Duke of Wellington) landed on Sjælland (Zealand) and bombarded Copenhagen into submission in August 1807. The British withdrew in October, taking with them almost all of Denmark's naval vessels.

If this second attack on Copenhagen was disastrous for the Danish state, what followed would prove more catastrophic still. On 16 August, the outraged Crown Prince Frederik declared war on Great Britain. Denmark's lucrative maritime trade was destroyed. Without a fleet, its sea communications with Norway (as well as with Iceland and the Færø Islands) were virtually cut off while the British navy made even movement between the Danish islands and the mainland hazardous. The situation became most acute for Norway, which even in the best of times could not grow enough grain to feed itself and thus needed imports from Denmark, and where the economy was most heavily dependent upon exports and seafaring. By 1809, Norway faced outright famine and serious unrest.

Meanwhile, in February 1808, ostensibly to force the Swedes to abandon their alliance with Britain and to join the Continental System, Russia declared war and invaded Finland. In actually, the Russians had long coveted Finland, which lay uncomfortably close to the imperial capital, St. Petersburg, just as the Swedes for strategic reasons had long sought to acquire Norway. In March, Denmark, as Napoleon's ally, likewise entered the field against Sweden. The Finnish field forces resisted valiantly in the east, while Gustaf IV Adolf concentrated much of his army in the west in hopes of at last seizing Norway from Denmark with British support, which failed to materialize. By the winter of 1809, the Russians had occupied all of Finland and were advancing into northern Sweden.

Never popular at best, Gustaf IV Adolf had been, if anything, more autocratic than Gustaf III, while his evident aversion to the Swedish and Finnish nobility had largely alienated them. He had meanwhile proven his deplorable incompetence in both diplomacy and war, leading to conspiracies against him. In early March 1809, Lieutenant-Colonel Georg Adlersparre on the Norwegian front, after arranging a secret armistice with the Danish commander, Prince Christian August of Augustenburg, marched on Stockholm at the head of an insurgent force. Before he could reach the capital, a group of officers seized and imprisoned the king on 13 March. They thereupon set up a provisional government, which summoned a Riksdag for the first time since 1800.

In May, the Riksdag deposed Gustaf IV Adolf and his heirs from the Swedish throne and elected his uncle King Carl XIII, subject to his acceptance of a new constitution that it prepared, which will be discussed in the

next chapter. As the new king was elderly and childless, it was then necessary to elect a successor.

Adlersparre and his supporters vigorously pushed for the election of none
other than Prince Christian August in Norway, even though Sweden was still
at war with Denmark. They cherished hopes that the prince, who was highly
popular with the Norwegians, would be prepared to capitalize on the growing discontents created by the war and the British blockade by raising an
insurrection that would lead to Norway's union with Sweden. In July, the Riksdag elected Christian August successor to the throne. The prince refused to
lead an uprising against Denmark, harboring instead an even more ambitious
plan to bring about a union of all three Scandinavian kingdoms under separate, liberal constitutions by eventually abdicating the Swedish crown to
Frederik of Denmark (since 1808, King Frederik VI).[13]

In September 1809, the Swedish government concluded peace with Russia at Fredrikshamn (Hamina), ceding all of Finland and the Åland Islands.
The loss was disastrous for Sweden, which thereby surrendered a third of its
territory and a quarter of its population. Rather than incorporating the conquered territory directly into the Russian empire, Tsar Alexander, who at that
point had liberal aspirations, chose to establish Finland as an autonomous
grand duchy under its own constitution (Gustaf III's constitution of 1772, only
slightly modified), with its own diet, institutions, and laws and with Swedish
still its administrative language, under the tsar's overlordship. Denmark made
peace with Sweden in December on the basis of the *status quo ante*, and
Prince Christian August departed for Stockholm, where he took the more
Swedish name Carl August. In January 1810, Sweden made peace with
France and formally entered the Continental System.

The new crown prince, Carl August, soon became highly popular in Sweden as he had been in Norway, but in May 1810 he suddenly died. While the
autopsy showed "apoplexy" as the cause of death, it was widely feared by the
Adlersparre faction that he had been poisoned by their rivals, the "Gusta-
vians," to restore the succession to the deposed Gustaf IV Adolf's son. These
rumors led to renewed unrest, culminating in June with the lynching of the
grand marshal of the court, Count Axel von Fersen, and further bloodshed
during the rioting that followed.[14]

A new Riksdag was summoned to elect another successor. The main candidates were at first Prince Christian Frederik of Augustenburg, brother of the
late crown prince, and King Frederik VI of Denmark, who now hoped to
unite all of Scandinavia under his rule. The impasse was broken when a new
contender suddenly announced himself from an unexpected quarter: the

Napoleonic marshal Jean-Baptiste Bernadotte in Paris. This quickly aroused hopes that under a proven military commander and with Napoleon's backing, Sweden might reconquer Finland when, as was already then expected, the Tilsit alliance collapsed and France and Russia once more went to war. The Riksdag elected Bernadotte as the Swedish successor in July. He arrived in Sweden in October and was formally adopted by Carl XIII as Crown Prince Carl Johan. Almost immediately, he made himself the real ruler of Sweden, proving to be not only a good military commander but an astute politician both at home and in the international arena.

Carl Johan belied the expectations of many of those who had supported his election. Swedish liberals and radicals quickly discovered that he was no longer the old Jacobin of his younger years but rather a strict man of order, who already by the next Riksdag in 1812, capitalizing on the growing reaction following the Fersen Riot, was able to interpret the new constitution in a decidedly more conservative manner than its framers had envisioned. Significantly, at this point, press censorship was reintroduced in Sweden.

More surprising yet was Carl Johan's reorientation of Sweden's foreign policy. Both Napoleon and most in the Swedish Riksdag who had voted for him in 1810 had confidently expected that he would undertake to regain Finland as France's ally in the near future. Here too, however, he was determined to follow his own course. As a hardheaded geopolitical realist of the Napoleonic school, he felt no sentimental attachment to Finland, which he realized would be hard to reconquer and harder still to retain in the long run. Nor was he prepared to be a dependent satellite of the French emperor, with whom his personal relations had been cool. Above all, as the elected successor to an unstable throne, it was essential that he be on the winning side in the great European struggle.

It was clear to Carl Johan—evidently even before his election—that Finland, if recovered, would always remain a liability, whereas to acquire Norway would consolidate Sweden's strategic position within defensible frontiers as well as his own popularity in Sweden. For these reasons, Carl Johan was quite prepared to let Finland go. At first, he played for time, realizing that so startling a reversal of expectations would be hazardous. But in January 1812, the French gave him the opportunity he awaited by reoccupying Swedish Pomerania in reaction to Swedish violations of the Continental blockade. The wave of indignation this aroused in Sweden allowed Carl Johan to embark upon what has been called his "Policy of 1812": to acquire Norway with the support of Napoleon's enemies.[15]

On 5 April 1812, Sweden concluded a secret treaty in St. Petersburg by which Russia undertook to provide a military force to support Sweden's acquisition of Norway, after which Sweden would contribute troops for a campaign against Napoleon. Both powers undertook, moreover, to guarantee each other's territory. Russia would henceforward be freed of Swedish threats to Finland, while Sweden's future sovereignty over Norway would likewise be assured.

Implementation of this plan was delayed by Napoleon's invasion of Russia in June, but in August, Carl Johan met personally with Tsar Alexander I at Åbo (Turku) in Finland to solidify their pact. In March 1813, Sweden concluded an alliance with Britain, which likewise guaranteed support for Sweden's acquisition of Norway in return for joining the war against Napoleon. In June, Carl Johan arrived in Germany at the head of his troops. Given command of the allied Northern Army, he played a decisive role in the campaign leading to his former master's decisive defeat in the Battle of Leipzig in October.

Rather than pursuing the retreating French, Carl Johan now turned his army, including its Russian contingents, against Napoleon's ally, Denmark, to claim his reward without further delay. Attacking through Schleswig-Holstein in early December, the Swedish and Russian veterans soon overwhelmed the Danish forces. On the night of the 14–15 January 1815, Frederik VI was compelled to accept the Treaty of Kiel ceding all of Norway to the king of Sweden. For Denmark, the loss was no less disastrous or less permanent that Sweden's loss of Finland five years earlier. The Danish kingdom relinquished the greater part of its European territory and nearly half its population.

Article 4 of the Treaty of Kiel is worth particular attention. In the original draft, Denmark was to cede Norway to Sweden in return for Swedish Pomerania and a monetary compensation. On Carl Johan's initiative, this was changed to specify that Norway was ceded to the king of Sweden to comprise a separate realm in union with Sweden ("un Royaume, et réuni à celle [*sic*] de la Suède").[16] The Swedish crown prince was astutely aware that the Norwegians would resolutely oppose outright annexation to Sweden. Already during Prince Christian August's secret negotiations with Georg Adlersparre and his supporters before the Swedish Revolution in 1809, certain influential Norwegians led by Count Herman Wedel-Jarlsberg had been prepared to raise an insurrection against Danish rule and to accept a union with Sweden, providing strictly that Norway be governed under its own constitution.

An undated letter from Wedel to a Swedish correspondent during the summer of 1809 would prove prophetic for the future. A union with Sweden, he wrote, "must come about in such fashion that Norway has its own representation on the basis of equality, its own laws, finances, etc. We have almost no nobles, and those we have must either content themselves with becoming like their fellow citizens or move to other places better suited to their exalted nature. Your constitution may be very good under present circumstances in Sweden, but it does not suit Norway, which will create entirely new institutions for itself."[17] It is worth noting that Count Wedel was himself one of only two titled noblemen in Norway. Increasingly concerned over the specter of separatism in Norway, Frederik VI sanctioned in 1811 the foundation of a Norwegian university and in 1813 a separate bank in Christiania.

Already in December 1810, shortly after arriving in Sweden, Carl Johan had secretly assured sympathetic Norwegians of his support for a union with Sweden under a separate constitution, and he made similar assurances thereafter. While most influential Swedes, including Carl XIII, strongly favored acquiring Norway, they envisioned its complete incorporation into the realm as it had been under Denmark, as Finland had been under Sweden, and as the frontier provinces Sweden conquered from Norway and Denmark had been in the seventeenth century. The crown prince thus astutely refrained from openly guaranteeing Norway's autonomy under a dynastic union before concluding the Treaty of Kiel in January 1814.[18]

In Norway, news of the Treaty of Kiel caused astonishment and outrage that the Norwegians themselves had played no part in determining their own future destiny. Despite their periodic discontents, the great majority of them had felt no real desire to be separated from Denmark. Encouraged by the Danish viceroy, Frederik VI's twenty-four-year-old cousin and heir apparent, Prince Christian Frederik, they now determined to take matters into their own hands while Carl Johan and his Swedish army were still engaged in the war against Napoleon well to the south. The prince at first hoped to assert his hereditary right to the Norwegian crown but was soon dissuaded by influential Norwegians. He was advised that through the Treaty of Kiel, Frederik VI had violated the sole restrictions on royal power under the *Lex Regia* of 1665: that the monarch could not change the dynasty nor cede any part of the realm. Thus, the Norwegians could rightly consider themselves to be in a state of nature, free to determine their own form of government and to elect their head of state.[19] Christian Frederik was, however, provisionally recognized as regent.

The prince called for elections for a national assembly, or *storting*, to draft a constitution, at which time all participants were invited to swear to uphold

and defend Norway's independence. The Storting convened on 8–9 April
1814 at Eidsvoll. Its 112 members were divided between the majority comprising an "Independence party" and a smaller "Union party" led by Count
Wedel-Jarlsberg, which considered complete independence a practical im-
possibility under present circumstances and thus favored a dynastic tie with
Sweden guaranteeing national autonomy. Both factions were in agreement
in following the good Swedish principle from 1809 of "constitution first,
then king."

The new constitution was approved, and Christian Frederik was elected
Norway's king on 17 May, after which the constituent Storting was dissolved.
The new form of government will be discussed at greater length in the next
chapter. Suffice it to say here that it was by far the most liberal in Europe at
the time of its adoption and showed influences from the American state and
federal constitutions, the French constitution of 1791, the Spanish junta's
Cadiz constitution of 1812, and indeed the Swedish constitution of 1809. Most
important for Norway's future, it was far more democratic in both franchise
and representation than Sweden's new constitution. A modified unicameral
legislature was elected by a wide electorate, including all landowners, features that were clearly intended at the time to mobilize the greatest possible
support for Norway's independence.

The euphoria surrounding 17 May soon gave way to serious concerns.
Until then, Crown Prince Carl Johan, commanding his Swedish army on the
Continent, could do nothing but issue periodic warnings to the Norwegians.
In April, however, Napoleon was at last defeated by the coalition forces, which
now entered Paris in triumph. By 28 May, Carl Johan was back in Stockholm
with assurances from his allies, now including Austria, of their backing for his
claim to Norway under the Treaty of Kiel. The Swedish army meanwhile
regrouped at home.

The ensuing months were filled with complex diplomatic maneuvering
on both sides. In June, Christian Magnus Falsen, one of the leaders of the
Independence party, issued an impassioned appeal for resistance to "true
French military despotism" under Carl Johan Bernadotte in favor of a free
and honorable Scandinavian union under the "Nordic" Christian Frederik.
Sweden's allies meanwhile made it clear that Norway could find no support
for its complete independence abroad despite much popular sympathy, particularly in Britain.[20]

By July, Christian Frederik was prepared to offer his terms for a settlement.
He would abdicate in favor of Carl XIII if the Storting met and sanctioned his

resignation, provided that Norway remain a separate kingdom under its own constitution. Carl Johan thereupon broke off negotiations, and on 26 July, the Swedish army invaded Norway. A few days later, he secretly offered his terms. Christian Frederik must abdicate and leave Norway. In return, Carl Johan was prepared to make a highly significant concession: that Norway be permitted to keep its existing constitution. Although he had repeatedly assured the Norwegians of separate status under a constitution of their own, he had heretofore refused to recognize the Eidsvoll constitution, since it had not been drafted under the rightful sovereignty of the king of Sweden according to the Treaty of Kiel.

The veteran Swedish forces greatly outnumbered and quickly outmaneuvered their Norwegian opponents. On 14 August, less than three weeks after the commencement of hostilities, Sweden and Norway concluded the Convention of Moss, confirming Carl Johan's terms.[21] In resorting to war, the crown prince avoided a negotiated agreement with a sovereign whom neither Sweden nor any other European power recognized as legitimate, proved Sweden's military superiority, and precluded any compromise that might have been imposed by his allies. In offering generous terms, he meanwhile hoped —like Tsar Alexander in Finland—not only to conciliate the Norwegians but also to win over liberal opinion abroad. For Norway, resistance—however brief—upheld the nation's honor.

The Norwegian state council convened a new Storting in Christiania on 7 October. Three days later, it accepted the abdication of Christian Frederik, who thereupon returned to Denmark—where he would later reign as King Christian VIII, from 1839 to 1848. On 20 October, the Storting voted to accept in principle a union with Sweden by a majority of seventy-two to five. The legislators thereupon proceeded to amend the constitution before formally electing the new monarch. Communicating with Carl Johan through a Swedish commission in Christiania, including members of the Swedish state council, the Storting not only resolutely rejected several proposals from the Swedish crown prince that would have significantly increased the authority in Norway of the union monarch but also curtailed some of the royal prerogatives included in the Eidsvoll constitution, as will be seen.

With the approach of winter and apprehensive that the congress of European powers about to convene in Vienna might intervene, Carl Johan found it expedient to give way, at least for the time being. Having firmly consolidated Norway's constitutional safeguards against arbitrary royal authority, the Storting "elected and recognized" Carl XIII as Norway's king on 4 November 1814.

Carl Johan at last made his entry into Christiania five days later. The Swedish Riksdag thereafter confirmed the union in February 1815, and the constitutional relationship was set forth in the Act of Union promulgated on 6 August 1815.[22]

This relationship would nonetheless remain an uneasy one. In declaring that the Swedish monarch was "elected and recognized," the Norwegian Storting left his position ambiguous, no doubt intentionally under the circumstances. To *recognize* his sovereignty implied that Norway acceded to terms imposed by Sweden and backed by its wartime allies. To *elect* him meant, on the contrary, that the Norwegians, through their Storting, freely acclaimed him as their king—with the underlying implication for the future that if they possessed the freedom to elect, they were also free to depose.

Already in February 1814, the Finnish-born Baron Gustaf Mauritz Armfelt, once Gustaf III's confidant, now an influential adviser to Alexander I in St. Petersburg, had foreseen that "Norway will be more of an encumbrance than a gain to Sweden." Carl XIII and much influential opinion in Sweden were sorely disappointed over the Convention of Moss and the ultimate form of the union after having hoped to incorporate Norway in the same manner as it had been under Denmark. In late September, Hans Järta, the principle author of the Swedish constitution of 1809, pondered the question: if "Sweden's and Norway's constitutional, moral, and economic conditions are not woven together early, what can, after a century or perhaps before, keep the Norwegian people from resuming the fight for independence it has now attempted?"[23] The future would prove how prophetic this anticipation would be.

2

The Civic Vision

THE TWO KINGDOMS that on 4 November 1814 came to form the Dual Monarchy differed greatly in their history, forms of government, and social structures. Sweden was an old political nation dating back to the Middle Ages. Even during most of the Kalmar Union period, the Swedes had managed to preserve their own self-rule. During the seventeenth century, Sweden had risen to the status of a European great power. The Swedes could pride themselves on venerable political traditions and administrative institutions.

Norway had meanwhile largely ceased to exist as a separate political entity under the Kalmar Union. By the early sixteenth century, it became administratively amalgamated with Denmark, and so it remained over the next three centuries. Only the dramatic events of 1814, which few Norwegians had earlier anticipated or desired, established Norway once again as a separate kingdom—in dynastic union with Sweden—with its own constitution, laws, and institutions. Yet, paradoxically it would seem, Sweden would be more obviously influenced by Norway during the union than Norway by Sweden. During the first half of the nineteenth century, the greatest Norwegian influence lay in the realm of political ideals.

To understand why this should be so, it is necessary to examine the constitutions of the two kingdoms and the underlying differences in their social structures. Although Gustaf IV Adolf had been deposed in 1809 for abuses of royal power, the new Swedish constitution of that year endowed the monarch with "undivided authority to administer" the kingdom. He was empowered to appoint and dismiss his ministers, who formed the *statsråd*, or state council, and in principle all other public officials—civil, clerical, and military—except for judges. In this respect, as well as in his authority to declare war, both offensive and defensive, and thus to employ Swedish troops outside of Sweden, his powers were even increased over what they previously had been. The monarch had widespread administrative authority, could propose measures to the Riksdag, and possessed an absolute veto over its legislation. As crown prince until 1818 and thereafter as king, Carl XIV Johan would exercise these prerogatives to the full.

The Riksdag nonetheless retained an essential role, for in it was vested the power of the purse: control over all taxation, loans, the state bank, and the national debt. Various special excises and tolls that formerly had provided standing revenue to the crown now became regular state revenues. The Riksdag was also given control over certain specific government expenditures. It shared with the crown the right both to propose and to veto legislation and convened every five years unless called by the crown for an extraordinary session between regular meetings.

The monarch was required to receive advice from his state councilors, or ministers, although not necessarily to consult with them as a group, which in practice generally meant that they dealt with him individually regarding their own areas of responsibility. While they were appointed and dismissed by the crown, they were also made accountable to the Riksdag, which could petition the crown for their removal for dereliction of duty by a special tribunal, the *riksrätt*, consisting ex officio of designated high officials. The dual accountability of the council would remain an Achilles' heel until the final breakthrough of full parliamentarianism in Sweden in the early twentieth century. The political forces in the field were now clearly the crown and the Riksdag.

Surviving corporate privileges, press freedom, and especially representation in the Riksdag aroused lively debate during 1809 but under the unsettled conditions of that time remained unresolved. In a climate of growing conservatism following the Fersen Riot of June 1810 in Stockholm, Crown Prince Carl Johan was able, exercising the monarch's administrative authority, to impose de facto press censorship at the Riksdag of 1812. Corporate privileges, particularly special tax benefits attached to manorial lands—even though commoners could now acquire such lands—would not be addressed for decades to come, much to the disgruntlement of the peasantry.

In April 1810, a proposal for reorganization of the Riksdag into a bicameral legislature with an upper house elected on the basis of substantial taxable property and a lower house based on population, although elected by voters qualified by property ownership, was passed as a constitutional amendment.[1] As such, this measure required passage by the two following Rikdags, but this failed to come about. The representation issue would thereafter remain the most intense and protracted controversy in Sweden's political life during the nineteenth century, opening the door to strong Norwegian influence.

The Riksdag thus remained divided into the four medieval estates of the nobility, the clergy, the burghers, and the (landowning) peasants, each of which voted internally before casting its vote in plenum. The votes of three estates were required to pass a proposal; and the vote of all four in three consecutive sessions, to amend the constitution. This disposition gave greatly disproportionate power to the small elites represented by the three higher estates, in particular the nobility, as opposed to the large peasant majority. Meanwhile, despite the leveling in 1789 and 1809 of all but their honorific privileges and separate representation in the Riksdag, the nobility would continue throughout the century to hold most of the higher civil, diplomatic, military, and court appointments.

This fundamental law was Sweden's fifth written constitution since 1643 and the fourth within the past century. While each was affected by the particular circumstances of the time in which it was framed, all reflected a complex social structure that had evolved since the Middle Ages; hence the elaborate system of checks and balances.

The nobility, still powerful and influential, was in fact a composite group. Relatively few could trace noble lineage back to the Middle Ages. Most descended from men, frequently of foreign origin, ennobled for military or civil service during Sweden's "Era of Greatness" in the seventeenth and early eighteenth century. Certain large entrepreneurs and even distinguished scholars had also been ennobled.[2] By European standards, the Swedish nobility was not wealthy. Aside from some manorial lords with large landholdings, most were primarily dependent upon state service, most often in the military, to support themselves in a modest but decent manner appropriate to their status. The nobility's political power therefore seemed essential to most of its members for preserving what remained of its privileged position. The Noble Estate included the heads of some one thousand noble families. Although not all chose to take part, their attendance and activity at the Riksdag was normally the highest among the four estates.

The other, elected estates likewise had corporate interests to defend. The clergy of the Lutheran state church had their livings and their traditional authority in the parish councils. Mindful of their vocation as shepherds of their flock, the Clerical Estate was generally mistrustful of newer currents of thought and politically conservative.

The Burgher Estate was elected by and represented men holding burgher rights in chartered towns. They too were a disparate group, including not only large merchants in Stockholm and Göteborg (Gothenburg) but also the far more numerous petty tradesmen and artisans organized in guilds. The estate was correspondingly divided in its political views. While it included many advocates of liberal reforms, its rank and file were highly solicitous of their established corporate privileges and trade monopolies. Although Stockholm, the center of liberal ideas, was far larger than any other Swedish town, its representation in the estate remained modest in relation to its population.

Peasants possessing freehold farms or holding crown tenancies elected their representatives to the Peasant Estate. Although, in principle, the estate jealously excluded landowners not of peasant origins to avoid outside influences in its deliberations, the leading peasant *riksdagsmän* were generally prosperous, some having purchased privileged manorial lands with their attached tax benefits. Already before the turn of the century, and especially at the Riksdag of 1809, the Peasant Estate had begun to play an ever greater political role.

The large majority of the population not belonging to any of the four estates meanwhile remained without direct representation in the Riksdag. They included a significant element known as the *ofrälse ståndspersoner*, or "non-noble persons of quality," including numerous entrepreneurs, such as iron-masters and manufacturers, public officials, rural landowners, professionals, journalists, and other intellectuals. Such unenfranchised members of the growing middle class tended to be strongly drawn to liberal and reforming ideals.[3] The majority of the peasant class, including manorial tenants, cotters, and landless laborers, was meanwhile ineligible for membership in the Peasant Estate.[4]

Norway's Eidsvoll constitution of 1814 was a straightforward statement of fundamental law. Sverre Steen found it reminiscent of the old Norse law codes in its simplicity.[5] As in the Swedish (and the American) constitution, authority was divided between an executive branch under the monarch, a legislature—the Storting—and a supreme court. At Eidsvoll, the monarch was given extensive powers, especially in foreign affairs, war and peace, the military forces, and the appointment of officials. He was advised by a state council whose members were excluded from the Storting but not permitted to resign, as in Sweden, in protest against royal policy. During the union, a deputation of the council led by a "minister president" was stationed in Stockholm when the king was in residence there.

The Storting, however, carefully circumscribed the powers of the crown granted at Eidsvoll during the fall of 1814 in preparation for dynastic union with Sweden to guard against any future threat of direct amalgamation with the Swedish realm. Crown Prince Carl Johan indeed hoped for a closer union from the start and pressed, through his Swedish commissioners, for the right to create nobles, to naturalize foreigners, to appoint subjects of one kingdom to positions in the other, and to dispose freely over the military forces of both kingdoms. All these demands were rejected by the Storting except the crown's appointment of its personal representative in Norway—the *statholder,* or *stathållare*—who could be either Norwegian or Swedish, the power to hold joint military maneuvers at stated intervals involving small Norwegian and Swedish detachments, and the authority to employ Norwegian regular troops outside of Norway—with the Storting's approval. Faced with the delicate circumstances of the time, the crown prince prudently avoided direct confrontation to await more favorable opportunities for revision in the future.

The principal differences between the Swedish and Norwegian constitutions lay in the legislative branch and the franchise. The Storting was organized—uniquely for its time—on the basis of a modified unicameralism. Common elections were held for all its members. After convening, the Storting itself elected one fourth of its number to serve as a *Lagting,* to review and confirm legislation passed by the remaining three fourths, which constituted the *Odelting.* If the Lagting twice rejected a proposal, it was voted on in plenary session at which a two-thirds majority was required for approval. Like the Swedish Riksdag, the Storting as well as the crown could propose legislation. The all-important difference lay in the veto. In Sweden, the monarch's veto was absolute. In Norway, it could be overridden if the Storting passed a measure in three consecutive sessions, which were held every three years.

The other great difference between the two constitutions concerned the franchise. Whereas in Sweden this required membership in one of the four corporate estates, in Norway it was based upon liberal, uniform qualifications. All males over the age of twenty-five, resident in the country for more than five years, who had owned or leased taxable rural property or had served as public officials or held burgher rights in towns with property valued at over three hundred *riksbankdaler,* and who swore to uphold the constitution possessed the right to vote. Stein Kuhnle has calculated that in 1814 they amounted to 45.5 percent of all Norwegian men over twenty-five years of age, or 10.3 percent of the total population, a far larger proportion at the time than in Sweden or in any other European constitutional monarchy.[6] Members of the Storting were to be residents of their districts, of which two-thirds were to be rural and one-third in the towns. Although this arrangement gave double weight to the small urban population, it nonetheless allowed the

Norwegian peasantry a potential majority in the Storting, which could give it a far stronger voice in politics than the Swedish Peasant Estate.

The Norwegian constitution contained a bill of basic civil rights, including—significantly—freedom of expression, in contrast to the de facto censorship imposed in Sweden at the Riksdag of 1812. Freedom of worship was permitted to all Christian subjects, although public officials were required to belong to the Lutheran state church. No new nobles could be created nor could manorial rights be granted. As in Sweden, public officials could be dismissed for cause following trial by a special tribunal, or *Rigsret*.[7]

Norway's far more liberal constitution reflected a much less complex social structure than Sweden's. The great difference was the virtual absence of a nobility, as has been noted. Hence, the constitutional prohibition against ennoblements and the creation of manors provided a guarantee against any future change in this regard. Norway lacked, in effect, those strong conservative elements that could have provided the basis for an effective upper house in the Storting.[8]

Whereas in Sweden the dominant social cleavage lay between nobles and commoners, in Norway it separated a thin stratum of bourgeois "persons of quality" and the vast peasant majority. Norway nonetheless experienced scarcely less social conflict than Sweden. During the later eighteenth century, there had been several peasant insurrections against the dominant class: the "Stril War" in the Bergen region in 1765, the Lofthuus Rebellion in southern Norway in 1786–87, the Hauge evangelical revival movement beginning in 1796, and local rioting during the wartime shortages in 1809.[9]

The Norwegian elite consisted in actuality of two basic elements: the town merchants and the public officials—civil, clerical, and military—both urban and rural.[10] While by no means socially exclusive and largely interrelated by marriage, each group had its particular objectives and values. Whereas the Stril War in 1765 was directed against the officials of the Danish crown, the following conflicts turned increasingly against the merchant oligarchy. The officials meanwhile became for a time more closely allied with the peasantry, who came to regard them as protectors of their interests.[11]

This alignment seems evident at the Eidsvoll constitutional convention, where the "Unionists" tended largely to represent the merchants and substantial men of wealth while the "Independence" party was led primarily by civil officials, clergymen, and military men and included most of the peasant representatives. That two-thirds of the seats in the Storting were apportioned to the rural districts—in effect, to representatives of the peasantry—was naturally motivated largely by the immediate need to mobilize the entire nation in its hour of peril. Yet, the public officials who dominated at Eidsvoll also counted on men of their kind being chosen in the future by the peasant electors in the rural constituencies to represent them in the Storting. Such indeed would generally be the case over the following decade and a half, even though peasant representatives, already at Eidsvoll, raised disquieting demands of their own that bore the seeds of future conflict.[12]

The Norwegian peasantry included the farmers, both freehold and leasehold, who were qualified to elect and represent their class in the Storting, as well as a sizable and growing element of cotters and landless laborers, who were ineligible. Farmholders of both kinds enjoyed substantial guarantees to their property rights and could be very well-to-do and influential in their neighborhoods. There was, meanwhile, much rural poverty, especially among the landless elements.[13]

In 1818, Carl XIII died and was succeeded in the Dual Monarchy by the crown prince. The new king, Carl XIV Johan, now felt the time had come to bring pressure to bear upon the Storting for changes to the Norwegian constitution to create a closer union of the kind he had felt it expedient to postpone in the fall of 1814. Two years before, he had confided to Queen Hedvig Elisabeth Charlotta: "I am especially gratified that the Norwegians are so poor, for this lets us hope that the two kingdoms will someday be truly unified, since Norway cannot exist independently." The next Storting, he was optimistically convinced, would demand a "firmer union," which he hoped might come about within three years and would be a "blessing for both Sweden and Norway."[14]

Carl Johan's hopes in this regard were encouraged at the time of his coronation in Trondheim by a peasant uprising in eastern Norway, which it appears at least he had covertly encouraged. Oppressed by high taxation and the declining timber trade during the hard post-Napoleonic years, the peasant insurgents called for abolition of the Storting and a return to a paternalistic government by the crown in the old Danish tradition. An attempted march on Christiania was quickly broken up, but the incident highlighted the smoldering conflict between the peasantry and the elite.[15] More than that, it may be considered prophetic regarding the crown's future dilemma: the monarch — and thus the union with Sweden — would ultimately have to find his primary support either among the governing elite or among the peasantry, while to alienate either would undermine the union's viability.

Carl Johan now pressed the Storting to grant the crown an absolute veto on all types of legislation, expanded powers to issue emergency decrees and to control the press, and the rights to deny naturalizations, to designate the speaker of the Storting, to appoint and dismiss members of the Supreme Court, and to create a hereditary nobility. He likewise sought to stipulate that the Storting would meet every five years rather than every three.[16] Acutely aware of the threat this program raised of the future "amalgamation" of the kingdoms, the Storting stood fast in defending the integrity of Norway's constitution and consistently rejected the royal proposals for its amendment.

In 1821, the Storting demonstrated its independence by voting for the third time to abolish titles of nobility altogether, thereby for the first time overriding the king's suspensive veto. It was fully aware that, as the Scottish visitor Samuel Laing would put it in 1837, in Norway "a body of titled and privileged persons could only subsist as placemen or pensioners."[17] The king considered this defiance so provocative that he contemplated a military coup but was discouraged by the reactions of the European powers he prudently sounded on the issue. When the Storting rejected his proposals in 1824, he mobilized both Norwegian and Swedish troops (the latter with live ammunition) and a Swedish naval squadron as a show of force but to no avail.

The Storting thereupon undertook in 1827 to clarify its powers regarding budgetary matters by bringing a state councilor—thus, indirectly, the crown itself—to trial before the Supreme Court and securing his dismissal for violation of the constitution, despite the king's protests that the court was not empowered to rule on constitutionality. This in turn encouraged a demonstrative celebration in Christiania that year of Norway's independence on 17 May, the date on which the constitution was promulgated in 1814, rather than, as Carl Johan wished, on 4 November, when the Storting had accepted the king of Sweden as its sovereign and thus consummated the union. The following year, the king again at least considered the use of force. In 1829, the celebration of 17 May, especially by students at the new university, so alarmed the Swedish statholder that he called in a local cavalry unit to break up the event on Christiania's main square, an incident soon magnified in the public imagination as an intolerable act of oppression.

Meanwhile, the king bowed to pressure from the European powers in 1821 for Norway to pay a share of the Danish national debt at the time of the separation in accordance with the Treaty of Kiel and in 1827 to grant compensation to British traders arrested for smuggling in the northern port of Bodø. These unpopular concessions made it painfully clear that foreign affairs in both kingdoms still remained the crown's prerogative.

From the late 1820s, Carl Johan came increasingly to realize that a direct confrontation with the Norwegians could only harm his position. As a son of the French Revolution and by now the only remaining "Napoleonide" on a European throne, he was keenly aware of the importance of public opinion. He had no real wish to rule by force, although he did once again briefly consider military intervention in Norway, when in 1836 the Storting again brought a state councilor to trial for violation of the constitution. But again the powers urged caution, and the king accepted a fait accompli.[18]

A more peaceful period began that year with the appointment as statholder of the Norwegian Herman Wedel-Jarlsberg, erstwhile leader of the Union party at the Eidsvoll Storting in 1814. Thereafter, Carl Johan would enjoy increasingly cordial relations with his Norwegian subjects during the latter years of his reign, up to his death in 1844. Indeed, no union monarch since has remained as popular in Norway. Oslo's main thoroughfare, leading up to his imposing equestrian statue before the royal palace, remains to this day named after him. Along it proceeds a great parade celebrating Norway's national day—each 17 May.

It is not our purpose here to retrace once again the complex history of the Norwegian-Swedish union but rather to survey visions of Norway and the impact they had in Sweden during the period. In the past, Swedes had paid little attention to their western neighbors except from a strategic point of view. During the eighteenth century, many Swedes traveled widely in Europe and the wider world, including the celebrated disciples of Carl von Linné (Linnæus), but few saw any reason to visit Norway.

Their generally patronizing attitude was perhaps well summarized by the ship's chaplain, Jacob Wallenberg, aboard a Swedish East Indiaman forced by the weather to put in to Bergen in 1769. The Norwegians he considered a benighted folk, under the heel of Danish despotism. "I could not hear their sighs," he wrote, "without thanking my lucky star that I was born a son of freedom in old Sweden." He continued in verse:

> Slavish in their ways of thought,
> Raised in shackles from their birth,
> Norway's folk toil 'neath the lash,
> Enjoying nought but the rights of oxen.
> . . . .
> Brother Northmen, join us now
> In the Swedish kingdom.
> Your kings shall in your place
> Receive our Pomeranians.[19]

Other voices in Sweden, however, expressed a different view. The ship carrying the Finnish-born naturalist Pehr Kalm, one of Linné's followers, to North America in 1749 was also compelled to put in to Bergen. The Norwegians he found to be a people of sturdy "Gothic" character, "with the old honesty and straightforwardness, for which the North, since time immemorial, has been so universally praised and admired."[20]

Eighteenth-century preromanticism nurtured a growing fascination with Nordic antiquity that, beginning in Britain and on the Continent, spread to Scandinavia itself. In this light, the seemingly unspoiled Nordic peasantry—above all in Norway—came to be seen as the embodiment of strength and rude virtues.[21] Georg Adlersparre and his friends, who in 1809 raised the banner of revolt against Gustaf IV Adolf and secured the election of Prince Christian August of Augustenburg as Swedish crown prince in hopes thereby of acquiring Norway, avidly desired the Swedes' "brotherhood with the Norwegian people, this simple, noble, strong, and serious folk."[22]

Disappointment was nonetheless great in Sweden over failure in 1814 to create a closer union with Norway under unquestioned Swedish control. Many would still have preferred to regain Finland rather than to have to deal with the stiff-necked Norwegians who dared to bid defiance to a proud old nation of warriors. J. A. Wadman, for instance inveighed against "that poverty-ridden, bullheaded, dissatisfied, demanding, and Swede-hating Norway, which is neither for us or against us . . . which hangs on old Sweden's back without ever being able or wishing to find its way to her heart." General Anders Fredrik Skjöldebrand, who like Wadman had fought in the Norwegian campaign, was filled with contempt for their poor showing in the field, combined with their cocksure braggadocio, and bitterly regretted Carl Johan's acceptance of their Eidsvoll constitution, which amounted to a "hidden anarchy." "Everything that could for all time separate the two nations," he wrote indignantly, "was included in the Act of Union."[23]

Yet, there were those who expressed a certain, even if grudging, admiration for the Norwegians' courage and determination. Queen Hedvig Elisabeth Charlotta described them in her diary as brave and virtuous, although childish in their unreasonable obstinacy. The Swedes, the poet Esaias Tegnér wrote more sympathetically to a friend in March 1814, should not "remind a noble people that it has been conquered and sold."[24]

Norwegian prejudices against Sweden were no less prevalent. The Swedish naturalist Sven Nilsson, traveling in 1816 from Christiania to Trondheim, was appalled upon being asked by a peasant whether "serfdom does not still exist in Sweden, whether the nobles on their estates are not still able to punish their peasants themselves, and whether the slightest infraction is not punished with the whip."[25]

The Swedish deputation that negotiated with the Storting during the fall of 1814 evidently consisted of persons sympathetic toward its constitutional principles. It appears indeed that it did not strongly oppose—and may even secretly have encouraged—the checks and balances the Storting managed to impose upon the crown out of apprehension over Carl Johan's autocratic propensities.[26] In the Riksdag the following year, Count Fredrik Boguslaus von Schwerin undertook to form a "loyal opposition" on the British model, which provoked the memorable outburst from Carl Johan: "Opposition, c'est conspiration!"[27] The small opposition in Sweden could make little headway in 1815, but it pointed toward developments in coming years and a growing appreciation for the Norwegian Storting's strict constitutionalism.

Opposition was initially strongest in the Noble Estate, with its old traditions of aristocratic constitutionalism. Specific grievances largely concerned Carl Johan's inept handling of economic matters and—more broadly—the overall power of the crown and its bureaucrats. This brought into relief the ineffectiveness of the Riksdag as a counterweight, resulting especially from its continued division into the four archaic estates. Hence, the question of representational reform gained increasing urgency. Representation had given rise to much debate and discussion at the constituent Riksdag of 1809–10 and had been ultimately put off because of its highly controversial nature. An unsuccessful proposal for representational reform was raised, as has been seen, at the Riksdag of 1815.

Support for a change in the system of representation at first reflected liberal ideals of British, French, and American origins, as well as older Swedish political tradition. While these remained important influences, by the 1820s, a new source of inspiration became increasingly evident: Norway's Eidsvoll constitution of 1814. Count Carl Henrik Anckarsvärd, a supporter of the revolution of 1809 who had since fallen out with Carl Johan, defended in 1828 the Norwegians' right to celebrate 17 May as their independence day, pointedly praising their wise constitution in comparison to the Swedish. A motion made by L. J. Dalman to the Riksdag's constitutional committee in 1829 presented the Norwegian constitution, as well as the failed Swedish representational proposal of 1810, as models for reform.[28]

Johan Gabriel Richert, Sweden's leading jurist, visited Norway in 1827 to study its penal system and to see its Storting in action. In May 1830, he together with C. H. Anckarsvärd published a proposal for constitutional reform. Although not specifically mentioned, it was clearly inspired by the Norwegian constitution. In its introduction, the proposal attacked the inefficiency of the four-estate system and the deplorable state of affairs it permitted to exist in Sweden. The authors appealed to "the common sense of the Swedish people and to Sweden's own experience in centuries past." They proposed somewhat vaguely that the state council be transformed from its present "collegial form" to "what is generally called a ministerial system," which would seem to imply some shift of its primary responsibility from the crown to the Riksdag.

At the heart of the Richert-Anckarsvärd proposal lay changes to the Riksdag's organization and the extent of the franchise. A legislature was to be elected in common elections, after which it would designate 75 persons to serve as its upper house, or *Pröfnings-Nämnd.* The latter body was not to be aristocratic in composition, for "any attempt to form an independent aristocratic element in a state in which the people neither recognizes nor wishes to recognize any aristocracy above it is and will forever remain fruitless."

The authors denied that they sought to extend the franchise as far as might be possible or "perhaps further than in any other country in our part of the world." Of the legislature's 175 members, 120 were to be elected indirectly by electors, 88 of them from rural districts and 32 from towns, while the remaining 55 were to be elected directly by those paying at least fifty *riksdaler* in taxes. Those who elected the electors must be resident in their own districts, own real property, or be taxed at a minimum of five *riksdaler.* Representatives were to be at least twenty-five years old, in good standing, and Christians.[29]

Anckarsvärd followed up this proposal in 1833 with a sharply polemic "political confession" in which he declared that "the Estates of the Realm, in their present composition in no way and from no point of view have any connection with the *Swedish people.*" In particular, he deplored the under-representation of the peasantry, "the representatives of simple, sound good sense," and their lack of contact in the Riksdag with the more enlightened and politically experienced elements within the other estates. Together, he pointed out, the "three privileged estates," which between them comprised 42,985 males, were represented at the last Riksdag of 1828–29 by 595 members, as against 122 representatives for a total male peasant population of 998,600, which bore the heaviest burdens for the public good.[30]

The Richert-Anckarsvärd proposal aroused much discussion despite press censorship. Liberals were further inspired by the revolutions of 1830 on the Continent and by the British First Reform Bill of 1832. Their ideals at this point are well expressed by a now forgotten book from 1833 by C. P. Agrelius, which above all evoked Norway's liberal constitution. The author traced the gradual loss since the Middle Ages of Sweden's ancient freedoms to a powerful aristocracy, "which like a mighty Colossus has weighed heavily upon the body politic and sought to oppose and stifle both the strivings of genius and material development." A "true" aristocracy he considered essential to the state, but it must be based on personal merit alone and act in accordance with the "general will." On this basis, he urged the adoption of a constitution essentially similar to the Norwegian, which, he held, would clear the way for a true union of the two nations, creating a greater Scandinavia of real weight in European affairs. He believed—or at least affected to believe—that Carl Johan would welcome a constitution in Sweden similar to that which he had sanctioned in Norway.[31]

While Swedish liberals and radicals by the early 1830s turned increasingly toward Norway for political inspiration, a fundamental shift in the political power base was getting underway there, following the excitement aroused by the July Revolution of 1830 in Paris. Although the constitution of 1814 had made a peasant majority in the Storting theoretically possible, Norway had in practice continued to be dominated by its elite class. With the bankruptcy of much of the old merchant oligarchy during the post-Napoleonic European economic depression, this elite had come to consist predominantly of the civil, military, and clerical officials of the state who both legislated and administered. The latter continued to hold ambiguous feelings toward the peasantry, regarding them in principle as bearers of the proud heritage of the nation's past yet mistrustful of their political ignorance and short-sightedness. All was well, from the elite's point of view, as long as the peasants followed the lead of their social betters in local affairs and elected them as their representatives in the Storting. Such was usually the case, despite occasional rumblings, up to 1830 when the peasantry began its own broad political mobilization.

The beginnings of this movement are largely ascribed to a well-to-do agitator of peasant origins, Jon Neergaard, who traveled widely throughout the land giving speeches and passing out copies of his booklet, popularly known as the "Ola-Book," in which he upheld the just demands of the "producing" *(nærende)* versus the "consuming" *(tærende)* classes and urged that the peasants elect their own kind to the Storting. Such demands found further, influential backing in new radical newspapers, especially Peder Soelvold's *Statsborgeren,* established in 1830, which rallied support for the peasantry among the more radical young intelligentsia, most notable among them the romantic poet Henrik Wergeland.

The accumulated grievances of the peasantry began to assume the contours of a simple, yet purposeful political program, aimed above all at bringing about "economy in the state" and control of local government by elected officials rather than appointed bureaucrats. Both objectives were perceived among the elite as potentially threatening to usher in the despotism of the masses. Economies in the state budget necessarily meant cutting back on the very expenditures upon which the elite depended for its livelihood: bureaucratic appointments, promotions, and salaries, the secondary "Latin" schools and the new university, and the church, military, and naval establishments. The peasants likewise sought to shift the tax burden from the land tax to tolls and excise revenues, which would fall most heavily on the urban population, and to abolish existing town monopolies on various trades and types of commerce. The free election of local officials would similarly undermine the authority and standing of rural persons of quality.

The elections of 1832 aroused great political agitation and returned twice as many peasant representatives to the Storting of the following year as at the last session—43—as opposed to 33 officials and academics, 2 large landed proprietors, 13 merchants, and 2 artisans.[32] The "Peasant Storting" of 1833 proved correspondingly radical. Aside from various state economies and adjustments in taxation, the greatest issue was that of communal self-government, which, while it aroused much heated debate, remained unresolved.

When a similarly composed Storting was elected in 1836, its manifest radicalism so aroused Carl Johan that in July he decreed its dissolution, creating a new crisis. Before dissolving, the Storting resolved to bring a royal councilor who had countersigned the royal decree to trial before the Rigsret. By fall, the king felt compelled to call a new, extraordinary Storting, which enacted local self-government and various economies in state, especially in military expenditures, and eliminated the land tax, even if now in a more sober and moderate spirit than before. The peasant representatives were gaining practical experience in political compromise and sophistication, qualities well exemplified by the leader that now emerged in their midst, Ole Gabriel Ueland.[33]

In Sweden, the political mobilization of the Norwegian peasantry during the 1830s aroused both enthusiasm, particularly among the Peasant Estate, and apprehensions, especially within the other estates, as will be seen. But there is another aspect to the peasant awakening in Norway: emigration to America, which after a modest beginning in 1825 got seriously underway by the late 1830s. Those who departed were on the whole well-to-do peasant farmers and even included some members of the intelligentsia. Their letters home and published accounts of America not only describe its material abundance but emphasize the social and political equality that prevailed there, thus highlighting existing inequities in the homeland.[34]

In this regard, too, the Norwegian peasantry inspired their Swedish brethren. Early Norwegian emigrant letters from America were not only widely published in Norwegian newspapers but found their way into the Swedish liberal press as well. The Norwegian impact upon the beginnings of the great Swedish emigration still awaits closer investigation, but it is clear that it was considerable. The first Swedish emigrant guidebook, published in Stockholm in 1841, consisted mainly of a translation of the Norwegian Ole Rynning's account of America from 1838.[35] Particular attention was aroused in both countries by a widely published letter from Illinois by the Norwegian peasant Gjert Gregoriussen Hovland from April 1835. He wrote, "I do not believe there can be better laws or arrangements for the benefit and happiness of the common man in the whole world. . . . The vote of the common man carries just as much authority as does that of the rich and powerful." There were no distinctions in dress or privileges. "The freedom which the one enjoys is just as good as that of the others." There were no passports and each was free "to engage in whatever business he finds most desirable."[36]

The retired regimental clerk Carl Friman and his five sons who emigrated to America in 1838 may be regarded as the true harbingers of the great Swedish trans-Atlantic migration. In 1842, one of the sons recalled how he and his family had read Hovland's letter in Sweden before undertaking their venture. In a letter from 1853, Carl Friman, now back in Sweden, expressed a widespread pessimism among the Swedish liberals over prospects in the Old World as compared with the New when he wrote that "in the land of despotism everyone is a despot as much as he can be and everyone is some poor devil's master. . . . Arrogance and oppression, jealousy, misery, vengefulness, and despair are the dominating features of life's tableau, everywhere there is wickedness and evil."[37]

The leader of the first group of Swedish peasants to the Middle West in 1845, Peter Cassel, was inspired in part by the letters from America of the Norwegian Hans Gasmann in Wisconsin, published in *Aftonbladet*, Sweden's leading radical newspaper. Like him, Cassel enthusiastically praised, in a widely publicized letter from Iowa in February 1846, the social and political equality in America, where there were "no such thing as class distinction . . . no counts, barons, or lordly estates." A Swedish peasant, "raised under oppression and accustomed to poverty and want," he continued, "here finds himself elevated to a new world, as it were, where all his former hazy ideas of a society conforming more closely to nature's laws are suddenly made real and he enjoys a satisfaction in life that he has never before experienced."[38]

In Sweden, the question of representation quickly came to the fore at the Riksdag of 1834–35, following a petition campaign encouraged by C. H. Anckarsvärd. The constitutional committee received no less than nine proposals for its reform, including some based on the Norwegian model. On 6 October 1834, Anders Danielsson, a veteran leader in the Peasant Estate since 1809, presented to his brethren a proposal evidently prepared behind the scenes by the radical nobleman Gustaf Hierta. This called for common elections in large districts to a common legislature, which in turn would elect a part of its membership to form an upper house, as in Norway. To those who justified the existing system of estates by historic precedent, Danielsson declared that

> this by no means proves their usefulness or their necessity. . . . new conditions and new attitudes toward society have developed that, so to say, have dissolved the interests of estates into the great and important interests of the nation. . . . It is clear that as long as some 200,000 peasant landowners have no more influence in the national representation than 30,000 taxable burghers, 1,200 heads of noble families, and around 1,500 enfranchised clergy, the greater part of the nation is entirely dominated by the capricious interests of the few.

Danielsson preferred voting rights without reference to estate but realized that such a change would be impossible under the constitution against the opposition of the other estates. He therefore proposed, to begin with, to "preserve the estates' right of representation but give the people the right to elect." All voters should thus be free to vote for candidates from any estate, while the number of peasant representatives should be double that of each of the other estates in a legislature of at most four hundred members. The secretary of the Peasant Estate thereupon read the paragraphs on suffrage in the Norwegian constitution.[39]

While such a radical proposal for its time was bound to be controversial, Danielsson and his peasant supporters seemed hardly prepared for the opposition they encountered within their own estate. Nils Strindlund argued that in Riksdag voting the peasantry would be "crowded out by persons of quality and others who cannot be considered real peasants. . . . Riksdag members of the Peasant Estate would no longer be able to make their voices heard or heeded, for how could it ever be possible that less enlightened peasants could hold their own against learned men from the other estates? . . . the Peasant Estate would, in a word, soon be like sheep among wolves." Several other peasant Riksdag members raised similar objections, and the Danielsson proposal died for lack of support.[40]

There was meanwhile considerable enthusiastic support for far-reaching representational reform in the other estates, in particular among the nobility. Debate within that estate during October 1834 shows the opposing positions and the basic assumptions about the probable political behavior of the broader masses that underlay them. Wilhelm Fredric Dalman—like Danielsson in the Peasant Estate—dismissed the conservative argument for a long and gradual evolution of the constitution. "We have seen," he declared, "how our brothers, the Norwegians, who after 300 years had no representation, needed no more than a few weeks to devise a system that perhaps is not perfect but is certainly better than our own." Lars Johan Hierta, editor of *Aftonbladet*, assured his fellow nobles that the Norwegian peasant representatives had shown their sound conservatism in steadfastly opposing Carl XIV Johan's attempts to graft onto their constitution "another element," that is, a nobility, "which I would not consider to *conserve*, but rather to *embalm*."

Baron Johan Albert Kanzow likewise pled eloquently for representational reform:

> Our Riksdags are regarded as evil rather than good and are seen as no more than taxation-machines. . . . And the reason . . . can be none other than that our representative body does not consist of the people. Certain guilds and corporations which are represented work in four separate chambers and usually pull in four different directions, from which it follows that no public spirit, unity, solidarity, or strength . . . can possibly be found there. The first condition for the people to realize its interest in its representation must, in my view, be that the people—that is, all classes of society, every mature and self-sufficient citizen—may, in some way or another, consider themselves to possess a voice in public affairs.

Kanzow offered the American republic as the prime example of such an ideal, with its strong public spirit, controls over elected public officials, and opportunities open to natural talent, which accounted for "the country's incredible progress in education and industry, to a broader freedom and prosperity among the lower classes, to the suppression of prejudices and arrogance, and ultimately to the forming of middle-class values, morality, that is, the moral element in society." "Such, in many respects," he added, "is the situation in our neighboring kingdom, Norway." As will be seen again, parallels between Norway and the United States came readily to mind in these years.

A weighty rejoinder came from Emil von Troil. In Norway, he pointed out, Storting representatives were not elected directly but rather by electors, one for each two hundred voters in towns and one for every one thousand in the country, since it was assumed that in the towns "there was a greater number of enlightened men than in the countryside." If common elections should be held in Sweden, he went on, "the peasant estate would be 27 times larger than the other estates taken together. I hold the greatest respect for that estate and believe it is necessary for it to comprise a part of the representation, but I would consider it neither beneficial nor reassuring for [our] independence and well-being to have a representation in which 97 to 98 percent were peasants." He feared that such a legislature could "easily be mislead by some cunning popular leader, whether a demagogue from the mob, who seeks to stir up rebellion to satisfy his ambitions, or a demagogue on the throne, who strives to lure from the people their freedom." Conditions in America were altogether different, he maintained, with no need to keep constant watch on a head of state who was elected for only four years at a time and where the separate states would surely rebel at the first sign of a coup by the central government.[41]

Lively discussion of constitutional reform continued, following the Riksdag of 1834–35, especially in the more radical papers, becoming particularly intense by the end of the decade with the approach of the next Riksdag. This is well illustrated by a number of articles in *Aftonbladet* during 1839. An unsigned report on 28 May told of Carl XIV Johan's recent visit to Christiania where the inhabitants, while showing all due respect for the monarch, celebrated 17 May and their free constitution. Under another form of government, the article commented, such a manifestation would be unthinkable, and an absolute ruler would impose his will by force. The anonymous author—most likely the editor Lars Johan Hierta himself—expressed admiration for the Norwegians' solidarity in upholding their constitution and invited comparison with the situation in Sweden:

> In Norway there is no *court* with all its hangers-on, no arrogant and impoverished *nobility* which must live at the state's expense and which thus, when it supports a royal proposal engages in a life-and-death struggle for its own bread, no *church* endowed with political power and dependent upon the court, no guildlike division of the state's present inhabitants into *estates*, so vulnerable to outside influences in their deliberations over the affairs of state.

Unlike in Norway, the writer concluded, any proposal for useful reform in Sweden was bound to be stifled by selfish corporate interests.

> *We* will require much struggle and travail to reach the point where the Norwegians were already a quarter-century ago. They needed only to *create*; our longest and hardest task will be to *clear away*, and this involves not only a multitude of harmful institutions but even more old prejudices, customs, corporate demands, superstitious fear of our fellow men, political apprehensions, childish fright, in a word an old sour dough inherited from a form of government that has been *éminemment monarchique*, despite all that has been *said* about freedom.

An unsigned article in the same journal dated 1 August 1839 again admired the Norwegians' lack of an encumbering "Old Regime":

> *Norway* is not blessed with a caste, of whom it may be said *par préférence* that "it has learned nothing and forgotten nothing," and Norway can thus *quickly* come to enjoy reforms once decided upon, whereas we, once they are decided and passed, must fight the same fight all over again if we wish to see *any* result of these decisions. Words and promises are easily bandied about, but simply attempt to demand their fulfillment and you are branded as a revolutionary! Thus it is stipulated and promised in the constitution that the offices of state, both high and low, shall be filled on the basis of the highest qualifications and skill, without regard to birth or estate. Norwegians and other foreigners must thus imagine that those who hold the highest positions in the state are the pick of Sweden's enlightenment, talent, and honor; and they must likewise imagine that these qualities are to be found almost exclusively among the high nobility!

Returning from a visit to Norway that year, C. H. Anckarsvärd came out on 10 August with a lengthy letter in *Aftonbladet* reconfirming his admiration for the Norwegian system of government, comparing the Storting's efficiency with the Riksdag's weakness and ineptitude, and pointedly praising the sober and responsible behavior of the Storting's peasant members. He still saw no reason to change the reform proposal he and Richert had presented nine years earlier.

> A unicameral system is also in my view the only just and suitable one. Norway has proven this in practice, and if any people has reason to honor its nationality, it is indisputably the Norwegians. Praise be to the Men of Eidsvoll as authors of the Norwegian constitution of the 17th of May! Would to God that Sweden had something similar! Praise be to Norway, which, through the constitution of the 17th of May has sheltered freedom, put to

flight almost everywhere in Europe, from whence she, hardened in the cold North, shall one day go forth throughout the world, to bring light to all peoples, at which time I hope she will even seriously seek a dwelling among us.

Both manifestations of the peasant awakening in Norway—political mobilization and emigration—aroused serious concerns among the elite classes in Sweden as well as in Norway. Richert, Anckarsvärd, and their following among the Swedish liberals had based their ideal of Norwegian political behavior upon the Storting elections from 1814 through the end of the 1820s, when the peasantry, as then seemed right and natural, had accepted the political leadership of the elite and elected a majority of public officials to represent them. Heartened by what they observed, Swedish liberals were encouraged to believe that common elections in Sweden as well would send educated and enlightened men to the Riksdag rather than an ignorant and tyrannical "peasant regime." With the political awakening of the Norwegian peasantry and their greatly increased representation and class-bound objectives at the Stortings of 1832 and 1836, liberals in Sweden, as well as in Norway, began to have some afterthoughts.[42]

It thus seemed all the more urgent to those who kept the faith to demonstrate by the end of the 1830s, in anticipation of approaching elections for the Riksdag of 1840–41, that the peasant representatives in the Storting had behaved soberly, moderately, and responsibly. An account in *Aftonbladet* on 1 August 1839 of Anckarsvärd's and Richert's recent visit to Christiania stressed in particular that they there had found "no trace of any ill-will toward the Swedes or any 'peasant rule,' or any signs of raw behavior in the Storting, as we have heard various enemies of the Norwegians claim; they have on the contrary found that all, with whom they spoke, consider the assembled representatives to be the core of the most enlightened and respected element in the land, which is just what one ought to seek in a [national] representation." In his own letter of 10 August to *Aftonbladet*, Anckarsvärd held that "the Norwegian cultivator or peasant fully justifies his place in the Storting, where he is in a position to receive from those possessing greater enlightenment needful guidance for his judgment in such matters as otherwise might leave him confused."

Representational reform became the burning issue at the Riksdag of 1840–41. Interest in Norway's constitution now reached its high-water mark. The three elected estates had meanwhile admitted representatives of certain categories of the "non-noble persons of quality." In 1828, the secular faculties of the universities of Uppsala and Lund and the non-noble members of the Academy

of Science had been allotted two places each in the Clerical Estate. At the
Riksdag of 1828–30, the iron-masters *(bruksägare)* of non-noble status had
been granted five places in the Burgher Estate. A considerably larger group,
the non-noble owners of former manorial tenancies *(frälsehemmansägare)*
had been made eligible for election to the Peasant Estate at the last Riksdag,
in 1835. While the total numbers were not great, the new elements represented
considerable wealth, learning, and experience and were in general strongly
committed to liberal reforms. Significantly, they now provided several of the
most able spokesmen for representational reform, including the Uppsala historian Erik Gustaf Geijer, the iron-masters Carl Fredrik Wærn and Johan
Teodor Petré, and the landowners Fredrik von Zweibergk and Per Sahlström.
Further liberalization of the same kind would add to the liberal forces leading up to the final demise of the old estate system in 1866.[43]

The representation issue appears repeatedly in the protocols of the different
estates and in the press during the Riksdag of 1840–41. C. H. Anckarsvärd, at
the height of his political power, chaired the constitutional committee, which
facing the issue head-on, presented a motion for common elections to be held
in large districts even more radical than the proposal he and J. G. Richert had
written ten years earlier, in 1830. It likewise recommended that in restructuring its Riksdag, Sweden adopt Norway's "middle way," which combined the
advantages of unicameralism with "at least one of bicameralism's, namely the
restraint of overly hasty decisions." In justifying these fundamental changes,
the committee pointed to the particular relevance of the Norwegian model
as suited to a brother nation whose "true strength," as in Sweden, lay in its
peasantry."[44]

Over the past decade, the Swedish peasantry had been inspired and
encouraged by the growing power of their brethren in the Storting, and strong
support was expressed in the Peasant Estate for representational reform based
on the Norwegian model. "In thus uniting the presently fragmented elements
of society," J. F. Dahllöf maintained, "our dear Fatherland would become as
fortunate as our brother kingdom, Norway." Per Hansson, who came from the
border province of Värmland, waxed enthusiastic over the remarkable rise in
prosperity among the peasants in Norway, "that poverty-ridden land," thanks
to its wise constitution.

If Norway' inhabitants, who now most resemble us Swedes in language,
customs, and way of life, and who inhabit the same peninsula as we,
although with a harder climate and less fertile soil, have been able to establish a fundamental law that leaves them free hands to adopt a wise
economy, which has had such an effect upon the country's prosperity,

should not we then, who are a people united with them, follow their norm rather than the examples of the constitutions of foreign countries, where conditions are altogether different than among us poor dwellers in the North, when it is a question of changing our form of representation?[45]

Per Sahlström also urged reform on the Norwegian model, "because this would in a constitutional sense bind us more closely to our brothers, the Norwegians, whose truly independent national life, ever since its beginning, we have warmly admired," and he warned that if their form of representation were not "grafted onto our system of government, this would cost us for all time all the possible and reasonable advantages of the union." Dahllöf went further. Fears had been expressed over the perils that might arise if changes were made. "I believe on the contrary," he stated, "that the danger would be great if this highly urgent change were not made. History shows us sufficient examples where, when the voice of nations was not heard and their rights were withheld from them, they have seized by force what was not freely given them." He compared in this respect the French Revolutions of 1789 and 1830 with the British Reform Bill of 1832.[46]

Fredrik von Zweibergk read a petition from the peasant voters in his district calling for a unicameral legislature "like Norway's," which gave some intimation of what might follow the election of a peasant majority. This included demands that state councilors who advised measures contrary to the constitution be dismissed, that no new appropriations be approved, and that "on the contrary," all appropriations be abolished or at least reduced by two-thirds, that all possible economies be made in government expenditures, that the military establishment and diplomatic corps be reduced, and that "all unnecessary court appointments and offices" be abolished.[47]

Sven Heurlin enthusiastically praised "Norway's constitution—that masterwork," which, he claimed with considerable overstatement, "is admired by all foreign powers." He declared himself prepared to face opposition within his own estate with "the Norwegian constitution in one hand and in the other a list of all the blessings it has conferred upon our brother-kingdom," and he was convinced that the outcome would be the same as when "Luther fought against the Popish superstitions."[48]

As in 1834, certain peasant representatives still remained fearful that the loss of an estate of their own would deprive them of any guaranteed voice in the political process. Måns Jönsson, for instance, complained in this vein of the rudeness and contempt with which "a peasant, who is and does not wish to be anything but a peasant, and who considers it his highest honor to be a peasant," was treated by members of the other estates. In particular, he was indignant over those in the Riksdag who "with liberal phrases on their tongues . . . seem to wish to reserve the right to express themselves for themselves alone." "In happy Norway," he added, "the peasantry presently sighs under heavy oppression by the official class and large numbers abandon their father's soil to seek their living in other lands. From such good fortune I pray that God will spare our peasantry!" By then, however, the majority in the Peasant Estate were prepared to accept a reform that would sacrifice their own secure estate to bring about the redress of their specific, concrete grievances.[49]

Admiration for the Norwegian model was strong in the Burgher Estate. Johan Teodor Petré, proprietor of Sweden's largest iron works, who was particularly opposed to the clergy's separate representation in the Riksdag, complained that the numerous critics of the Norway's constitution had not allowed themselves the benefit of a close examination. "They generally declare, purely and simply, that what is suitable for Norway is altogether inappropriate for Sweden. And inquiry ends at that point." They failed, moreover, to consider "the political importance of strengthening the [Swedish-Norwegian] union with similar forms of government." H. D. Helsingius held that the Norwegians had wisely taken to heart that "most of Sweden's national misfortunes had in large part derived from Sweden's aristocracy." This lesson he considered to be reflected in their constitution, which established "a fully democratic constitutional monarchy, with the two classes mixed together [in the Storting], or if you will, reinforced with teachers of religion and public officials."[50]

The iron-master Carl Fredrik Wærn delivered an impassioned argument for representational reform on the Norwegian model. He praised the Norwegians' staunch loyalty to their form of government and continued, "a constitution that is loved with such enthusiasm is that which the [Riksdag's] Constitutional Committee has taken as its pattern." He spoke of "how easily Norway's machinery of government moves and the golden harvests, sprung from the seeds of freedom, [which this] has brought, even in a material sense, to that people who are united with us." He pointed in contrast to the lack of support for the constitution in Sweden. The comparison, he held, would continue to arise at every Riksdag:

> The aristocratic element among us will be shaken to its foundations, while one would sooner be able to uproot the Norwegian people than deprive them of that freedom, which is the highest goal for the strivings of the civilized nations. . . . I should not be misunderstood as desiring any amalgamation between the [two] peoples. No, I consider it highly fortunate that

Freedom's genius can find a special asylum among the mountains of Norway, if ever she should be abandoned by [our] thoughtless descendants or driven out by force. Soon she would be seen again upon the bordering mountains and Svea would once again call her to her motherly bosom.[51]

Petré thereafter argued against in any way compromising the reform proposal and urged, "Let us rather follow Herr *Wærn's* advice, 'neither to despise the common folk nor to fear the powerful.' If Norway's . . . beautiful and rational system of representation only has time to become rooted in the hearts of the Swedish people, the so-called 'Norwegian craze' will no longer be branded as un-Swedish and the Constitutional Committee's proposal for restructuring will be warmly embraced by the true friends of the fatherland."[52]

The reform proposal had ardent supporters in the Noble Estate as well. Arguing against the alternative of a truly bicameral system, Nils Rudolph Munck af Rosenschöld declared that this would mean the people's representatives had "sanctioned their own impotence, [for] a bicameral system is . . . not only the symbol of discord but rather discord itself." More important, he too held that a system like Norway's would clear the way for a closer union of the northern kingdoms, like the German Confederation, eventually even including Denmark, and that this would be altogether natural for "children of the same house." "The time, I presume, is already past," he declared, "when peoples were slaves subject to the whims of rulers, when only a word from them was needed to turn peoples sympathetic toward each other into the bitterest of enemies."

The young Carl Axel Mannerskantz, attending his first Riksdag, had "now seen this many-headed Hydra at close quarters," convincing him all the more of the need for a unicameral legislature as the only cure for the "paralysis" into which Sweden had fallen. The open and concealed enemies of reform, he warned, must realize that "for all their wrongly applied, so-called historical theories, the Swedish people will rise up en masse for what it now aspires to, regardless of what it aspired to centuries ago, for this people, long mired in indifference, has now awakened to full consciousness. It will no longer be leashed, [but] is determined vigilantly to uphold its most sacred rights."[53]

If Norway provided the shining ideal of the more radical proponents of representational reform, it was the counterideal of its conservative opponents. The more moderate among them were often prepared to recognize that the Eidsvoll constitution was well suited to actual conditions in the new Norwegian kingdom but emphatically denied its relevance for Sweden, an ancient monarchy with a complex society and proud traditions from the past. In the Noble Estate, Baron Mauritz Klingspor, for instance, declared:

No warm friend of freedom can fail to admire the Norwegians' calm but determined and uncompromising constitutional stance, no one [can] be blind to their country's constant material advancement. But even fully recognizing this and accepting that the Norwegian institutions are excellent for Norway, nothing more than geographical proximity speaks for their adoption in Sweden. It is truly remarkable how two nations, living under the same sky, sharing the same occupations, can be so different from each other in customs, manners, and way of life. The reasons are to be found in their political antecedents.

As Norway had long had no powerful nobility, resident monarch, or court, there was, Klingspor claimed, "now hardly any greater similarity between the Swede and the Norwegian than between the Englishman and the Neapolitan." "Since the Norwegians can scarcely be persuaded to accept Swedish institutions," he went on, "many consider it necessary [for us] to adopt theirs as the only way to bring about an amalgamation of the two nations." Klingspor insisted, however, that a healthy relationship between the two peoples was best assured by "preserving the institutions that best correspond to the differing national types. Thus now and in the future the union between them ought to be federative only."

Gustaf Nordenskiöld meanwhile held that the liberals' unbounded admiration for a unicameral system was based on a mere quarter-century's experience in Norway under particularly favorable circumstances, and above all, that Sweden, compelled by its geographical position to bear the heaviest burden for the common defense, stood as a "protective wall" for Norway.

More vehement in his opposition to change, Gustaf Herman Ehrenhoff saw the constitutional committee's proposal as a monstrous attempt by a "liberal tyranny" to deprive the nobility of its indispensable, independent political role. The hunt was on, and "we should be on our guard, for the hunters have supporters within these walls"—that is, within the Noble Estate itself. "Have we ceased to be part of the Swedish nation? This is undoubtedly how they wish to regard our existence, for we are in the way. . . . And if we succumb to this fearful outcry, the day will come when the 'liberated,' on behalf of the nation, will demand our fortunes and forbid us to tread the soil that our forefathers' lives and blood have consecrated. . . . No, gentlemen! It is now the duty of the Noble Estate not to give way to the unrest of the times."[54]

Outside the Riksdag, the conservative newspaper *Minerva* was particularly acerbic toward the Norwegians, especially the peasants, considering them a hive of Jacobins and ridiculing their constitution. "If in the midst of that chaotic night some star revealed itself on the firmament, [if] some evidence of reason, good sense, and objectivity could be discovered amid that formless mass of wild ignorance, it would be in the nature of things that we should draw attention to it."[55]

Svenska Bondens Tidning, a paper directed toward peasant readers, had in its turn denounced on 4 August 1836 efforts by Swedish conservatives to arouse dissension between Swedes and Norwegians in hopes of discrediting projects for constitutional reform.

> Such attempts are to be discovered particularly among those who have long sought to mislead us Swedes into believing that we, in direct opposition to the traditions of our fathers, ought to hate a manly, independent people and should rather dress ourselves in the long caftans of the East [i.e., autocratic Russia], under which one curtsies as easily as one bows! What would these gown-peddlers, who connive between the Caftans [Russians] and the Blue Jackets [Swedes], rather see than disunity between Sweden and Norway?[56]

Despite a compromise attempt to revise the constitutional committee's proposal by introducing somewhat more restrictive voting requirements, only the Peasant Estate voted in favor of it. The Noble, Clerical, and Burgher Estates meanwhile voted to table the matter until the following Riksdag.[57]

It is interesting to see how both liberals and conservatives in this debate pointed to parallels—positive or negative, as the case might be—between Norway and America. "I draw the honorable speaker's attention to Norway," Dahllöf declared in the Peasant Estate in October 1840, "where, according to the unanimous opinion of objective observers, the peasants are far superior to those in Sweden, regarding both education and prosperity. Attention has also been called to the United States of North America and the situation there in 1838. It is known, however, that the situation of the farmers in North America is especially fortunate and that the Swedish peasantry, compared with them, are to be pitied in more ways than one."

When another speaker in the same estate pointed to widespread corruption in the American elections of 1838 by an "aristocracy of wealth," Sven Heurlin denied that such a thing should be possible in Sweden. The conservative Måns Jönsson meanwhile warned that the merging of peasants into a commonly elected legislature would result in something like the tumultuous proceedings in "American congresses." In the Noble Estate, Gustaf Nordenskiöld held that election of Riksdag members by province *(län)* would resemble the American system and would promote local particularism. This was not a problem in America, he held, because the separate states existed before they formed their union and because a strong central government was unnecessary there since neighboring Mexico and Canada did not threaten its existence. L. J. Hierta's *Aftonbladet,* which throughout this period was outspokenly enthusiastic about Norway, was no less outspoken in its admiration for the American republic.[58]

The examples given here should demonstrate the powerful impact of Norway and its constitution during the 1830s and early 1840s upon Swedish political debate. Many more such examples could doubtless be mined from the dozens of stout volumes of Riksdag protocols for each of the four estates, as well as from the back files of the newspapers during those years. By that time, most politically involved Swedes recognized the need to reform their archaic system of representation in the Riksdag, but opinion was much divided as to what should take its place. While the radicals, especially in the Peasant Estate, warmly espoused the Norwegian system with at best little modification, most tended to prefer some type of truly bicameral system with separate elections based on differing but relatively high voting qualifications for an upper and a lower house, whether on the British, French, or American model. Die-hard conservatives meanwhile held out for the preservation of the existing system.

As time passed, international, as opposed to Norwegian, influences gained increasing weight in the ongoing debate over representational reform.[59] The essential, underlying question was how to create a uniform and equitable system that would still protect the rights and interests of the wealthy, educated, and socially prominent elements of society. This was the basic dilemma facing both liberals and conservatives throughout the Western world during the "long nineteenth century."

Already by the mid-1830s, some Swedish liberals who had initially admired Norway began to feel apprehensive over the rising power and populist political objectives of the peasants in the Storting. The smaller and more moderate peasant contingent at the Storting of 1839 allayed some of this anxiety, but by the Storting of 1845, the peasant representatives had become both more numerous and more assertive. The impact becomes increasingly evident at the Swedish Riksdag of 1845, which as before failed to enact representational reform.

By the mid-1840s, the split between the peasantry and the elite in Norway was becoming ever more acute. Swedish visitors to Norway were sobered by the bitter complaints they heard from Norwegian officials against the peasants in the Storting. O. I. Fåhræus, who was with Oscar I's entourage in Christiania in February 1845, wrote to his brother, "Norway's [system of] representation is here the object of bitter complaints by all reasonable people, who in perspective foresee grave national calamities as its results; but the peasants persist, as they do with us, since they have—for good or evil—gotten a taste for the tree of knowledge." "Whoever has had the honor of making the Storting's closer acquaintance," Henning Hamilton, another member of the entourage, wrote to a friend in March 1845, "and seen with what contempt this legislative assembly is held by all the more cultivated persons in this coun-try, is not especially tempted to hasten the reform of [Sweden's] system of rep-resentation." The former Norwegian state councilor Severin Løvenskiold wrote at this time to the king that "intelligence and fortune now seek the pro-tection of the crown, which is supported by these important elements of bour-geois society." In the same spirit, the prominent Norwegian jurist Bernhard Dunker wrote that "the enlightened part of the nation cannot recognize the national assembly [i.e., the Storting] as its representative."[60]

Swedish liberals were meanwhile taken aback by Norwegian peasant oppo-sition to liberal as well as to conservative ideas and by expressions of offensive national egotism in Norway. W. F. Dalman, who admired the Norwegian constitution and saw in it needed support for the advance of liberalism in Sweden, pointed out sharply that Norway had Carl XIV Johan to thank for its freedom, since he could have refused it, but that it would be too much for Norway to expect full equality within the union. "And it ought certainly to mean more in a national sense to be a Swede than a Norwegian. Read his-tory! On what page does one not find the Swedish name—where other than in the sagas does one find the Norwegian? What did Norwegian national 'feel-ing' amount to under the Kalmar Union? What did they do when Gustaf Vasa liberated Sweden?" In 1845 and 1846, L. J. Hierta in *Aftonbladet* considered the American constitution preferable to the Norwegian, although he still con-sidered the latter more practicable for Sweden.[61]

In 1844, Carl XIV Johan died and was succeeded by his son, Oscar I, who was initially liberal in his views and was understood to favor representational reform. Events, both in his own kingdoms and elsewhere in Europe over the next few years, however, turned both him and much of Swedish and Nor-wegian opinion in an increasingly conservative direction. The European rev-olutions of 1848–49 caused widespread alarm in the North, especially following rioting in Stockholm on 18–19 March 1848 that took several lives and that was inspired by the February revolution in Paris.

In 1847, a small working-class socialist organization, *Skandinaviska Säll-skapet*, appeared in Stockholm with the bookseller Pär Götrek as its leading figure. It espoused ideals drawn from Étienne Cabet, as well as from Karl Marx and Friedrich Engels, whose *Communist Manifesto* Götrek translated into Swedish in 1848. In April 1848, the society petitioned the king to grant the vote to workers. A far larger workers' movement, including landless farm laborers, was organized by Marcus Thrane in Norway in late 1848 and reached its height by 1850. Thrane was imprisoned in 1851, released in 1858, and emigrated to America in 1863.[62]

European events in 1848 meanwhile also increased liberal demands for Riksdag reform. Realizing that at least some appearance of concession was necessary, Oscar I and his ministers presented a royal proposal to the Riksdag held that year for a markedly conservative representational reform, counting on its rejection by the Peasant Estate at the following Riksdag, as indeed was the case in 1851. In 1854, the conservative Carl von Hartmansdorff came up with a voluminous proposal for parliamentary and governmental reorganization, which likewise led nowhere. By that date, the question of representational reform had dominated the political agenda for some twenty years, during which over fifty proposals had been made in the Riksdag without result. Over the next decade, the matter rested as attention turned to other national concerns.[63]

The views of outside observers regarding Sweden and Norway add further perspective to their political interaction during the earlier decades of the union. The United States first established a diplomatic presence in Stockholm in 1814, but its representation was sporadic up to 1854. Their reports show the first American envoys to have been largely ignorant of Norway and the nature of its union with Sweden, but by the 1840s, they reveal an increasing awareness of the two kingdoms, the differences between them, and the Norwegian inspiration to the Swedish liberals. After the Riksdag's rejection of the royal reform proposal in 1851 and the onset of the Crimean War in 1853, the envoys' interest tended to turn to other matters. Coming from a young republic with a constitution and a society widely considered to resemble the new Norwegian nation, the American diplomats not surprisingly tended to show a warm appreciation for Norway and a more reserved attitude toward Sweden, surely deriving largely from Swedish liberals with whom they associated.

Already in March 1827, John Appleton, following J. G. Richert's return from Christiania, had reported to Washington how "under the influence of free institutions and a liberal Government, all the elements of public prosperity [in Norway] are acquiring daily more life and expansion." In February 1845, George Lay described Norway's political advantages of having neither nobility nor an absolute royal veto and its economic benefits under a free regime, which had promoted a much more vigorous recovery since 1814 than had occurred in Sweden. "The commercial and lower classes [in Sweden]," his successor, Henry Ellsworth, wrote the same month, "are continually excited by the comparison of their unhappy situation with that of their Norwegian neighbors, who are prosperous beneath the care of a mild and indeed almost republican Government."

In August 1850, Francis Schroeder found representational reform the "all absorbing point of interest" in Sweden, but he now judged its prospects to be dimmer than they had been three years earlier. In November that year, he wrote of the "wretched character of the Swedish representation," which surely could not last, due to the connection with Norway. "The progress of the world," he went on, "is no longer a secret in the forests and along the distant lakes of Sweden. In the furthest recesses a light has penetrated. The tardy Swede beholds with envy the growth and thrift of his Norwegian brother, and the germ of enlightened liberty, native to the heart, must sooner or later mature, for at last it has nourishment." When in January 1851 the defeat of the royal proposal was clear, Schroeder reported:

> The Swedish jealousy of the liberal institutions of the sister kingdom is exceedingly marked. The two nations are so dissimilar in political creed and prejudices that an embittered feeling on the part of the Swedes I believe to be increasing. Norway is destined to have effective influence in the affairs of Sweden, and attempts on the part of the Norwegians at this time for yet more freedom than they already possess, are viewed in this country in the worst light and with positive anxiety.

By September 1851, Schroeder commented wearily, "No great reform of any kind can in fact be hoped for in Sweden which shall originate within its own borders." After Louis-Napoleon Bonaparte's coup d'état in France in December 1851, Schroeder saw Norway as the only remaining inspiration to reform in Sweden: "But for the union with Norway, Sweden would seem destined to be among the last holds in Europe of a well-nigh arbitrary rule. The enlightened constitution of Norway, sustained there by the prevalence of almost republican feeling, may be in the connection with this country, perhaps the best counterpoise that shall remain to Sweden against a Russian influence that enters much into the councils of the Government." Had Carl XIV Johan succeeded in overcoming the resistance of the Storting and the Norwegian people to changing their constitution, he added, this "would have undermined the best hope that now appears to remain to Sweden—that which is built upon the existing character of the Union."[64]

Three foreign travelers—a Scot and two Americans—likewise provide insights into the Dual Kingdom. Perhaps the most celebrated and controversial outside observer in the region during the earlier nineteenth century was the Scotsman Samuel Laing, a staunch doctrinaire liberal who lived in Norway between 1834 and 1836. After publishing a warmly enthusiastic account of that country, its inhabitants, and its form of government, he visited Sweden for a few months in the summer of 1838, providing the basis for his far more critical volume, much of which was devoted to unfavorable comparisons with Norway.[65]

The Norwegians, in Laing's view, presented to the philosopher "the singular spectacle of a nation emerging suddenly from under the hand of an uncontrolled and absolute sovereign power, with their civil liberties and social arrangements so well adapted to their condition, and so well secured by their ancient laws, that the transition from despotism to democracy was unmarked by any convulsion, or revolutionary movement, or important changes in the state of society or property." Remarkably, they alone, in their constitution, had achieved in practice the high ideals of the French Revolution. The basis of Norwegian liberty and equality Laing saw in what he considered an essentially even distribution of property, more even indeed than in many parts of the United States. "If there be a happy class of people in Europe," he wrote, "it is the Norwegian bonder [*bonde*, or peasant farmer]. He is the owner of his little estate, has no feudal duty or feudal service to pay to any superior. He is the king of his own land, and landlord as well as king."[66]

Anticipating conservative skepticism, Laing was at pains to point out that there was no lack of respect between social classes in Norway—at the very time when in fact deep fissures were becoming ever more evident between the elite and the peasantry—yet, it enjoyed "a much more democratical body politic than that of the United States." Of the ninety-six members of the Storting of 1836, he maintained, there were nearly sixty "who from their professions, must have enjoyed the best education which the country affords, and must be among its most able men," while only thirty-seven (obviously peasants) "may be presumed from their occupation, not to have the habits of business, although they are likely to possess great natural talents and judgments."[67]

The Norwegians proved meanwhile, according to Laing, that "a press as free as that of the United States, may exist without scurrility or brutal violation of the sanctity of private life. Such newspapers as the American people read would not find editors in this country." Articles freely printed in Norway would incur censorship and prosecution in Sweden.[68]

In sum, wrote Laing, "Sweden is still under its ancient regime; while Norway is practically in advance of the age in the enjoyment of institutions favourable to political liberty." Sweden's desire to amalgamate Norway was, in Laing's opinion, largely motivated by the needs of its numerous nobility "for an office or function yielding a subsistence suitable to their rank," a need made more pressing by the loss of Finland. If the Swedes meanwhile had little understanding of Norway, it was in part because so few of them traveled there in comparison to the numerous visitors from Britain and Germany. He claimed to have encountered only two "Swedish travellers of the higher class," while Swedes of the lower classes had much more direct contact with Norway.[69]

"Sweden," Laing wrote in his account of that country, "with her splendid court, and her numerous and powerful nobility and clergy, forming distinct orders in her social structure, and distinct legislative bodies in her constitution, must present a curious contrast to the simple and democratic Norway." Here, he noted greater poverty in both town and countryside, despite Sweden's having a larger population and greater resources than Norway. There were many signs of rural poverty, while Stockholm, despite its striking natural beauty, appeared run-down and dilapidated. Laing found little opulence. Even most of the nobility were poor, "living from civil or military employments with small pay; or on their farms in great obscurity and poverty." For the common people, poverty meant "absolute destitution." On reentering Norway, he immediately found far greater comfort and prosperity.[70]

The root cause for this paradoxical contrast Laing found in the unequal distribution of property in Sweden. As in most of Continental Europe, this still consisted not only of "land and the products of industry," as in Britain, but also of legal corporate privileges and monopolies. Under such a system, "the exercise of industry is property as well as its produce." This amounted to nothing less than an "appropriation by a part of the community, of what we in our social state consider the common right of every individual to the free exercise of his own industry." In Sweden, the privileged included not only the hereditary aristocracy, officers, and members of professions "but the tailor, the shoemaker, the smith . . . in short, every man exercising any craft, trade, branch of industry, or means of living." From this, it followed that "the constitution and civil rights of the nation mean here the right of corporate bodies to meet in a legislative assembly without reference to the mass of the community, on whom they prey."[71]

Laing went to great lengths to demonstrate—on the basis of official Swedish statistics—"the singular and embarrassing fact, that the Swedish nation, isolated from the mass of the European people, and almost entirely agricultural or pastoral . . . is, notwithstanding, in a more demoralised state than any nation in Europe." In support of this claim, he reported high levels of criminality and illegitimate births.[72] This moral depravity ultimately resulted, in his view, from "the great pressure of the upper privileged classes upon the time, labour, and property of the lower; in the servile condition, in a word, of the mass of the population. . . . It is clearly no defect in the physical condition of the Swedish people that produces this extraordinary moral state. It is a defect in their civil and political condition." It was the result of "bad government, bad legislation, bad social arrangements." "The people of the noblest character in modern history, who have made the greatest sacrifices for religious and civil liberties," Laing soberly observed, "are now far behind the rest of Europe in institutions and government suitable to their intelligence as individuals. If Gustavus Vasa were to rise from the dead, he would not recognise a modern Swede in spirit or character."[73]

At the top of this corrupted and impoverished nation, wrote Laing, "a knot of old nobility, a century behind the age they live in, and unable to appreciate the importance of public opinion in these times, surround the King, and advise measures more suited to the court of France before the revolution, than to the nineteenth century." The government meanwhile strove to control opinion through press censorship, which was in theory free under the constitution but in fact constrained by the "temporary" emergency measure of 1812. Hierta's *Aftonbladet*, Sweden's leading liberal newspaper, had been suppressed no less than twenty-four times but constantly reappeared under slightly changed titles; at present, it appeared as the "Twenty-Fifth Aftonblad."[74]

King Carl XIV Johan, Laing claimed, was highly unpopular in Sweden, while he enjoyed the staunch loyalty of his Norwegian subjects, who identified him with what they valued most, "their constitutional and national independence." Despite the reactionary advice of the Swedish aristocratic cabal, he had shown good sense in avoiding outright conflict with Norway. Laing thus made the provocative proposal that Carl Johan relinquish Sweden to Prince Gustaf of Vasa, son of the deposed Gustaf IV Adolf and legitimate heir to its throne, while retaining Norway for himself. In the face of so much opposition, "the Bernadotte dynasty can scarcely hope to hold both crowns." "The total independence of Norway and of her means of defense, and their total separation from Swedish interests, objects, or intrigues," he concluded, "appear in this view the true policy of the European powers."[75]

Laing's books received widespread press coverage in Britain, where there were strong sympathies for Norway. But they did not go unanswered. In 1840, Count Magnus Björnstjerna, the Swedish-Norwegian minister to Great

Britain, brought out an anonymous booklet in English defending Sweden and the union against Laing's criticisms. His arguments provide an illuminating presentation of the Swedish conservatives' political philosophy of the time, just as Laing gives a classic statement of the ideas of contemporary liberalism. Laing's true purpose, Björnstjerna wrote, was to espouse the cause of democracy against aristocracy. "He has devoted his pen to this social movement, which, after accomplishing the destruction of feudalism, and conquering kings, will most assuredly not be restrained in its march either by the middle classes or by the rich." He was thus one of the "thousand instruments of destruction, sapping on all sides the foundations of the social edifice."[76]

Björnstjerna argued that the Norwegian Odelting was not a true upper house. Being elected by the total membership of the Storting, it was powerless to act independently and thus to protect the nation against the "greatest misfortunes." World history, he wrote, "confirms in its every page that a national representation, formed in *one* democratical chamber, will, besides its frequent mistakes, always be *despotic*, and will, by its single position against royalty, get into *conflict* with it, which must necessarily lead either to *absolutism*, or, what is still worse, to *anarchy*." He cited various political philosophers from Aristotle to François Guizot and Alexis de Tocqueville to prove his point.[77]

As Laing attributed Norway's well-being to its broad property distribution, Björnstjerna produced figures to show that property was even more widely distributed in Sweden.[78] Norway's admitted prosperity derived, he maintained, not from its form of government but from its union with Sweden, which bore the expenses of defense and of the court. Whereas Norway had for five centuries been a "mere *province* of Denmark," in union with Sweden it had become an "independent kingdom." Its grievances were "trifling" compared with the immense benefits of the union. The two kingdoms, he continued, "have everything requisite to confirm their union. . . . England and Scotland were under the same kings during a *century* before their union took place; it is not more than a *quarter* of a century since Sweden and Norway made this first step, and we hope it will also be conducive to a future closer union between the two nations for the prosperity and benefit of both."[79]

On statistical grounds, Björnstjerna took up the cudgels against Laing's allegations of Sweden's moral depravity, producing figures to demonstrate that crime and promiscuity were not more prevalent there than in other European lands—including Norway.[80] He defended the Swedish nobility, in a land that had never known true feudalism and where the peasantry had always remained free, and he held that while the nobles were powerful, they had always been the defenders of Swedish liberty.[81]

If all was admittedly not what it should be in Sweden, Björnstjerna claimed, this was due to its government now being *too* democratic. The constitution of 1809, which raised the Peasant Estate to full equality with the others, had replaced a "limited *aristocracy*" with an "almost illimited *democracy*." Laing had held that "democracy is not sufficiently developed in Sweden," Björnstjerna wrote. "But if we are unfortunate enough to have Mr. Laing against us, we happily have the history of mankind for us." Arguing the "decline of morality by the increase of democracy," he gave as examples Britain after the First Reform Bill, France, and worst of all, the United States, where lynch law and anarchy reigned. Sweden was an old civilized country, whereas Norway resembled America, "issued quite fresh from Nature's bosom."[82] He concluded by ridiculing Laing's contention that Sweden should revert to the house of Vasa while Norway remained under the "present dynasty."[83]

Laing immediately responded contemptuously to this anonymous "pamphlet," which he rightly suspected to emanate from official circles in Sweden, and stoutly reiterated his charges against that country and his admiration of Norway. "The practical workings of the legislative machine in the Norwegian constitution," he proclaimed in the third person, "is held my Mr. Laing to be worth all the master-mind nostrums and theories of speculative philosophers, from Aristotle, Bacon, and Jeremy Bentham, down to this pamphleteer." On later occasions, Laing likewise found occasion to criticize Sweden. In retrospect, it would appear that in provoking Laing's counterattacks and the attention this aroused abroad, Count Björnstjerna did more harm than good to Sweden's reputation in his effort to refute the Scotsman.[84]

Two Americans, Charles Loring Brace and Bayard Taylor, visited Sweden and Norway, both in 1857. While their accounts are largely filled with picturesque descriptions of landscape and folklife, they offer some interesting insights into the union. Brace, who previously had written about Germany and Hungary, was a fervent admirer of the Vikings of old, to whom he ultimately attributed "what of good is at this day to be seen in England and America." He meanwhile gives some intimation of the increasingly conservative trend in Scandinavia, as elsewhere, when he compared the comparatively cool reception he now received as an American with the enthusiasm he had encountered in Europe five years earlier.[85]

As a patriotic American with strong democratic sympathies, Brace admired the Norwegian form of government. He nonetheless declared, "Norway has been so thoroughly travelled and described of late years by English tourists, that I have bestowed much less space and investigation on its peculiarities than on those of Sweden, which is yet a somewhat fresh field." In Norway, he met numerous Englishmen, largely wealthy salmon fishermen, who he believed had tended to corrupt the moral character of the Norwegian peasants as they previously had corrupted the Swiss. Some of his more interesting encounters were meanwhile with visiting Norwegians emigrants from America who professed to find Norway discouragingly backward.[86]

Brace regarded the Swedish constitution as awkward and absurd with its four estates, considering that America had trouble enough with its two houses of Congress. Yet, he found the Swedes more interesting and far more genuinely hospitable than the Norwegians. "In no country," he declared, "can a peasantry so independent, honest, and virtuous be found." He was particularly impressed with the peasants of Dalarna province. "Give such an intelligent population as the Dalecarlians, good common schools, and they will be able to accomplish anything. There is excellent stuff in the character of the people." And bestowing his highest praise, he wrote, "The country is the New England of Sweden."[87]

Bayard Taylor, by this time a prolific and popular writer of travel accounts, was highly enthusiastic about Scandinavia and inhabitants. "The Norwegian constitution," he declared, "is in almost all respects as free as that of any American state, and it is cheering to see what material well-being and solid progress has followed its adoption." Yet, he admitted that while he had come to Scandinavia prejudiced in favor of the Norwegians, he had changed his view. Like Brace, he became more kindly disposed toward the Swedish people. "The Swedes," he wrote, "have all the honesty which the Norwegians claim for themselves, more warmth and geniality of character, and less selfish sharpness and shrewdness." The most common Norwegian trait he found to be "an excessive national vanity, which is always on the alert, and fires up on the slightest provocation. Say anything you like, except that Norway in any respect is surpassed by any other country." The Swedes' greatest fault was a strong tendency to depreciate their own country and character. "This habit of detraction is carried to quite as great an extreme as the vanity of the Norwegians, and is the less pardonable vice of the two. . . . The more I see of the Swedes, the more I am convinced there is no kinder, simpler, and honester people in the world."[88]

Looking ahead, the long conflict over representational reform in Sweden would finally end after much heated debate and public controversy when all four estates — as the constitution required — passed the Riksdag Reform Bill in December 1865, which received royal sanction and went into effect in 1866, establishing a fully bicameral system. Each of the two chambers was to be equal in competency and authority, but their members were to be elected separately, according to a complex formula.

The First Chamber, intended to serve as a conservative bulwark, was to be elected indirectly by the twenty-four provincial councils, whose members in turn were elected by more highly taxed persons who cast multiple votes apportioned according to wealth. Only some six thousand men in Sweden could qualify for membership in the First Chamber on the basis of stiff property qualifications, resulting, in Sten Carlsson's view, in an upper house that was "more aristocratic than the Noble Estate itself."

The Second Chamber was to be elected directly by men meeting lower, but still substantial, property qualifications, amounting to some 5 percent of Sweden's total population and around 20 percent of its adult males. This was scarcely an increase from the percentage before the reform, and indeed some eleven thousand freeholders were disenfranchised on the basis of the new property qualifications. In contrast, Stein Kuhnle calculated, as previously noted, that in 1814, 10.3 percent of Norway's total population, or 45.5 percent of its men, had been enfranchised under the Eidsvoll constitution.

The new Swedish system was hardly democratic. Yet, the Riksdag Reform of 1866 is a momentous landmark in Sweden's history. The venerable medieval system at last came to an end. Class replaced caste in the election of its legislature. Democracy would follow in due course.[89]

Carl XIV Johan had sought to cement the union by changing Norway's constitution along conservative lines. The Swedish liberals of the 1830s and 1840s, at the other end of the political spectrum, had argued for a more democratic representation in Sweden in part because they believed that creating a legislature more similar to Norway's would strengthen the union. Although King Carl XV, who succeeded Oscar I in 1859, sanctioned the reform in 1866, he had serious misgivings about this "great leap in the dark," as Benjamin Disraeli would describe the British Second Reform Bill of the following year. Nonetheless, the Norwegian professor Lorenz Dietrichson at the Royal Academy of Art in Stockholm, who was on close terms with the king, claimed in his memoirs that Carl XV told him repeatedly, both at the time and later, "that it was not least concern for Norway, the hope that a more modern constitution in Sweden, more closely related to the Norwegian, would contribute to bringing the peoples closer together in understanding and cooperation, that determined his attitude toward the representation question."[90]

Ultimately, it would be impossible to assay with any real accuracy the impact of Norway and its constitution upon the reform of the Riksdag in Sweden.

Even without the union of the two kingdoms or any influence from across the Keel, the ongoing processes of change would sooner or later have compelled the Swedes to recast their medieval Riksdag in a manner reflecting new economic and social conditions. Both Sweden and Norway, moreover, shared the common heritage of Western political philosophy.

Yet, there can be little question that throughout the debate over constitutional reform in Sweden, and especially during the 1830s and 1840s, Norway was the touchstone before all others. It was first and foremost visions of Norway that inspired the bright hopes of radicals and liberals—and the fears and forebodings of conservatives. That in the end the representational reform of the Riksdag enacted in 1865 was distinctively different and more conservative than Norway's Eidsvoll constitution of 1814 over a half century earlier reflected in high degree a process of testing political ideas against the practical example of Norwegian political life and evaluating their applicability to Sweden's differing circumstances.[91]

It meanwhile seems evident that the relationship to Sweden had its impact upon Norway's political evolution by producing a more democratic franchise and representation to promote national solidarity in time of crisis in 1814 than surely would have come about under more peaceful circumstances. In this way, the Norwegian elite rallied the nation and enjoyed solid support in its determined defense of the constitution against Carl XIV Johan's efforts to change it. But ultimately, common voting rights and the two-thirds majority in the Storting for the rural districts would undermine their status and authority.[92]

Göran B. Nilsson has pointed to effective Norwegian influences in the area of specific practical reforms in Sweden, especially during the period 1840 to 1860 when relations between the two kingdoms were most cordial. The Norwegian law of 1836 establishing communal self-government provided a pattern for similar legislation in Sweden in 1843 and 1862. Poor relief in Norway inspired the Swedish Poor Law of 1871. Abolition of guild monopolies, free trade, toleration of dissenting religious sects, increasing rights for women, penal reform, and a variety of specific administrative reforms all took place first in Norway and thereafter in Sweden. In time, the Norwegian temperance movement, agricultural credit banks, folk high schools, societies for domestic tourism, sports, and much else would inspire similar developments in Sweden. If research on Norway's influence upon Swedish constitutional reform has remained limited, its impact in these more specific administrative, humanitarian, and associational spheres has received less attention still. Much remains to be done in these areas and, we may hope, will in time be done by Swedish and Norwegian scholars.[93]

To be conservative regarding representation in the Riksdag by no means implied opposition to specific practical reforms. Conversely, the illiberal prejudices often revealed by both Norwegian and Swedish peasants confronted old liberals in both countries with a growing dilemma: What was ultimately most important, genuinely representative government or truly enlightened reforms? Indeed, most of the forward-looking measures briefly referred to above were enacted in Sweden before the Riksdag Reform of 1866, largely realizing the program the liberals of the 1830s and 1840s had hoped to make possible through more democratic representation. In 1866, the "last symbol" of the old corporate structure was finally swept away, according to Johan Norberg. But the sequence of reform was unanticipated. "The reform marked the end, rather than the beginning, of a remarkably intense change of system."[94] As was true in Norway during the same period, it was the work of a progressive administrative, commercial, and intellectual elite that over the next two decades or more would become largely eclipsed by the landed magnates and well-to-do farmers who came to dominate, respectively, the Riksdag's upper and lower chambers.

To contemporary Swedes, not least those whose particular interests were affected, pervasive Norwegian influences were surely more evident then than they are now. Faced with a major reorganization in the navy during the 1840s, a Swedish officer complained bitterly about "those damned Norwegians who are supposed to lay down the law for us in everything!"[95]

3

High Noon and Decline
of the Union

B Y MIDCENTURY, direct Norwegian political influences were on the decline in Sweden. Having been strongly inspired by the Norwegian model, Swedish liberals were becoming increasingly convinced that reform of parliamentary representation would have to find a solution corresponding more closely to Swedish realities. Henceforward, the most powerful impulses coming from across the Keel would be cultural. But before these can be considered in context, it is necessary to survey the ongoing vicissitudes of the union down to its demise in 1905, particularly in view of the characteristically close association of culture and politics during the nineteenth century.

The period between 1836, when Carl XIV Johan appointed Herman Wedel-Jarlsberg as the first Norwegian statholder in Christiania, down to around 1880 may be considered the high noon of the union, despite occasional disputes. Improved relations between the two governments were built largely during these years upon a de facto alliance between the Norwegian and Swedish official classes faced with the rise in both kingdoms of what appeared to be alarmingly radical and democratic forces.

Apprehensive over the growing political power of the peasantry, the Norwegian elite was increasingly prepared to consider at least some renegotiation of the union to create a smoother working relationship with Sweden and the monarch. In 1839, Carl XIV Johan appointed a joint union committee to propose possible revisions. It presented its report in 1844, but under Oscar I, who succeeded his father that year, nothing came of it. The new monarch, however, showed much good will toward his Norwegian subjects.[1]

Carl XV, whose reign began in 1859, was likewise well disposed toward Norway. In 1865, he appointed a new joint committee to consider revision of the union, which worked over the next two years to produce a proposal for a joint council of state *(statsråd)* to deal with common concerns, combined defense forces, and joint diplomatic and consular officials responsible to a foreign office under the control of neither the Riksdag nor the Storting. The British historian T. K. Derry has pointed to similarities in this proposal both to the North German Confederation of 1866 and to the Austro-Hungarian *Ausgleich* of 1867.

The proposal was approved by the Riksdag committee and evidently would have passed in the Riksdag. It was presented to the Storting in 1868 and came up for debate at its next session in 1871. There was strong support for strengthening the union in the Norwegian committee, and the ministry was initially confident that it would pass. But the opportunity that might at this critical juncture have created a more lasting union was lost. The peasant leader Ole Gabriel Ueland, who had supported the proposal on the committee, died in 1870. It came under increasing fire from a growing coalition of forces and in 1871 was decisively defeated in the Storting.[2]

The conciliatory attitude in leading circles in both kingdoms had been reinforced by the Scandinavianism, or the Pan-Scandinavian movement, warmly espoused especially by university students and other intellectuals in the Nordic countries during the middle decades of the century.[3] The cultural impact of this movement will be considered in the next chapter. It offers, meanwhile, a prime example of the interaction of culture with politics, for Scandinavianism also had its political implications.

As previously noted, there had been a growing sense of a common Scandinavian destiny already by the 1790s, which had briefly given rise during the Swedish succession crises during 1809 and 1810 to short-lived visions of a union of the three Nordic kingdoms.[4] Such political ambitions fell into abeyance after 1814. By the 1840s, they began once again to revive. The impetus now came from Denmark. The duchies of Schleswig (Slesvig) and Holstein, with their predominantly German population, grew increasingly restive under Danish rule and agitated for greater autonomy. Danish patriots, well aware of sympathy throughout Germany for the Schleswig-Holsteiners, looked to their fellow Scandinavians in Norway and Sweden for backing. In 1848–49, the Germans in the duchies rose up in an armed insurrection, drawing much support from the Germanic Confederation. Many Swedish and Norwegian volunteers joined the Danish forces, and four thousand Swedish troops were sent to the island of Fyn to ward off any German attempt to cross the Little Belt.

The intervention of the European great powers led to the London Conference of 1852, which in effect restored the status quo in the duchies.[5] But some kind of durable political alliance among the three Scandinavian kingdoms became ever more Denmark's hope for the future. Sweden meanwhile had its own political agenda. Hopes of regaining Finland had not yet died out in leading Swedish circles, and the outbreak of the Crimean War in 1853 seemed to offer a long-awaited opportunity for its recovery. The British and French fleets controlled the Baltic and attacked Russian fortifications in Finland. With tacit royal approval, Scandinavianist and anti-Russian sentiments flourished in Sweden. In November 1855, Oscar I abandoned the policy of rapprochement with Russia begun by his father over forty years earlier by entering into a convention with Britain and France guaranteeing the territorial integrity of the Dual Kingdom, obviously against the possible threat of Russian aggression. This was understood to clear the way toward direct involvement, but the war ended shortly thereafter. Relations with Russia would henceforward remain strained at best.[6]

Oscar I was increasingly committed to a Scandinavianist stance, as was his successor in 1859, Carl XV. A new and brighter vision now arose on the Scandinavian horizon. Frederik VII of Denmark had no male heir. This opened up the possibility that an agreement might be reached whereby the Danish crown might devolve after his death to the king of Sweden and Norway. The idea was encouraged by Danish national liberals in response to new unrest among the Germans of Schleswig-Holstein. On his own initiative, Carl XV promised the Danish government in July 1863 the support of twenty thousand Swedish and Norwegian troops in the event that the Germanic powers invaded Schleswig—although not Holstein, with its entirely German population—in anticipation of an eventual union of the crowns.

The Norwegian response to Scandinavianism had meanwhile been divided and ambiguous. Unlike Denmark and Sweden, Norway had no foreign policy considerations involved other than its own territorial integrity. On the one hand, a possible tripartite union of the three kingdoms might appear to weaken Norway's position in relation to the two wealthier and more populous nations and could increase the dangers of entanglement in foreign conflicts of no real relevance to Norway's own interests. On the other hand, as one of three united kingdoms, Sweden's relative standing might be reduced, thereby enhancing Norway's position.[7]

Hostilities over Schleswig-Holstein broke out early in 1864 between Denmark on the one side and Prussia and Austria on the other. Carl XV faced a humiliating debacle. The Norwegian council was prepared to join in an intervention, subject to the Storting's approval, only in the highly unlikely event that at least Great Britain, among the great powers, also took part—which it did not. The Storting went further by passing a resolution opposing any political connection with Denmark.

The king's Swedish ministers were divided, but encouraged by the action of their Norwegian colleagues, the majority opposed intervention by Sweden alone in the Danish-German conflict. Behind their refusal lay not only sober *Realpolitik* but also political calculation: by forcing the king to back down, they showed their determination to gain greater control over foreign policy and thereby to reduce significantly the royal prerogative Carl XIV Johan had secured for himself. In this, as in other respects, the Norwegian example had a significant political impact in Sweden. As Göran B. Nilsson has observed, the crisis showed who really decided foreign policy: the powerful bureaucracy in both countries, who in this instance interacted closely.[8]

The Danes fought bravely in 1864 against the combined Prussian and Austrian onslaught but were soon compelled to make peace, relinquishing to the Germanic Confederation Danish sovereignty over both duchies, including a sizable Danish population in northern Schleswig. Following the Austro-Prussian War two years later, Schleswig-Holstein was incorporated into Prussia, and in 1871, into the new German Empire. Only in 1920, after World War I, did Denmark recover by plebiscite the Danish part of North Schleswig.

The debacle of 1864 was the deathblow to nineteenth-century political Scandinavianism, although its cultural manifestations, together with efforts at practical cooperation between the Nordic lands, continued on. The frightening military might and imperial ambitions of Bismarck's Prussia encouraged for a time Swedish-Norwegian efforts to create a closer union and thus greater security for the peninsula, although in the end to no avail.

The Danish episode was a sobering reminder to Carl XV of how little control he had over his Norwegian kingdom. His endorsement of Riksdag reform in 1866 was, it would seem, motivated largely by the lingering hope of creating a closer union between his two domains. The restrictive and weighted voting requirements it established caused widespread disillusionment in Sweden. Norway, with its more democratic franchise, still remained an ideal for Swedish liberals and radicals aspiring to further reforms.

Ill and disillusioned, Carl XV died in 1872 and was succeeded by his ambitious younger brother Oscar II, who had been ostensibly raised as the "Norwegian prince," was warmly attached to Norway, spoke its language fluently, and adopted as his motto "the welfare of the brother peoples." He received a splendid coronation in Trondheim cathedral and a royal reception in Christiania. On the latter occasion, the conservative historian Torkel Halvor Aschehoug declared, "Sweden is our comrade in a political union that has been witness and contributor to the progress of the past century, the most fortunate Norway has known. Our fathers accepted this union as a necessity. We, the present generation, have learned to value it as a blessing from heaven."[9] It seemed the auspicious beginning of a new era in the union's history. Ultimately, it proved to be the final phase.

There were two basic causes for the failure to create a closer union around the middle of the nineteenth century. The one involved the relations between the two kingdoms, the other concerned internal developments within each, above all in Norway. The first was the conflicts that periodically arose between Norway and Sweden over questions—often of an essentially symbolic nature—that all too painfully reminded Norwegians of their de facto subordinate status within the union. Examination of these controversies has largely dominated the historical literature on the union on both the Norwegian and the Swedish sides.

Regarding discord within the Dual Monarchy, the question of the Norwegian flag is a notable case in point. In 1821, the present flag with a blue cross superimposed upon a white one against a red field was devised. Until 1830, however, Norwegian merchant ships were required to fly the Swedish flag south of Cape Finistère as protection against the Barbary pirates to whom Sweden paid a tribute. Oscar I established uniform regulations for both kingdoms in 1844: henceforward, both the Swedish and Norwegian flags were to include the union insignia combining the Swedish and Norwegian colors in the upper left quarter. To Norwegian patriots, the union mark—or "herring salad," as it came to be contemptuously called in Norway—was a constant, nagging reminder of their country's dependence on the larger kingdom. Similar irritations included, for instance, the Norwegian quartering incorporated into the Swedish national coat-of-arms and the numbering of the union kings according to Swedish practice.

A question with more serious implications for the union concerned the position of the statholder in Norway. According to the revised Norwegian constitution of 1814, he served as the king's personal representative in Norway during the king's absence and could be either a Swede or a Norwegian. The first statholders were Swedish. Then, following a vacancy of several years, Carl XIV Johan appointed the Norwegian Herman Wedel-Jarlsberg to the post in 1836 as a measure of conciliation after his confrontation with the Storting that year. From that time forward, political expediency effectively ruled out the appointment of any more Swedish statholders. This meant in essence that the Swedish government no longer had any official envoy in Norway—its most important means of presenting its viewpoints in union matters there—corresponding to the Norwegian minister of state who attended the king in Stockholm. Sweden was, as Sam Clason has put it, thereafter less adequately represented in its sister kingdom than in any other country.[10]

The statholderate, which remained vacant after 1856, was nonetheless by its very existence a reminder of Norway's subservience to Sweden, giving rise to repeated controversies. In 1859, following Carl XV's accession, the Storting, with the king's discreet encouragement, passed a bill abolishing the statholderate. This unilateral action stirred up a storm in influential Swedish circles dissatisfied with the union as it had become, who perceived in it a serious threat to Sweden's vital interests.

Anticipating such a move, Count Carl Henrik Anckarsvärd, who in the 1830s and 1840s had championed the Norwegian constitution, demanded in the Riksdag's Noble Estate that Sweden revise the Act of Union to keep Norway in its proper subordinate position under the Treaty of Kiel. Norway, he complained, enjoyed the benefits of the union without bearing its burdens. While he claimed still to admire Norway's constitution, he held that it should never stand in the way of Sweden's rightful preeminence. "The prevailing spirit in Norway," he declared, "seems to be that Sweden is a kingdom united with Norway," whereas "it is Norway that is united with Sweden."

Although Anckarsvärd's attack called forth several rejoinders in defense of the Norwegians, the point was made, and Wilhelm Fredric Dalman, a one-time liberal comrade in arms, made specific proposals for revising the union in Sweden's favor. This maneuver was clearly intended to prevent Carl XV from sanctioning the Storting's abolition of the statholderate, thereby asserting the Riksdag's political power, and the well-meaning but weak-willed king backed down. The political scientist Nils Elvander has perceived in this episode the beginnings of a schism between the "cultural-national," Scandinavianist form of liberalism that had previously held sway and a growing "state-national" liberalism that would play an increasing political role, while becoming progressively more conservative in orientation, down to the end of the union.[11]

The issue was finally resolved, although in a manner that left resentment on both sides of the Keel, in 1872. Upon succeeding to the throne that year, Oscar II, as a means of creating goodwill, decreed the abolition of the statholderate. This time the Riksdag reacted against the king rather than the Storting, maintaining that he was not empowered to act on its own in this matter, although having made the point, it thereupon itself passed a bill finally abolishing the position. From the viewpoint of Swedish internal politics, this was yet another case of the legislature seeking to limit royal authority.

For Norway, the Riksdag's behavior over the statholderate spoiled what had been intended as a magnanimous gesture from the throne. Previously, union conflicts had pitted the Storting against the monarch. Now, the Swedish Riksdag made clear its view that not only the Act of Union of 1815 but the Norwegian constitution itself was subject to its review and effective veto where union—that is, Swedish—interests were involved and that the union monarch could not act freely as the king of Norway. The conflict aroused intense resentments in Norway and led, more than anything else, to the rising opposition to the proposals of the joint Norwegian-Swedish commission for revision of the Act of Union that by 1871 brought about their resounding defeat in the Storting.

The British historian T. K. Derry has written regarding the statholder controversy and by implication the imbroglios in general that periodically disturbed the union:

> The details of such a dispute make tedious reading, and are likely to convey the impression that the Norwegians were not merely legalistic but petty-minded. The instinct, however, was a sure one, which taught the nationalists, throughout the period of their union with a neighbour state possessing greater wealth, population, and prestige than their own, to cling to every formal evidence of equality. Otherwise, there would be a tendency to drift into a closer relationship with the stronger state which, for better or worse, the nationalists sought to avoid.[12]

The most substantial matter of dispute, and that which in the end would prove the rock upon which the union would founder, was the control of foreign affairs. Both the Swedish constitution of 1809 and the Norwegian constitution of 1814 had delegated this power to the crown. As long as Carl XIV Johan lived, there could be no disputing this principle. Initially, he worked through the Swedish foreign ministry and diplomatic service. While Norwegians could hold diplomatic posts, they were nominated by the Swedish state council. The king's handling of the matter of the Danish national debt and the Bodø crisis meanwhile caused much dissatisfaction in Norway during the troubled 1820s, making painfully clear the Norwegians' dependence in foreign matters affecting themselves. In 1835–37, as part of his more conciliatory line, Carl XIV Johan was prepared to grant significant concessions: In foreign policy matters concerning the union as a whole or Norway alone, Norwegian state councilors were to be consulted, while the appointment and dismissal of consuls, who were to take a special oath as Norwegian officials, was entrusted to the combined state councils.[13]

Ultimately, however, the power of the crown in foreign affairs was curtailed by the Norwegian constitution's limitations on the employment of Norwegian troops outside the kingdom without the Storting's approval, which had so ignominiously put an effective stop to Carl XV's ambitious plan to support Denmark against the German powers in 1864.

If recurrent controversies raised obstacles, a deeper-lying cause for the failure of the sister kingdoms to develop a closer union may be found in the dynamics of Norwegian internal politics. Since 1814, it was the official elite that had drafted Norway's constitution and had determinedly and skillfully defended it against all attempts to revise it. By the 1850s, alarmed by the European revolutions of 1848–49, the Thrane labor movement, and the political power of the peasantry, influential members of the official class were prepared to contemplate a closer union with Sweden that would strengthen the forces of conservatism in Norway. This tendency was furthered by a new and more aggressive generation of leaders from the official class who favored more active government under an elite drawn from the intelligentsia and looked more to practical results than to abstract legal theory, above all in economic development. Its foremost representative, Frederik Stang, emerged by 1848 as indisputably the strongest figure in the government over the next thirty-five years, with only five years' interruption.[14]

A revealing sign of changing times was the statue of Carl XIV Johan promoted by the socially prominent Norwegian Carl Johan Society founded in 1856 and inspired by the earlier Swedish Carl Johan Society from 1848. The statue was paid for through public subscription in Norway beginning in 1864 and was unveiled in 1875 before the royal palace at the head of Carl Johan Avenue in Christiania. It was erected, according to the Norwegian historian Alf Kaartvedt, "with clear political intent, as an homage to the union with Sweden and to the union's founder." It will be recalled that Carl XIV Johan, after becoming king in 1818, had carried out a determined offensive to amend the Norwegian constitution to create a closer union. His staunchest adversaries at that time had been the very official elite whose sons now idealized the first Bernadotte as the strong man of order with visionary progressive ideals.[15]

That such should be the case reveals how the political domination of the official class was coming under increasing pressure from rival forces by the early 1870s. The peasantry had steadily gained in political experience and sophistication. After Ueland's death, the more sophisticated and aggressive

Søren Jaabæk became their leader in the Storting. Radical members of the intelligentsia grew increasingly restive and found their champion in the charismatic Johan Sverdrup, who was first elected to the Storting in 1851.

By 1869, Sverdrup formed a working alliance with Jaabæk and his peasant following, which accepted Sverdrup's leadership on larger issues in return for the satisfaction of specific peasant demands. Beginning with the Storting of 1872, Sverdrup went on the offensive against the conservatives by securing the first passage of a bill to seat the ministers, or state councilors, in the Storting, thereby bringing them under its control. By 1880, this became law when passed for the third time, thereby overriding Oscar II's veto. Sverdrup then secured passage of a resolution to assert the Storting's supreme authority over the ministry.

As it affected the principle of the separation of powers, this resolution amounted to an amendment to the constitution, which raised a crucial question. While for ordinary legislation the royal veto could be overridden after passage by the Storting in three consecutive sessions, the Norwegian constitution was unclear as to whether the king's veto was absolute in the case of constitutional amendments. Plausible arguments could be raised on either side, with the ministry and its conservative supporters defending the absolute veto and the liberal and radical opposition upholding the suspensive veto for all forms of legislation. On this point turned Norway's whole relationship to Sweden within the union. If the Storting were free to change the constitution at will, Norway would in principle henceforward be free to determine its own future, even though few Norwegians then envisioned ending a union that would recognize their rightful place in it.

In discouragement, Frederik Stang resigned as premier in 1880 and was replaced by Christian Selmer, a determined defender of the absolute royal veto on constitutional change. Thereafter, Sverdrup and his supporters mounted an intensive campaign to arouse public opinion over the issue.

The old officialdom, with its bastion in the state council of ministers, was increasingly dependent on the king and the more conservative Swedish government for backing. On the other side, the rising forces of democracy with their stronghold in the Storting strove to keep the powers of the council and the crown, and Swedish political influence, in check.

But far more was involved. The struggle between liberals and conservatives now became a veritable *Kulturkampf* between conflicting worldviews by the early 1880s. Conservatives strove to uphold tradition and established authority, and they found powerful support in the church, the bureaucracy, the military and naval officer corps, the law courts, the university faculty, and much of the press. "In Christiania they are now saying quite openly it would be better to be Swedish than to submit to Norwegian peasant rule," the radical poet Bjørnstjerne Bjørnson wrote in June 1880 to a Swedish confidant. "The great merchants and officials believe that it is a Norwegian natural law that they should hold power."[16]

Liberals and radicals meanwhile looked to new cosmopolitan ideals of personal freedom, scientific positivism, progress, and evolution. They drew their principal support from most of the peasantry under Jaabæk's lead, the more radical intelligentsia, and the rising commercial classes.

Increasing attention was now being directed toward social problems, not least by a new generation of writers and artists. Conventional education, marriage, the family, the role of women, conditions among the working classes, business ethics, the church, the bureaucracy, prevailing aesthetic standards—all came under increasing criticism. On the cultural scene, realism carried the day with a long series of social novels, dramas, and paintings, as will be seen. The radical Christiania intellectuals became passionately engaged. Voluntary sharpshooter corps were organized on the liberal side to stand watch over Norway's liberties.

Conservatives denounced their opponents as godless, ruthlessly destructive, and immoral. Liberals and radicals condemned the conservatives as obscurantist, reactionary—and subservient to aristocratic Sweden. During the statholder crisis of 1859–60, the Swedish Riksdag had been prepared to create bad blood in Norway as the price for increasing its own power vis-à-vis the monarch. By the early 1880s, Sverdrup and his following in the Storting were prepared to antagonize Sweden for the same purpose. The bitter ideological battle in Norway separated friend from friend, father from son.[17]

In the crucial Storting elections of 1882, in which a far larger part of the electorate took part than ever before, the Sverdrup coalition gained control of the Storting. In 1884, it took the decisive step. Employing the device that had been used most effectively by the political elite to defend and reinterpret the constitution during Carl XIV Johan's time, the Storting impeached Selmer and most of his colleagues on the council before the special tribunal, or Rigsret, which sentenced them to loss of office.

Oscar II tried for four months to form a new ministry of similar complexion but in the end had to accept one headed by Sverdrup and supported by the Storting, thereby tacitly at least accepting the principle of ministerial responsibility to the legislature rather than to the crown. From that time forward, ministers increasingly were members of the Storting.

The king was in a high state of agitation and indecision during the Norwegian constitutional crisis. He wavered from one viewpoint to another. Some within his court encouraged him to carry out a coup to break the deadlock.

Knowing of the European powers' desire to preserve stability in the North and their apprehensions that Norway might set a dangerous example by becoming a republic, Oscar II secretly sounded out Prince Bismarck in Berlin, who admonished him to stand fast against the Storting and, it appears, for a time considered a German intervention. On the other, the king was cautioned against any forceful solution by his Swedish ministers, who in effect smoothed the way for the breakthrough of parliamentarianism in the sister kingdom. While the king had carried on his strictly personal diplomacy in deepest secrecy, there was no lack of rumor in Norway that he was appealing for foreign support against his own Norwegian subjects, creating further distrust for the future.[18]

The ministerial crisis meant the effective end of the official elite's dominance in Norway, at least in principle. Henceforward, there could be no looking to the crown or to revision of the union to reinforce its position, even though persons from the old families have ever since continued to play a prominent part in Norwegian politics and public life.[19] Beginning in 1884, the Sverdrup coalition formally organized as the *Venstre*, or Left, party, although the name had already been in use for several years, while the conservatives coalesced as the *Høyre*, the Right. From that time on, organized political parties would dominate Norwegian politics.

The rise of Sverdrup and his coalition and the ministerial crisis of 1884 had fateful consequences for the union with Sweden. Sverdrup and his allies were able to mobilize the full force of exuberant Norwegian patriotism in their struggle for a more democratic regime against the conservatives, whom they could brand as pro-Swedish and prepared to compromise Norway's independence. Their position was further enhanced by a modest suffrage reform that year. This was a bitter irony for the official elite, which was thus hoisted by its own petard, having itself established a popular franchise and limited the crown's powers in 1814 and having since served as the staunch guardians of Norway's constitutional liberties. The crown and the union thus remained the only real restraints to the power of the Storting, and they were now depicted as "foreign" by the democratic and nationalistic forces in Norway.[20]

In appealing to Norwegian nationalism, the Sverdrup coalition found its leading ideologue in the radical nationalist historian Ernst Sars at the University of Christiania. Its most eloquent spokesman, both at home and abroad, was meanwhile Bjørnstjerne Bjørnson, who by then was widely renowned as both a poet and a publicist. More prominently than anyone else in his time, he embodied the close union of culture and politics, as will be discussed more fully in the following chapters.

While Bjørnson during these years held to the ideal of a Norwegian-Swedish union, he determinedly opposed the alliance of Norwegian conservatives with the court and the government in Sweden. Although he had shown sympathy toward the earlier Bernadotte monarchs, he had soon come to mistrust Oscar II. At the same time that Bjørnson deeply admired the Swedes and their glorious past, he wrote to a friend in 1880, "I am unshakably opposed to a Swedish king's or Norwegian or Swedish reactionaries' attempts to make an England-Scotland out of Sweden-Norway, that 'closer union' they speak of."[21]

During 1879–80, Bjørnson, together with Sars, Sverdrup, and others, found in the old question of the flag a weapon to turn against their political opponents on both sides of the Keel and launched a campaign for the exclusive use of the "pure" Norwegian flag, cleansed of the union insignia, which they condemned as a humiliating symbol of subjugation. For Bjørnson, the issue was above all a means to arouse what he called "*Selvstændighedens Æresfølelse*"—the sense of national pride and honor that only freedom could give—among his people, who after centuries of foreign domination he considered all too inclined toward the indifference and thrall-like servility of a vassal kingdom. "If we were offered victory [in this struggle] today," he wrote to his good Swedish friend Sven Adolf Hedlund, editor of the liberal *Göteborgs Handels- och Sjöfartstidning*, in May 1879, "I would say, for God's sake, no! Through this cause we must first discover how poorly off we are when it comes to feelings of freedom and honor. . . . Only then will the work begin to realize the promise of freedom that lies within our constitution and national character."

Inspired by the historian Sars, Bjørnson saw in the decline of the medieval Norwegian nobility both the cause of Norway's loss of independence in the fourteenth century and the essential precondition for its rebirth as a democratic society after 1814. As the old aristocracy had merged with the landowning peasants, this had created a peasant aristocracy that had kept alive its pride and traditions of local self-rule until the end of the Danish regime. These were the qualities that Bjørnson saw it as his mission to inculcate throughout the land.[22] Both publicly and in letters to his Swedish friends, Bjørnson insisted that his crusade to instill national pride among his compatriots did not imply any hostility toward Sweden or, despite his sharp criticisms of the king and his entourage, toward a union rightly conceived. In one of his finest speeches, at Lilliestrømmen in June 1881, he proclaimed: "The more independently and freely both peoples develop, the more firmly the union stands. . . . Long live Norway! Long live the union with Sweden."[23]

The time was not yet ripe, however, to make an issue of the flag. The campaign to remove the union insignia stirred up a storm of opposition and some rowdy behavior in Norway, especially in the capital. A motion to abolish the union flag was defeated in the Storting in June 1879, and an attempt to revive the issue the following year received no support there. Agitation nonetheless continued over the following years. In 1898, the Storting resolved for the third time the adoption of the "pure flag" except for military purposes, overriding the royal veto.[24]

The Riksdag reform in 1866 produced a new political polarization in Sweden. The First Chamber became a strongly conservative aristocratic and plutocratic stronghold. The Second Chamber soon came to be dominated for over a decade by the *Lantmannaparti*, or Farmers' Party, organized in 1867 somewhat paradoxically under the leadership of Count Carl Posse, an erstwhile outspoken opponent in the former Noble Estate of the representational reform. The rapid rise of the Swedish Farmers' Party in turn provided inspiration to the political Left in Norway under Sverdrup and Jaabæk in its struggle against the old official elite.[25]

Direct contact between the two "people's parties" came about by the early 1870s, with the initiative coming from Sverdrup and promoted by Bjørnson and his close friend from that time forward, S. A. Hedlund in Göteborg, who played the leading role on the Swedish side. The Sverdrup party likewise had a valuable intermediary in the prominent Norwegian timber merchant in Stockholm, H. R. Astrup (later a Storting member and state councilor), who enjoyed close relations with the Riksdag men in the *Lantmannaparti*.

Prospects for cooperation—including the Danish *Forenede Venstre*, or Left Alliance—raised high hopes of an informal yet effective Scandinavian alliance on the Left to bring about true democracy in the North. The Swedish *Lantmannaparti* shared with the Norwegian peasant bloc its goals of strict government economies and control over state officials. Efforts were made, again largely on the initiative of Sverdrup and his party in Norway, to coordinate action in both the Storting and the Riksdag.[26]

Bjørnson's voluminous correspondence with people in Sweden sheds light on this relationship. Already in 1860, during the first statholder crisis, he had envisioned a Scandinavian people's movement against the old establishments, but little had then come of it. In October 1871, during the second statholder crisis, Bjørnson wrote to Count Posse seeking the support of the *Lantmannaparti* and envisioning close cooperation between the two agrarian parties. Both, he maintained, pursued the same goals. "We have felt your victory to be our own," he wrote, and the Swedish Farmers' Party would also have cause "to feel that our victory is yours." To Hedlund, he urged in May 1872 that

> mutual help can lead our common cause to victory. . . . And this common cause is not the dreams of kings and merchants and defense contracts, but our uniqueness as children of the same father and mother, what we must do to preserve it, develop it, so that it can realize its mission for itself and for European democracy, which cannot, I am convinced, find peace in any way until we have, with our higher morality, lawfulness, and faith, shown how it is to be done.

Bjørnson's letters to his Swedish associates are filled with admonitions and sound at times as though they emanated from the headquarters of an allied army.

Following a visit to Stockholm, Bjørnson wrote to Hedlund in April 1873, "The Swedish Riksdag farmers are not as clever or well instructed as ours, generally speaking, but how high do they not stand above them in simple courage, in broad-minded humanity! It was inspiring to associate with them."[27]

The cooperation Sverdrup, Bjørnson, and their party had put their hopes in was put to the real test in 1884 when, together with Swedish liberals, the *Lantmannaparti* gave powerful support to the Norwegian Left during Norway's constitutional crisis. One of its leaders, Liss O. Larsson, wrote to a Norwegian colleague, "We see clearly that the struggle concerns Sweden just as much, for if Norway can be ruled *in opposition to* its freely elected representatives, the same [fate] awaits us."

Oscar II was highly apprehensive over the backing he could count on in Sweden and vainly sought assurances of support from leading members of the Farmers' Party that dominated the Riksdag's Second Chamber. Its position was made unmistakably clear in April that year when the prominent Norwegian radical Viggo Ullmann visited Stockholm to agitate on behalf of the Sverdrup coalition. A banquet was held in his honor, attended by over one hundred *Lantmannaparti* Riksdag members and numerous supporters. The king was deeply incensed but duly impressed—as, apparently, was Bismarck, who dropped any further thoughts of intervention. In June, as has been seen, Oscar II gave way and accepted a Sverdrup ministry. The role of the Swedish Farmers' Party would appear to have been crucial, and this episode was its high point as a political force in Sweden, before it became increasingly fractionalized.[28]

The establishment of ministerial responsibility in Norway far preceded its implementation in Sweden; not until 1917 would it be fully confirmed there. The Norwegian example meanwhile did not fail to stimulate liberal efforts in that direction, not least with regard to foreign affairs. In practice, if not in theory, the foreign ministry became ever more susceptible to pressures from the Riksdag, which in 1885 resolved that the Swedish premier and another state councilor should take part with the foreign minister in consultations on foreign matters. The liberal Adolf Hedin—a warm admirer of Norway—went further and introduced legislation in the Riksdag that placed foreign affairs under parliamentary control. As the foreign ministry was still Swedish, however, this meant that management of the union's foreign relations came more firmly than before under specifically Swedish control. Such a development could not but lead to mounting dissension with Norway over what remained the most substantial bone of contention between the two kingdoms.

Management of foreign policy, especially its consular functions, was of more than academic interest to the Norwegians in view of their large and rapidly growing merchant marine, which by the late nineteenth century was far larger than Sweden's and heavily engaged in the carrying trade between foreign ports. There were differences as well between Norwegian and Swedish trade policies, especially when Sweden in 1888 established protective tariffs while Norway continued to favor free trade. To what degree the existing consular system may actually have been harmful to Norwegian interests is open to question.[29] Still, it was widely perceived to be so in Norway, as well as being a central issue of national prestige.

The ever-powerful voice of Bjørnstjerne Bjørnson continued both to lead and to reflect opinion in Norway as the crisis deepened. In a speech in 1889, he launched the term *storsvensker,* roughly translated "Great-Swedes"—an obvious allusion to the *Gross-Deutsche* in Germany—to depict what he and the Norwegian Left regarded as the reactionary, chauvinistic, and aristocratic clique, with its atavistic dreams of Sweden's past military and imperial glories, that dominated the Swedish court, government, and high society. The epithet quickly gained currency among both Norwegian and Swedish liberals and radicals, who moreover were apprehensive about the increasingly "Prussian" tone of the Swedish court and official elite since the German victory in the Franco-Prussian War in 1870–71. Bjørnson meanwhile continued throughout to express his great faith in the fair-minded "Swedish people" as his compatriots' natural allies in the common struggle for justice and democracy.

In his celebrated poem "Den—!" from 1892, Bjørnson called publicly for an end to the existing union, to be replaced by a defensive alliance. The idea was, however, by no means new. As early as 1872, he had written to S. A. Hedlund, "If the union cannot eventually provide the most complete equality, then it must be dissolved." When Norway stood entirely free and equal beside Sweden, he now declared in his poem,

> then canst thou give thy hand to thy brother.
> The pact that we now are plagued with
> We hate and damn.

It was his firm conviction that only by demonstrating their national pride and self-respect in stoutly defending their rights could the Norwegians hope to win true respect from the Swedes.[30]

From the Swedish viewpoint, the security of the entire peninsula had been from the beginning the paramount consideration—the union's very raison d'être—that above all required a unified foreign and military policy. The Swedes were ever aware of the ominous vicinity of the Russians to the east and had long resented the Norwegians' unwillingness to bear their share of the burden of defense. There was, to be sure, a respectable build-up of Norway's forces just prior to the Danish-German War of 1864. Following the constitutional crisis of 1884, however, the Storting, under Sverdrup's *Venstre* ministry, in 1885 substantially reduced the number of troops of the line—which under the constitution could be deployed outside the country with the Storting's approval—to only eighteen thousand, while correspondingly increasing the reserve forces whose use was strictly confined to Norway. This change received royal sanction in the expectation that Norway would in return modify its constitutional restriction on the use of the reserve outside the country— that is to say, in Sweden—for the common defense of the peninsula. The Storting's conspicuous failure to do so caused widespread disillusionment in Sweden. Norway, it was felt, unjustly refused to bear its rightful share of the common defense, which raised questions among Swedish conservatives about the continued value of the union.[31]

The Norwegians, being somewhat less exposed, largely failed to understand fully the Swedes' fears of the Russian menace. To increase the monarch's power over Norway's military forces again raised their suspicions of reactionary and militaristic machinations to "amalgamate" Norway with Sweden. "For you," Bjørnson explained to Hedlund in 1881, "the union offers security, for you are larger, for us it is . . . a constant danger and struggle." "We have no desire to become Swedish cannon fodder," he wrote to a Swedish radical in December 1894.

Bjørnson and those of like mind on both sides of the Keel mistrusted the king and the chauvinistic *storsvensker* whom they believed dominated him. Instead, they put their faith in the idealism of the two peoples under that true popular sovereignty, which, as Bjørnson had told Hedlund in 1881, was the ultimate goal of his life's strivings. When a Swedish correspondent recognized the Norwegians' just demands within the union yet expressed the widely shared fear that an independent Norway could not by itself withstand Russian domination, Bjørnson wrote confidently to him in November 1896, "The day shall never come, whether we remain within the union or leave it, when we would lose our reason to the point where an attack on Sweden would not also be understood as an attack on Norway." This ideal would be reiterated by others in Norway even as the union broke down in 1905. Bjørnson meanwhile set forth his credo in an article in Christiania's liberal *Verdens Gang* in June 1899:

> I have since my youth been a Scandinavianist. I have always held to this, both when the idea was triumphant and when it was ridiculed. But I have never understood Scandinavianism as other than an association *[Forbund]* between independent peoples. Nor has any other Scandinavianism been possible. . . . For me and those like me, Scandinavianism was and is a higher union, more just than that now existing between Swedes and Norwegians. . . . Under one king, under two, under a republic, through good days and bad, [our] association must endure![32]

In 1890, negotiations were begun between the two governments to set up a joint council of ministers to handle foreign affairs. But these broke down over Swedish insistence that Sweden's foreign minister remain head of the foreign office. Matters were not helped in this strained situation when the Swedish premier, Baron Gustaf Åkerhjelm, blustered about "talking Swedish" to the Norwegians from a position of military strength. It was ironic that Åkerhjelm, whose mother was Norwegian, who spoke the language perfectly, and who was normally considered friendly toward Norway, should have allowed himself to be so carried away, thereby committing a blunder that compelled him soon after to resign.[33]

Conservative Swedish nationalists, with the historian and chancellor of Uppsala University Oscar Alin in the forefront, meanwhile uncompromisingly proclaimed Norway's necessary subordination to Sweden on both juridical and strategic grounds. Sweden, Alin wrote in 1896, could, if need be, manage by itself as it had in its past days of greatness. Nevertheless, he asked:

> Do we consider it consistent with Sweden's honor that we quite simply let go of what at the beginning of the century we gained for ourselves through bloody sacrifice and the loss of provinces [i.e., Finland] dearly gained? Shall anyone whomsoever be permitted to deprive us of what we have won? Are we prepared to see the fruits of our last great political act collapse as a failure? How after such weakness in this matter would Europe—and Norway—regard and treat us concerning other [matters]?

Alin moreover feared—with the Russian colossus in mind—that an independent Norway would be unable to escape "Poland's fate," thereby bringing misfortune both to itself and to the rest of Scandinavia.[34]

By 1891, there were alarming rumors that Sweden might seek to settle the crisis by force. The Storting, under a new radical Left ministry, nonetheless resolved in 1892 to establish a separate Norwegian foreign minister, on the argument that since the Act of Union did not specifically mention control of foreign affairs, it was a purely Norwegian matter. When Oscar II vetoed this plan, ostentatious military preparations were made on both sides. By 1895, however, the Norwegian government felt compelled to give way and accept new negotiations with Sweden.

That matters were not pushed to the breaking point either in 1891 or in 1895 was due not only to Norway's military unpreparedness but also to divided counsels at the top. Crown Prince Gustaf favored strong measures. Kaiser Wilhelm II vigorously urged Oscar to stand firm and use force if need be, although he refrained from any overt offers of German support. His influence was persuasively counteracted by Queen Sophia, supported by the young Prince Eugen.[35]

Once again, there was vocal backing for the Norwegian position from Swedish liberals and radicals both inside and outside the Riksdag. In March 1891, the British minister in Stockholm wrote to his government of apprehensions that the "extreme Radical Party" in Norway was in collusion with Adolf Hedin and the Swedish radicals. "In fact," he went on, "to my mind . . . there is more to fear of the Swedish and Norwegian Radicals combining to do away with the Monarchy, than of the two nations carrying on their dispute so far as to break up the union." The liberal *Dagens Nyheter* echoed the political conflicts of the 1830s and 1840s when it held that the Swedes should follow the Norwegian example. "Either Norway must become aristocratized," it declared, "or Sweden must become democratized" and thereby catch up with the times. In September 1895, the liberal Riksdag member and historian

Hans Forssell wrote in *Stockholms Dagblad* that while the tactics of the "Great-Swedes" united Norway, they divided Sweden, since their true aim was nothing less than Norway's subjugation.[36]

The imbroglio, however, did not pass without creating dissension in Norway as well, some of it apparently covert. In March 1895, the British minister reported that he had learned from "a Norwegian statesman" of a secret plan to be submitted to the king for him to appoint a "ministry to carry on the business of the country, to be supported, if necessary, against the Storthing [*sic*] by a coup d'état in which only Norwegian troops would be used."[37]

Hjalmar Branting, leader of the fledgling Swedish Social Democratic party, was particularly outspoken in condemning the dispute as an artificial distraction created by the Swedish ruling class, which felt "that the ground is burning under their feet." He went so far as to hint darkly that "perhaps down among the broader masses someone may get the idea of taking judgment into his own hands and with a bullet seek, without orders, to prevent tens of thousands of bullets being fired upon command to mutilate and kill friends and brothers," for which remarks he was tried for incitement to violence.[38] What role Branting and the Swedish working class may have played in this instance would be hard to estimate. But fear of social revolution was real among the upper classes during the late nineteenth century.

At the same time, many influential intellectuals, with the author Ellen Key—daughter of a leading member of the Farmers' Party—and the painter-writer Richard Bergh in the van, raised their voices in protest against any thought of hostilities. In June 1895, Key wrote proudly to Bjørnson of great demonstrations throughout Sweden "for universal suffrage and peace in Norway." Another devoted Swedish friend, Ann-Margret Holmgren, wrote him in December that war was now surely unthinkable, since the great masses in Sweden would have no part of it. That the Swedish ministry could even contemplate such a course, she said, "was shameful and unworthy of a Scandinavian people."

Bergh wrote to Key in 1898 that "only if each land goes forward separately and grows strong in its own way can the North as a whole become strong." The following year, Key, attacking "Great-Swedish patriotism," declared it both nobler and wiser for Sweden to accept the demise of the existing union in favor of a freely negotiated treaty of amity and defense than to perpetuate a "monstrous" historical injustice. Circumstances were no longer what they had been in 1814; "on the contrary, forms of government are broken down by the strength of life, of growth, of development." From this perspective, she concluded, "Norway, as compared with Sweden, is like a vigorous and ambitious youth, shackled to one that at present is as though paralyzed."[39]

In Norway, the crisis of 1895 had meanwhile provided a painful lesson in military weakness, thanks largely to the severely restrictive military budgets that had been imposed by Venstre—the very party that had pushed hardest for a separate consular system. In 1897, the Riksdag allowed the last of the reciprocal Swedish-Norwegian tariff agreements that had been in effect since 1817 to lapse in keeping with its protectionist policy, thereby harming various Norwegian business interests.[40]

The Storting now carried out military reforms and increased defense expenditures. Beginning in 1900, fortifications were constructed along the exposed southeastern border with Sweden. At that very time, a new, aggressive Russification program in Finland caused mounting fears of future Russian aggression in Sweden, which undertook to bolster its defenses against its old enemy to the east. Sweden alone was fortifying the far North for the defense of the entire peninsula, while the Norwegians in turn were fortifying themselves against Sweden. Nothing caused so much bitterness as this reflection.[41] Old fears of a possible war on two fronts revived.

In this increasingly belligerent situation, the Norwegian Left became divided over how aggressively to push the issue. In March 1893, Bjørnson broke with the radical Left and its policy of the "clenched fist." It would be impossible to fight, he wrote in Verdens Gang, against half of Norway and all of Sweden.[42] Moderate liberals, among them Bjørnson, in 1903 joined with conservatives in a coalition, the Samlingsparti, dedicated to finding a peaceful resolution of the foreign policy question through ongoing negotiation within the framework of the union. Such a resolution now seemed increasingly vital in these circles, faced as they were both with the evident Russian threat posed by the Russification campaign then at its height in Finland and the rising tide of socialism following Norway's establishment of universal manhood suffrage in 1898. The "Pure Left" (Rene Venstre), for its part, now pushed for nothing less than dissolution of the union when the time was ripe.

In 1899, Sigurd Ibsen, son of the playwright and Bjørnson's son-in-law, prepared what appeared to be a promising plan for separate consular establishments combined with a single diplomatic staff for the two kingdoms. A new union joint commission was established, and its prolonged negotiations at first seemed promising. There followed what the Norwegian historian Erik Rudeng has described as the union's brief "Indian summer," at least until the

construction of Norway's new border fortifications aroused mounting apprehension on the Swedish side. But this last effort at conciliation was spoiled
in November 1904 by the Swedish premier E. G. Boström's last-minute insistence on six clauses that once again would have confirmed Norway's dependent position under the union.

This final blow put the Pure Left in an unassailable position. Sweden
could be squarely blamed for the breakdown of negotiations. Norway now
could—and must—proceed to break the tie. Any Norwegian who opposed
such a course could be branded as unpatriotic and as the lackey of an impe-
rialistic Sweden. The Right—*Høyre*—and the moderates were backed into
a corner. Much as many of them might have wished in principle for a continued union under more acceptable conditions, they realized that with the
failure of negotiation they had played their last card. Their very survival as a
political force in the next elections left them no choice but to join in bringing about the union's dissolution.[43]

In March 1905, a new coalition government headed by Christian Michelsen came to power, which in May secured passage of a resolution in the Storting establishing a separate Norwegian consular service, in full expectation
that Oscar II would veto it. When the king did so, the ministry relegated its
powers to the Storting, thereby effectively resigning, despite the king's formal
refused to accept its resignation.

The outgoing ministry rightly counted on Oscar's inability to replace it
with a new one, which gave the Storting the opportunity to take the final step.
On 7 June 1905, it unanimously resolved that "the union with Sweden under
one king is dissolved in consequence of the king's ceasing to function as king
of Norway."[44] Oscar was profoundly mortified. As a gesture of conciliation,
the Storting thereupon offered the Norwegian throne to a prince of the house
of Bernadotte. Secretly, Bjørnson—the old republican—and his friends in
both countries apparently sought to promote the candidature of the king's
youngest son, Prince Eugen, an outstanding painter who had broad contacts
with intellectual and artistic circles in Norway, thereby once again illustrating the intimate linkage between culture and politics.[45]

While the declaration of the nation's complete independence caused wild
jubilation in Norway, it created a serious internal crisis in Sweden. Sympathy was widespread there for the aging monarch who had thus been humili-
ated, and indeed such feelings, if not openly expressed, were not lacking in
Norway as well. Kaiser Wilhelm II of Germany admonished Oscar II to oppose
force with force, while avoiding any outright offer of support. Swedish ultra-
nationalists and conservatives clamored for military action to force the Nor-

wegians back into subservience. C. A. Reuterskiöld wrote, for instance, to the editor of the conservative *Göteborgs Aftonblad* on 19 June: "I go about in chronic rage and despair over the decadence in Sweden and impudence in Norway. . . . a *war* is the *only* thing that could now arouse and unite a people lulled to complacency by peace. I *want* war, but it will not come . . . unless Norway attacks. Let us do what we can to provoke this." Foreign diplomats urged caution. The Norwegian government made military preparations.[46]

The Norwegian nationalists had meanwhile long cultivated public opinion in favor of their position abroad. Notable in this regard were Bjørnson's numerous articles in the foreign press. Bjørnson tended to regard the alleged Russian menace as a bogey manipulated by reactionary *storsvensker* to distract both Swedes and Norwegians from domestic and union concerns. The series of articles he wrote for the Russian newspaper *Peterburgskie Vedomosti* beginning in 1896, which sought to justify a distinctive and more conciliatory Norwegian foreign policy line, aroused particular resentment in Sweden. Early in 1905, the world-renowned Arctic explorer Fridtjof Nansen wrote a series of articles for the London *Times*, which his celebrated Swedish counterpart, Sven Hedin, the explorer of the wastes of Central Asia—a staunch conservative not to be confused with the radical *Adolf* Hedin—did his best to counteract in the foreign press.[47] Norway by 1905 enjoyed far greater sympathy abroad than Sweden.

The Norwegian government could once again count on widespread support in Sweden itself. Already in 1893, Prince Eugen, who had strongly liberal sympathies, had written from Christiania to a friend that he would not regard an amicable dissolution of the union as a "great misfortune," especially when compared with the "monstrosity" that presently existed. The initiative should nonetheless come from Sweden itself through conviction that it was morally right rather than through "exhaustion." Liberal leaders such as Adolf Hedin and Karl Staaf had been consistently outspoken in their pro-Norwegian views, as were various liberal newspapers. During the crisis in 1905, liberal and radical intellectuals made a public appeal for peace. During that summer, August Strindberg published articles in the Norwegian, Danish, and German press justifying the Norwegians' dissolution of the union.[48]

Perhaps more seriously, the growing Social Democratic and labor movements in Sweden became intensely involved, holding massive rallies in support of the Norwegian cause. The union conflict concerned only the bourgeoisie, the Social Democratic newspaper *Brand* proclaimed, and in the present crisis, it revealed greater hostility toward Sweden's working class than the Norwegian people ever did. In speeches held at labor rallies in Stockholm in March and April, Adolf Hedin pointed to a more radical solution: "Sweden's workers hold the power to impose an absolute veto against a war between Sweden and Norway. They should now prepare to express this veto." The socialists and labor unions responded by calling publicly for their adherents to refuse military service in the event that war between the brother peoples should break out.[49]

The Swedish political scientist Evert Vedung has pointed to the paradoxical alignment of political forces in the two kingdoms by 1905. In effect, the Norwegian Right and the Swedish Left had found in the union reinforcement for their respective political objectives. Meanwhile, the aggressively nationalistic Norwegian Left and Swedish Right—much as they detested each other's political principles—had in common their opposition to the political forces that they perceived the union as upholding. As the liberal Swedish *Karlstads-Tidningen* recognized in 1905, "The Norwegian Left and the Swedish Right have worked like two cogwheels in breaking down the union."[50]

Conservative nationalists in Sweden had indeed seriously considered terminating the union following the establishment in 1884 of ministerial responsibility in Norway and especially the Storting's restrictive military reform the following year, both of which seriously curtailed the power of the crown in the sister kingdom. "The advanced liberal tendencies of the Norwegians," the British minister wrote from Stockholm in 1891, "are highly offensive to the Conservative Swedes, who fear the example may lead to their own discomfiture." Nonetheless, when Curry Treffenberg proposed dissolution in the Riksdag's First Chamber in 1893, his motion found no support.

At the height of the consular crisis two years later, the ultraconservative nationalist, Rudolf Kjellén, known as the "father of geopolitics," was prepared to let the Norwegians go—but only in return for the cession of a sizable part of southeastern Norway. "Then," he maintained, "we will have shown that we still possess national strength and through this action heightened [our] national feeling more than hundreds of unions. . . . Then we would have Norway in our hand for the future: a pledge, to be returned if Norway, once it has tired of this masquerade, can offer us real guarantees for a true and fair union." Crown Prince Gustaf and Oscar II himself seem to have speculated during the summer of 1905 that the Norwegians would establish a republic that ultimately would fail, bringing Norway once again back into a union with Sweden.[51]

That more than national spirit and *Realpolitik* was involved is revealed by Kjellén in an article in the conservative *Göteborgs Aftonblad* in December 1899. "We, the champions of nationalism in this country," he wrote, "are fighting on two fronts: in part against a united Norway, in part internally, against those elements of society that, rightly or wrongly, feel themselves disadvantaged in our political life and who therefore in a patriotic Swedish victory over Norway are unable yet to see anything but the 'upper class's' triumph over themselves."

By the winter of 1905, the moderate conservative Harald Hjärne of Uppsala University declared in the conservative *Svenska Dagbladet*, on purely pragmatic grounds, that the defunct, existing union ought to be dissolved and replaced with an effective defensive alliance between two fully sovereign and equal kingdoms.[52]

In the final crisis, nevertheless, their natural inclinations did not prevent Swedish conservatives from seeking for reasons of both security and prestige to preserve the union nor Swedish radicals from defending the Norwegians' right to dissolve it. The Social Democratic *Brand* could now gloat that "the conservative Swedish papers, which during recent years have so often and so strongly called for dissolution of the union, should now have been satisfied. But no, *this* was not their view. It was Sweden that should make the break, otherwise it would not be proper. . . . Norway's forceful and self-confident action was in no way a blow against Sweden and the Swedish people, but rather against the braggardly and puffed-up Swedish court camarilla."[53]

Under the circumstances, saber rattling on both sides may have been mainly for the sake of appearances. A military confrontation would have been a highly risky undertaking. For Sweden, it could at best only perpetuate for a time an essentially moribund union while it ran the risk of provoking a ruinous internal crisis. The influential writer Verner von Heidenstam warned in a personal public appeal that internal dissension in Sweden threatened to create a "new and dissatisfied Norway in Sweden."

Returning from Norway in March 1905, Crown Prince Gustaf had urged that Sweden itself propose a "separation in good faith" to leave the least possible bitterness, "rather than [our] being, so to speak, kicked out of the union." The initiative must, however, come from the Riksdag, since the king was bound by oath to uphold the union of 1814. The Riksdag failed to act on this suggestion, and Oscar II faced the inevitable with resigned dignity, renouncing any intention of seeking to preserve the union by forceful means. Only thereafter did the Riksdag follow suit, accepting dissolution of the union, subject to conditions that would make the separation a bilateral agreement. It demanded that the Norwegian government confirm the will of the people through a plebiscite, to confirm that the Storting's action truly reflected the will of the majority in Norway and not simply that of a political faction. The Riksdag also demanded that Norway's provisional government negotiate the details of dissolution with the Swedish government to settle practical details.[54]

The Norwegian plebiscite of 13 August 1905, in which some 85 percent of the electorate took part, showed a majority of 367,149 to 184 in favor of ending the union. In retrospect, it may nevertheless be wondered how well this result reflected the various shades of Norwegian opinion. Following dissolution, various Norwegians privately expressed their regrets to Swedish friends. But such regrets, one imagines, must have been more for the union as it had existed in happier times during the mid-nineteenth century—or especially for what it might have become, had the final negotiations been carried out in a genuine spirit of conciliation. Quite aside from the pressures of the moment, few were prepared to vote to preserve the union as it was, or threatened to become, by the spring of 1905. The historian Yngvar Nielsen declared that while he had always been among the union's staunchest supporters, during its final months, he, with most others of like mind, had suffered bitter disillusionment and had come to accept its dissolution. Events, he wrote, had "destroyed old ideals, but in return created new and greater ones."[55]

Negotiations in Karlstad during the summer dealt primarily with military questions. The bargaining was hard and at times heated, with Sweden shrewdly employing the diplomatic ace the Storting had given it by offering the Norwegian throne to a Bernadotte prince. By deliberately delaying its response, Norway was kept officially deprived of a head of state, without which foreign powers refused to recognize its independence or offer support. Ultimately, the Norwegian government was prepared to accede to Swedish demands to demilitarize the border, which involved the demolition of fortifications constructed at great expense since 1900 and aroused widespread indignation in Norway as a parting reminder of the Swedish will to dominate. Details concerning transit rights, the special privileges of the nomadic Lapps in the far north, and arbitration of future disputes were also worked out.[56]

Although there was much strong sentiment on the Left for establishing a republic, when Oscar II at last rejected a Bernadotte candidature, the Storting offered the Norwegian crown to Prince Carl of Denmark. He was crowned as King Haakon VII, thereby emphasizing the continuity of Norwegian kingship since the Middle Ages.

It is meanwhile worth noting that the mother of the new Norwegian king was the Bernadotte princess, Louise, and that in 1929 Princess Märtha of Sweden, a granddaughter of Oscar II, would marry the Norwegian crown prince, later Olav V, and become the mother of the present King Harald V of Norway.

Ultimately, the only way for Norway to attain full equality with Sweden was to establish its full independence. Hard feelings lingered on both sides. Nonetheless, there was also great relief. "An entire people constitutes itself a national assembly, all voices are united as one," Bjørnson wrote at the height of the crisis. "In hopes of peace, a powerful invocation is heard: My brother, our friendship is threatened by the relationship we find ourselves in. Let us find freer guides to working together." "May we leave each other at a time when we may once again find one another," August Strindberg wrote in the Norwegian *Nationaltidende* in July. "[May we] discover each other again, and when we have forgotten the bitterness become friends anew; for friendship can exist only between free men." In his speech renouncing the Norwegian throne, Oscar II declared, "May God give Sweden strength and unity to regain what it may lose through a dissolution of the union."[57] Both kingdoms could now devote themselves to putting their own houses in order, and a new beginning was now possible for ongoing Nordic interaction in the time to come.[58]

Carl XIV Johan, the former French field marshal Jean-Baptiste Bernadotte, was elected successor to the Swedish throne in 1810, brought about the union of Norway and Sweden in 1814, and reigned over both kingdoms with a strong hand from 1818 to 1844. (Portrait by Emil Mascré, 1843, Rosersberg Palace. Courtesy of Svenskt Porträttarkiv, Stockholm.)

Oscar I, who succeeded his father in 1844 and reigned until 1859, at first inspired liberal
hopes but became increasingly conservative and opposed to representational reform in
Sweden. (Portrait by K. T. Staaf, 1858, Gripsholm Palace. Courtesy of Svenskt Porträttarkiv,
Stockholm.)

Carl XV, who reigned from 1859 to 1872, possessed a sanguine, romantic nature and strong aesthetic interests. By 1864, his hopes for a broader Scandinavian union under Swedish leadership failed to materialize. While skeptical toward Swedish representational reform, he at last sanctioned it in 1866. (Portrait by A. J. G. Virgin, 1873, the Royal Palace, Stockholm. Courtesy of Svenskt Porträttarkiv, Stockholm.)

Oscar II, the younger brother of Carl XV and a former naval officer, reigned longest over the Dual Monarchy, from 1872 to 1907. Sentimentally attached to Norway, he nonetheless opposed the growing movement there toward democracy and greater autonomy until Norway unilaterally seceded from the union in 1905. (Portrait by Edvard Perséus, 1880, the Naval College, Näsby. Courtesy of Svenskt Porträttarkiv, Stockholm.)

The Norwegian professor Lorenz Dietrichson lectured on Danish and Norwegian literature at Uppsala University in 1859–62, held posts at the National Art Gallery and the Royal
Academy of Art in Stockholm in 1866–75, and served as the leading mediator of Norwegian culture in Sweden. (Pen sketch by Fritz von Dardel, date unknown. Courtesy of
Kungliga Biblioteket, Stockholm.)

The liberal nationalist poet and publicist Bjørnstjerne Bjørnson was the most influential and controversial opinion-maker in Norway during the second half of the nineteenth century. In Sweden as well as Norway, he was idolized by liberals and radicals and vilified by conservatives. (Portrait by Erik Werenskiold, 1900. Photo: Dowic Fotografi. Courtesy of Statens Museum for Kunst, Copenhagen.)

The dramatist Henrik Ibsen, who spent much of his career outside of Norway, shunned political involvement, although his plays had a profound influence on Swedish literature and viewpoints from the 1860s through the 1880s. (Portrait by Erik Werenskiold, 1895. Photo: J. Lathion. ©Nasjonalgalleriet, Oslo.)

AVG·STRINDBERG
FVRVSVND · JVLI · 1899 · RITADT AT HAN
CAMLE VÄN

The Swedish author and dramatist August Strindberg was initially influenced by Ibsen and Bjørnson but became alienated from both and led the way by the mid-1880s to a growing reaction in Sweden against exaggerated and uncritical admiration for Norwegian culture. (Portrait by Carl Larsson, 1899. Courtesy of Nationalmuseum, Stockholm.)

The poet Verner von Heidenstam took the lead by the late 1880s in creating a Swedish national romanticism in literature and the arts in reaction to the prevailing realism, which he portrayed as characteristically Norwegian. (Portrait by Oscar Björck, 1900. Courtesy of Göteborgs Konstmuseum, Göteborg.)

Vossevangsdalen, a romantic Swedish view of Norway in the early nineteenth century, anticipates the later idealization of that land by both Norwegian and Swedish artists. (Engraving by M. G. Anckarsvärd, from C. J. Fahlcrantz, August Anckarsvärd, and Michael Gustaf Anckarsvärd, *Samling af Svenska och Norrska Utsigter*, Stockholm, 1830.)

From Hjelle in Valdres (1841) by Norway's greatest romantic landscape painter, Johan Christian Dahl, expresses the Norwegians' growing pride in their ancient rural culture and magnificent natural surroundings. (Photo: J. Lathion. ©Nasjonalgalleriet, Oslo.)

Peasant Wedding at Hardanger (1848) by Adolf Tidemand, who painted the figures, and Hans Frederik Gude, who painted the scenery, is the quintessential Norwegian work in the Düsseldorf style of genre and landscape painting and one of the great icons of mid-nineteenth-century Norwegian national romanticism. (Photo: J. Lathion. ©Nasjonalgalleriet, Oslo.)

Sunday Morning in Blekinge (1883) by Bengt Nordenberg is representative of the work by Swedish artists who flocked to Düsseldorf to study following a widely acclaimed Norwegian exhibition in Stockholm in 1850. A characteristic genre painting clearly influenced by the Norwegian Düsseldorf style, it was painted at a time when many Norwegian and Swedish artists were already being drawn to Paris and French realism. (Courtesy of Malmö Konstmuseum.)

The Emigrants (c. 1870) by S. V. Helander, one of the lesser-known Swedish Düsseldorf artists, recalls an earlier painting of the same motif by the Norwegian Tidemand and illustrates Norwegian influence not only on Swedish art but on the growing Swedish emigration to America. (Courtesy of Nordiska Museets Arkiv, Stockholm.)

Norwegian Fjord in Moonlight (1872) by the most outstanding of the Swedish Düsseldorf painters, Marcus Larson, reveals the powerful fascination Norway's dramatic landscapes exercised on the Swedish imagination, especially during the third quarter of the nineteenth century. (Courtesy of Nationalmuseum, Stockholm.) (*Opposite*)

Norwegian Landscape from Valdres, an anonymous engraving, is from the Swedish Scandinavianist and Old Norse enthusiast Peter August Gödecke's widely read and influential travel account "En resa i Norge," in *Land och Folk* (1873).

Thor's Battle with the Giants (1872) by Mårten Eskil Winge represents the school of historical painting in Sweden, contemporaneous with the Düsseldorf group, that was devoted to the saga age as well as to dramatic scenes from more recent Swedish history. (Courtesy of Nationalmuseum, Stockholm.)

This engraving of the twelfth-century Borgund stave church is by the painter Johan Christian Dahl, who later took the lead in organizing the Norwegian Society for the Preservation of National Monuments, in 1844. (From J. C. Dahl, *Denkmalen einer sehr ausgebildeten Holzbaukunst aus den frühesten Jahrhunterten in den innern Landschaften Norwegens*, Christiania, 1836–37.)

"Storstugan II," the summer home of physician Carl Curman in Lysekil, photographed in 1880, exemplifies the vogue in Sweden during the 1870s and 1880s for building in the Old Norse style, inspired by medieval stave churches and traditional peasant building traditions in Norway. (Courtesy of Nordiska Museets Arkiv, Stockholm.)

The Military Society Masquerade Ball in Stockholm, photographed in 1869, featured costumes designed by August Malmström, the painter par excellence of Nordic antiquity. From the 1860s to the 1880s, masquerade balls with Old Norse themes were highly fashionable in Sweden. (Courtesy of Stockholms Stadsmuseum, Stockholm.)

From Telemark (1883) by Erik Werenskiold, one of the Norwegian painters inspired by French *plein air* realism during the 1870s to break with the romanticism of the Düsseldorf school, nonetheless reveals a deep feeling for its characteristic Norwegian motif, while anticipating the twilight mood of the following years. (Photo: J. Lathion. ©Nasjonalgalleriet, Olso.)

Our Daily Bread (1886) by the Swede Anders Zorn, who began as a realist, shows a scene from his native Dalarna, toward which he felt a strong local patriotism as well as pride in his own peasant roots. (Courtesy of Nationalmuseum, Stockholm.)

The Water Spirit (1874), an early version of a theme to which the artist would later return, was painted by the Swede Ernst Josephson in Eggedal, Norway, with a Norwegian peasant as his model and anticipated the flowering of a new romanticism in Swedish art by the 1890s. (Photo: Ebbe Carlsson. Courtesy of Göteborgs Konstmuseum, Göteborg.)

Summer Night (1886) by Eilif Peterssen was painted at Fleskum, where a group of young Norwegian artists one memorable summer established the long Nordic twilight as a characteristic theme in Scandinavian turn-of-the-century painting. (Photo: J. Lathion. ©Nasjonalgalleriet, Oslo.)

Nordic Summer Evening (1899) by Richard Bergh is perhaps the ultimate expression of fin de siècle Swedish national romanticism with its mood of quiet pensiveness and underlying melancholy. Prince Eugen stood as the model for the man in his friend's painting. (Photo: Ebbe Carlsson. Courtesy of Göteborgs Konstmuseum, Göteborg.)

Early Spring at Ballingsta (1891) is an intimate Swedish landscape by Prince Eugen, who was inspired by Norwegian painting and truly discovered the Nordic landscape while painting in Norway in 1889 and 1890. He later became the principal link between Swedish and Norwegian artists of his time. (Courtesy of Nationalmuseum, Stockholm.) (*Opposite*)

Midsummer Dance (1899) by Anders Zorn, who had become one of the most celebrated exponents of Swedish national romanticism by the 1890s, is suffused with pride in Sweden's ancient peasant culture and with nostalgia as the sun sets upon the old ways of life, even in tradition-rich Dalarna. (Courtesy of Nationalmuseum, Stockholm.)

Autumn (1909) by Helmer Osslund expresses exhilaration over the opening of Sweden's vast northern wilderness, which inspired the founding of the Swedish Tourist Society in 1885. (Courtesy of Nationalmuseum, Stockholm.)

The Victors' Ships Return from Svolder by Erik Werenskiold is from *Snorres Kongesagaer*, the widely read 1899 translation of thirteenth-century Icelandic sagas of the Norwegian kings that glorifies the Viking and Early Christian Middle Ages as Norway's historic age of greatness and continues to inspire national patriotism, in part because of its evocative illustrations by leading Norwegian artists. (©2001 Artists Rights Society [ARS], New York/BONO, Norway.)

Frognerseteren Restaurant outside Christiania, photographed in 1890, was designed by
Holm Munthe and was an outstanding example of the culmination of the Old Norse
"dragon style" of architecture in the 1890s. (Courtesy of Riksantikvaren, Oslo.)

Gustaf III Receives the Antique Statues from Italy (1896), a mural by Carl Larsson in the grand staircase at Stockholm's National Museum of Art, proudly celebrates Sweden's cultural brilliance and refinement during the eighteenth century, when Norway remained in a period of national eclipse under Danish domination. (Courtesy of Nationalmuseum, Stockholm.)

A private villa in Gävle shows the winsome grace of Swedish national romantic domestic architecture around 1900, reflecting the tasteful neoclassical style of a century earlier, in contrast to the Old Norse "dragon style" in Norway. (Courtesy of Eva Eriksson, Bromma.)

The Stockholm Law Courts Building, designed by Carl Westman and built in 1909–15, illustrates the proud reassertion of the simple and massive "Vasa" style from Sweden's sixteenth- and seventeenth-century age of greatness. (Courtesy of Stockholms Stadsmuseum, Stockholm.)

Part Two

Culture

4

The Cultural Vision

I N 1814, Norway had become a political, but not yet a cultural, nation. During the first decades of its new existence, its national consciousness was concentrated above all upon its constitution and its political life. But if it was no longer a part of the Danish state, it was still very much a Danish cultural province. "In Christiania they regarded Copenhagen as Norway's real capital," the visiting Swedish scholar Sven Nilsson wrote in 1816, "which is not strange considering that they have been so recently liberated from it." The town was "more Danish than Norwegian," in Nilsson's view, "in appearance, language, and attitudes." Bergen showed strong German influences and Trondheim English ones, reflecting their established trade patterns, he observed, and in Trondheim he noted that English was often spoken among members of the prominent merchant families.[1]

Christiania, which now emerged as the capital of the new nation, offered a slender cultural base at best. A town of some thirteen thousand people in 1814, it was at the time smaller than Bergen and confined to an area of only around six hundred square meters. Aside from the medieval Akershus castle, the cathedral from 1697, and the cathedral school, all its other buildings were originally built for private use. Up until 1849, a single-story former merchant's compound popularly called "Anker's Palace" served as the royal residence. The Storting met in the cathedral school until 1866, and the new government bureaus and university sought out such accommodations as they could find in town.

The contrast with Stockholm, with its population of some seventy thousand, its magnificent royal palace, resplendent court, public buildings, stock exchange, opera, theater, academies, and opulent private residences, was striking, as it was in other ways with Sweden's old university towns, Uppsala and Lund. According to August von Hartmansdorff, secretary to the first

Swedish statholder in Norway, a visit to Stockholm would be as great an experience for a Norwegian as a visit to Paris for a Swede. The Norwegian visitor who could compare the Swedish capital not with Christiania but with Copenhagen as it had been in its glory before the Napoleonic wars might not, however, be so greatly impressed.[2]

Christiania's new status nonetheless brought constant growth and development over the following decades. Construction of the neoclassical royal palace began in 1825 and was at last completed in 1848. During the 1840s, a broad avenue that to this day bears Carl Johan's name was laid out, connecting the palace with the town, and along it the capital's main public edifices were constructed. These included the Stock Exchange in 1826–28, the university complex in 1841–54, the Storting building (by a Swedish architect) in 1861–66, and the National Theater, which opened in 1899.[3]

Cultivated Swedes, who prided themselves on their urbane and cosmopolitan refinement and liked to refer to themselves as the "Frenchmen of the North," generally considered the Norwegian ruling class ignorant and uncouth at the beginning of the century. Queen Hedvig Elisabeth Charlotta wrote in her diary for September 1814:

> That nation, however capable it may be, lacks all civilization, the diffusion of which the Danish government constantly sought to hinder. The Norwegians have taken on the poorer characteristics and unrefined manners of the English although not the English merchants' knowledge and sophistication. In addition, the Norwegians love to drink and smoke, and lack any concept of a refined social life. Art and science are unknown, the women have no style. . . . The Norwegians are in general grossly uneducated.

In November, she wrote of their absurd conceitedness and went on:

> Wealthy Norwegians are merchants. Norway is a nation of merchants. Every Norwegian devotes himself to commerce and strives to become rich. This takes up all his time, so that he has no chance to develop a profession or cultivate the fine arts. The situation is altogether different in Sweden. Here the crown has often shown its interest in enlightenment, belles lettres, science, and the arts, which have then been supported and encouraged. This was especially the case most recently with Gustaf III.

"The greatest crudeness still prevails in that land," the poet J. A. Wadman declared at the time. "We shall see whether the sun of new-gained freedom can warm those peasant hearts, which until now, under Denmark's fatherly scepter, never learned to beat for any virtues other than a larger herring catch or smuggling along the coasts." In his memoirs written in the 1830s, General Anders Fredrik Skjöldebrand, who had visited northern Norway in 1799 and had taken part in the campaign and negotiation of the Convention of Moss there in 1814, showed great contempt for the Norwegians for their ignorance and their national conceit. "The Norwegians," he wrote indignantly, "who can only look back to deeds from the ancient obscurity of the saga age . . . who during more enlightened centuries vegetated under Danish despotism and never took a step toward recovering their freedom . . . consider themselves nobler and more valiant than all other nations." The Swedes he meanwhile considered all too modest about their glorious past. The early Swedish statholders and their staffs in Christiania generally felt as though they were in social and cultural exile.[4]

Swedish skepticism regarding breeding and higher culture in Norway did not prevent those with romantic sensibilities from idealizing Norway's magnificent nature, the stirring Old Norse past, and the presumed virtues of the Norwegian peasantry, attitudes largely absorbed indirectly by way of British and Continental romanticism.[5] Sven Nilsson, traveling in Norway in 1816, reflected this view when he wrote of the peasants of the Dovre region, "These mountain-dwellers are fortunate people; they receive from their herds all that they need, their life is almost nomadic. Many vices that thrive in towns, particularly larger ones, are unknown to them. Courage, honesty, and hospitality are the main traits of their character." They were, in his view, progressively more corrupted the closer they lived to towns, "the proximity of which is always harmful to the peasantry." Even Queen Hedvig Elisabeth Charlotta imagined the lower classes in Norway to be the best part of the nation.[6]

The romantic attitude of the time is reflected in Swedish art. For all his later bitterness and contempt for the Norwegians, Skjöldebrand, an accomplished amateur artist, published his dramatic lithographs of landscapes in northernmost Norway in 1813. Sweden's leading romantic landscapist, Carl Johan Fahlcrantz, together with August and Michael Gustaf Anckarsvärd, brought out a popular series of engravings of striking scenery from both Norway and Sweden in 1830, replete with towering mountings, deep fjords, and plunging waterfalls, typically with idyllic farmsteads and picturesque peasants in the middle distance.[7]

Comparisons between the new but largely undeveloped Norwegian kingdom and the expanding young American republic again come readily to mind. To its liberal admirers, America—like Norway—offered a dream of primitive innocence in grandiose surroundings, of sturdy and independent cultivators of the soil, of freedom and equality, and of a better tomorrow. To conservative skeptics, it presented a nightmare of unbridled egotism, crass materialism, ignorant self-satisfaction, and cultural desolation.[8]

Historically, the normal course of state formation has been that cultural precedes political nationalism. In Norway, the challenge was, on the contrary, to fill out the new political framework by recovering—and in large degree creating—a distinctive national culture and identity.[9] During the first decades after 1814, inspiration came primarily from the established Nordic cultural nations. Danish influences naturally remained strong. The eighteenth-century Danish classical canon at first continued to dominate Norway's modest literary scene, and Danish actors held the stage up to midcentury. Clinging closely to the Danish heritage helped educated Norwegians to mark their distinctiveness vis-à-vis their Swedish partners within the union.[10] But new romantic impulses now came not only from Denmark but, for the first time, from Sweden as well.

The beginning of the nineteenth century was a time of intense cultural creativity in both Denmark and Sweden, the golden age of Scandinavian romanticism. In both lands, the new wave not only reflected invigorating influences from Great Britain and the Continent but expressed a defiant reaction to the traumas and defeats both kingdoms had suffered during the Napoleonic wars. In Denmark, Adam Oehlenschläger and Nicolai Frederik Severin Grundtvig looked back to heroic pre-Christian Nordic antiquity for solace and inspiration in dramatic tragedies and epic verse set in the Viking age.

In Sweden, enthusiastic young romantics in Uppsala organized a Gothic League (*Götiska Förbundet*) in 1810, whose spirit is best represented by the poets Esaias Tegnér and Erik Gustaf Geijer, which was likewise devoted to promoting the glories of the ancient North, seeking thereby to revitalize their nation for the challenges ahead. Together, Tegnér and Geijer set the dominant themes for a distinctive Nordic romanticism. Tegnér—like Oehlenschläger—extolled the robust virtues of the Viking age, above all in his epic *Frithiofs saga*. Geijer idealized both the hardy Viking and the sturdy peasant landowner, notably in his *Vikingen* (The Viking) and *Odalbonden* (The yeoman), showing how the latter was the former's worthy successor.[11]

For Swedish as well as Danish romantics, Norway was of central importance. There lay Scandinavia's most sublime scenery and most archaic ways of life in remote mountain valleys and along distant fjords. The history and lore of the Viking age were, thanks to the medieval Icelandic sagas, better preserved for Norway than for the other Scandinavian lands, except for Iceland itself. Here, the past seemed closest to the present. Norway thus stood, in the eyes of Danes and Swedes, as the living monument to the Old Nordic heritage.

Underlying this veneration were two fundamental assumptions: that this heritage was most faithfully preserved among the contemporary Scandinavian peasantry and that, while it lived on most vividly in Norway, it was common to all of Scandinavia. It was thus altogether natural, for instance, that a Norwegian should be included among the original members of the Gothic League in Uppsala and that both Oehlenschläger in his drama *Hakan Jarl* and Tegnér in his epic *Frithiofs saga* should chose Norwegian subjects and settings. Geijer's peasant landholder likewise reflected a common ideal.

Norwegians could thus draw inspiration from both Swedish and Danish romanticism to devote themselves to their own rich past and folk culture. According to the Norwegian literary scholar Kristian Magnus Kommandantvold, the cultural tide within the Dual Monarchy flowed from Sweden to Norway at least up to the middle of the nineteenth century. *Frithiofs saga* from 1825 in particular achieved a veritable cult status in Norway, as witnessed, for instance, by the popularity of the names of its main characters, Frithiof and Ingeborg, in Norway as well as in Sweden. As a historian as well as a poet, Geijer also inspired interest in Norway in the country's past and peasantry.

The poet Henrik Wergeland was particularly well-read in Swedish literature and a warm admirer above all of the Swedish romantic poets; Örjan Lindberger holds that Sweden meant far more to Wergeland than Wergeland to Sweden and that indeed Swedish inspiration was of fundamental importance to his work. Bjørnstjerne Bjørnson fondly recalled how in his childhood his mother had often read to him from *Frithiofs saga*, which left a profound impression. He had also been an avid reader of Swedish history.[12]

In Norway, romantic influences were meanwhile slow to assert themselves in literature. The first clear manifestations of a Norwegian national cultural awakening are rather to be sought in the realm of art, above all in landscape painting. The great central figure in this regard was Johan Christian Dahl, who was trained in Copenhagen and who from 1824 was a professor at the Dresden Academy of Art in Saxony, since Norway could at the time offer no real training and little profitable employment for artists. Dahl nonetheless frequently visited his native land on sketching trips, resulting in vast romantic Norwegian mountain landscapes. He was meanwhile influential in establishing the Norwegian Society for the Preservation of Historical Monuments (*Foreningen til norske Fortidsmindesmærkers Bevaring*) in 1844, whose work would in time provide inspiration for new building in traditional Norwegian vernacular styles. As a painter, Dahl had his Norwegian disciples, the best-known being the talented Thomas Fearnley, who was partly of English descent and who also spent much of his short life abroad, and Peder Balke, painter of Norway's far north, both of whom also studied for a time at Stockholm's Royal Academy of Art. Like Balke, others such as Johan Flintoe, Jacob Munch, or Mattias Stoltenberg worked mainly in Norway, seeking such patronage as they could, including commissions from Carl XIV Johan and his successors.

As yet, Norwegian artists did not seek to portray heroic figures and scenes from Nordic antiquity as a number of their Swedish colleagues, such as the painters Nils Jakob Blommér or Carl Wahlbom or the sculptor Bengt Erland Fogelberg, strove with varying success to do. Nor did they depict the cozy domesticity of the Biedermeier age as did contemporary Danish painters, such as Christoffer Wilhelm Eckersberg or Constantin Hansen. In the world of Scandinavian art, the romantic landscape was their particular forte, and here they were able to provide stimulus to their neighbors.

By the 1840s, Norwegian artists found a new source of inspiration in the German Düsseldorf school of genre painting. Several studied at Düsseldorf's art academy, most notably Adolf Tidemand, who first arrived in 1837 and was appointed a professor there in 1845, and Hans Frederik Gude, who arrived in 1841 and thereafter served as a professor in Düsseldorf, Karlsruhe, and Berlin. Tidemand specialized in picturesque scenes from peasant life featuring colorful holiday folk dress and archaic interiors, while Gude was primarily a painter of romantic landscapes and seascapes. In 1848, the two collaborated in painting *Peasant Wedding at Hardanger*, one of the veritable icons of Norwegian national romanticism, showing a festive, brightly clad wedding party crossing the choppy fjord by boat, with an ancient stave church, against a backdrop of towering, snow-clad mountains, in the distance. Under Gude's inspiration, several Norwegians, such as August Cappelen and Lars Hertervig, devoted themselves to evocative landscapes of their native land.[13]

Genre painting from peasant life received a strong stimulus from the collections of colorful old Norwegian folktales brought out beginning in 1842 by Peter Christen Asbjørnsen and Jørgen Moe, which aroused great enthusiasm for the old Norwegian traditions preserved orally over the generations in peasant lore.[14]

In the same vein, Ludvig Mattias Lindeman, following earlier Danish and Swedish examples, traveled around Norway collecting over a thousand traditional folk melodies. A vogue for Norwegian folk music was, however, above all created by the violinist, composer, and impresario Ole Bull, best remembered in America for his failed Norwegian settlement at Oleana, Pennsylvania, in 1852–53. Building upon his immense popularity as a performer, he played his artful arrangements of traditional folk melodies to enthusiastic audiences both at home and abroad. In addition to Bull, Richard Nordraak and Halfdan Kjerulf adapted and made generous use of folk melodies and musical idioms in their compositions, soon to be followed by Edvard Grieg, Christian Sinding, and Johan Svendsen.

Elaborately costumed representations of festive scenes from peasant life became vastly popular by midcentury in fashionable salons and on the stage of Ole Bull's Norske Teater in Bergen, the first truly Norwegian theater, which opened in 1850. An amusing episode illustrating the gap between the genteel adaptation of folk tradition of the time and the real thing was a performance that year of a play, *Fjeldstuen* (The mountain cottage), by Henrik Wergeland, in which Bull brought in real peasants to dance in the wedding scene. The lads swung the lasses so vigorously, according to a contemporary account, that "their skirts flew straight out in the air. It then became apparent that these dancers were in traditional dress both inside and out. But traditional dress unfortunately did not include—pantaloons!"[15]

The portal figure in Norwegian national romantic literature was Henrik Wergeland, perhaps Norway's greatest lyric poet of the century and an outspoken protagonist in cultural debate. Whereas the defense of the country's constitutional rights was directed against political pressures, real or perceived, from Sweden, the assertion of its distinctive natural culture and identity involved its liberation from lingering Danish cultural hegemony. Wergeland proudly asserted Norway's cultural independence and wrote dramas and verse celebrating its imposing landscape, proud medieval past, and genuine folk character, while vocally supporting the political strivings of the peasantry to create a more democratic society. To mark his nationalist and populist stance, he made generous use of Norwegian vernacular idioms in his language. Toward Sweden, meanwhile, Wergeland had mixed feelings. Although a proud Norwegian patriot, he warmly admired Swedish romanticism and the Swedish language. He also came genuinely to admire Carl XIV Johan, who appreciated his talent and appointed him Norway's national archivist, a post for which he was unfortunately ill suited.

Wergeland was by no means unopposed in his time. His bitter rival was Johan Sebastian Welhaven, the head of a group of young intellectuals in Christiania who proudly called themselves the "Intelligence Party" and indignantly rejected what in their view was Wergeland's dangerous populism and narrow cultural chauvinism. While no less patriotically Norwegian, they were apprehensive over the political rise of the peasant masses and the vulgarization of Norway's culture before it had the chance to mature as a part of the wider European cultural world. Wergeland and the "Patriots" turned "inward," as Anne-Lise Seip has expressed it, whereas Welhaven and the "Intelligence Party" turned "outward." The fierce polemic battle between popular national and higher cosmopolitan culture brought to the surface tensions within Norwegian society and cultural life that would run throughout the period of the union and beyond. At the heart of this controversy there lay— and still lies—the difficult question of how narrowly or broadly to define what was authentically "Norwegian." That Wergeland's younger sister, Camilla, was passionately in love with Welhaven made the men's personal rivalry all the more complex. Under her later married name, Camilla Collett would herself become a novelist and a pioneer of Norwegian feminism.[16]

The writing of history played a central role in the creation of a Norwegian national consciousness. Norway's heroic era had been the Viking and the Christian Middle Ages up to the decline of the fourteenth century, celebrated in song and saga. Wergeland and others regarded the Danish domination that followed as Norway's "lost centuries," a time of profound stagnation at last ended by the national revival after 1814.

This view of the past became basic to the work of the country's most important historians during the earlier nineteenth century, Jacob Rudolf Keyser and Peter Andreas Munch. Reviving a theory first presented by the eighteenth-century Norwegian scholar Gerhard Schønning, they maintained that the Norwegians were of a distinct and different origin than their Scandinavian neighbors, having migrated into the peninsula from the north and the east. The kindred *Svear*, or Swedes, had meanwhile entered central Sweden from the east. Together they overcame and dominated in pre-Viking times the Teutonic "Goths" in southern Sweden and Denmark, who had come into the region from the south. This theory carried the implication that the Norwegians represented the purest of the old Scandinavian stock.[17]

More controversial and provocative yet was their theory that the old, pre-Christian Nordic *(Norrøn)* culture was uniquely Norwegian in origin and that the saga literature was written in an originally distinct and separate Norwegian language and its later Icelandic variant. As Keyser stated categorically, "There is . . . every reason to assume that just as the Norwegian branch of the [Germanic] race was that which kept itself freest from intermixture with other peoples, it consequently possessed the richest and purest traditions from the origins of the race." For P. A. Munch, it was a matter of defending from encroachment what rightly belonged to his nation, in particular against Danish claims: "No proprietary right is more greatly respected among nations than that which each nation has to its historic memories. To deprive a nation of these is almost as unjust as to deprive it of a part of its territory. And such a despoliation is doubly unjust when it affects a nation like Norway, which has so few historic memories that it cannot afford to lose any whatsoever, no matter how insignificant, to say nothing of the best that it possesses." Both Denmark and Sweden, he held, had gained sufficient glory for themselves during their more recent histories.[18] In this manner, Keyser and Munch sought to assert the Norwegians' uniqueness and innate superiority to both their Scandinavian neighbors, who politically and culturally had in more recent times dominated Norway, and they stoutly opposed their claims to a shared Old Norse heritage.

It was ironic in this regard that much of the romantic enthusiasm for the Old Norse saga age in Norway had, as has been seen, previously drawn inspiration from both Denmark and Sweden. The Keyser-Munch theory meanwhile directly challenged the authority of the venerable *Ynglinga saga*, originating with the Norwegian skald Tjodolf of Hvin around A.D. 900 and recorded in the Icelandic chronicler Snorri Sturlason's *Heimskringla* in the thirteenth century. According to this account, the Asa folk, led by their chieftain Odin, had come from their legendary homeland, Great Svithiod, presumed to lie somewhere near the Black Sea, to their new Svithiod in Sweden via Germany and Denmark before expanding into Norway. Uppsala, according to the saga, had been the seat of the early Asa kings and the central cult place of the ancient North.[19] The *Ynglinga saga* had been, and remained, a fundamental article of faith to most educated Scandinavians. "Svithiod" remained a favored poetic designation for Sweden, especially among the Swedish romantics.

The claims of Norwegian historians to an exclusive Norwegian Old Norse culture caused great chagrin and aroused much criticism in both Denmark and Sweden. In a review of a work in 1879 by the strongly nationalist Ernst Sars, *Aftonbladet* in Stockholm sourly commented:

> It appears in many places as though he wished to mention Sweden and Denmark only to thank God that his land is not like those publicans. The sea has been no hindrance for communications between Romans, Franks, and peoples of all kinds, not even for Irish cultural influences, but rather for any similarity with Denmark. The mountains that do exist have not separated southern from northern Norway, but the mountains that do *not* exist are [presumed] to have acted as a Chinese wall against Sweden.[20]

Glorification of Norway's medieval age of greatness did not, on the other hand, preclude a growing appreciation of Carl XIV Johan among Norwegian conservative historians. The monarch who during the 1820s and the early

1830s had been seen as a constant threat to the constitution could now in ret-rospect be conceived as the founder of Norway's regained nationhood.[21]

While Asbjørnsen and Moe popularized the oral traditions of the Norwe-gian peasantry, Pastor Eilert Sundt carried out extensive studies of their material culture and living conditions. In part, these brought to public atten-tion serious social problems of poverty, drunkenness, and promiscuity in rural areas. Sundt meanwhile provided the growing vogue of enthusiasm for folk-lore and folklife with a wealth of carefully observed ethnographic detail, heightening an overall impression of the continuity of a uniquely Norwegian, archaic way of life reaching back over the "lost centuries" of Danish rule to the saga age itself.[22]

It was a fundamental dilemma, at a time when language and nationality had come to be regarded as virtually synonymous, that the Old Norse tongue had died out as a literary language by the sixteenth century and had been replaced in educated and official Norwegian circles by standard Danish. Wergeland sought to assert a national distinctiveness by deliberately intro-ducing into his writings characteristically Norwegian idioms, a practice that was much criticized by his rival Welhaven and the "Intelligence Party." Asb-jørnsen and Moe had similarly "Norwegianized" the language of their folk-tales. Ivar Aasen, a self-taught scholar of peasant background, took a far more radical approach. Regarding the existing Norwegian peasant dialects, espe-cially in the west, as survivals from the Old Norse, he set about deliberately to create through a synthesis of these dialects a "new-old," authentically Nor-wegian language, *Landsmål*—"the language of the land"—coming out with a grammar book in 1848, which was soon followed by a dictionary.

Landsmål stirred up a profound cultural conflict, which to some degree continues even today. To fervent nationalists and populist political radicals, as well as in rural districts with strong traditional antipathies toward the rul-ing elite and suspicion toward its refined cosmopolitan culture, it represented a true liberation from foreign cultural hegemony and an expression of Nor-way's national uniqueness and independence. To most members of the edu-cated classes, the bureaucracy, church, and educational establishment, *Landsmål* was an artificial creation that threatened to isolate Norway from the ongoing currents of Scandinavian and Western culture. Much of the more devout peasantry had meanwhile come to regard the old Danish as an almost sacral language in church and thus showed a marked coolness toward *Landsmål*. Looking ahead, *Landsmål*, with the powerful backing of *Venstre*, would achieve equal status with Dano-Norwegian in the elementary schools in 1892.

The alternative approach to nationalizing the language was a gradual modification of Dano-Norwegian through the introduction of purely Norwegian words and grammatical forms and the respelling of words in accordance with characteristic Norwegian pronunciation, ultimately resulting in what is presently called *Riksmål*. This had been Wergeland's practice, and it would be followed by Bjørnstjerne Bjørnson and most other Norwegian writers down to the present. Its leading protagonist during the nineteenth century was the philologist Knud Knudsen. During the twentieth century, there has been a tendency for the two forms of Norwegian to become increasingly similar, pointing toward the gradual evolution of a common *Samnorsk*.[23]

Norwegian patriotism by no means excluded warmly Pan-Scandinavian sentiments. It has been seen in chapter 3 that Scandinavianism had its political aspects. At the same time, it built—as had its antecedents in the late eighteenth century—upon the firm conviction that Danes, Swedes, and Norwegians descended from common stock, spoke variants of an original *Norrøn* tongue, and shared the same fundamental cultural traditions and values. Most educated Norwegians, like their brethren in the other Scandinavian lands, therefore had misgivings about the efforts of the more extreme Norwegianizers to erect barriers against their neighbors. Thus, for all their differences, both Wergeland and his rival Welhaven combined Norwegian patriotism with the ideal of a wider Scandinavian community. Looking back at the end of the century, their countryman Lorenz Dietrichson recalled the Scandinavianist enthusiasm of his youth:

> To preserve our national characteristics, but without suspicion, to seek without pettiness to become one with our kinsmen in all we had in common in a cultural community, which with three-fold strength could make its voice heard in the European arena and which—if and when it should reach maturity—could through circumstance lead forward even to an outward political union and thus make the North a power which need fear no great power, that seemed to us well worth devoting our life work to. There was greatness of spirit in the way in which the peoples of the North—and not only the youth—at that time regarded each other that gave our young lives meaning. . . . National feeling and Scandinavianism [went] hand in hand.

Dietrichson nonetheless here implies that at least for Norway, both cultural and political Scandinavianism posed the dilemma that the least populous, least culturally developed, and least independent of the Nordic lands might all too quickly be overshadowed by its more dominant neighbors.[24]

The first clear manifestation of Scandinavianism following the end of the Napoleonic wars was a meeting in 1829 of Swedish and Danish university students in Lund, at which Esaias Tegnér crowned Adam Oehlenschläger with a laurel wreath and declared that the old national enmities in the North were now dead. By 1842, regular meetings of students from Lund and Copenhagen began, which soon broadened in scope to include other universities. Student meetings were held in Uppsala in 1843, Lund and Copenhagen in 1845—with the earliest Norwegian participation—Christiania in 1851 and 1852, Uppsala in 1856, Copenhagen and Lund in 1862, Christiania in 1869, and Uppsala in 1876.

The jubilant student meeting in Uppsala in 1856 was of particular importance to Norwegian Scandinavianism. It was here that Dietrichson was inspired to devote himself to Norwegian-Swedish cultural exchange. It was also here that Bjørnstjerne Bjørnson, who heretofore had been mainly active as a journalist, was, by his own account, inspired to become a poet.[25]

Of Bjørnson, it has been said that if he was not the greatest Norwegian poet of the nineteenth century, he was the greatest Norwegian. Ernst Sars declared that Norway's history after 1814 could best be described as a "poetocracy," in which the first chapter should be entitled "Wergeland" and the second, "Bjørnson." In time, Bjørnson—like Wergeland, his revered role model, before him—was often referred to as the "uncrowned king of Norway."[26] His intense political engagement on the Norwegian Left has already been examined in the preceding chapter.

Bjørnson was in agreement with P. A. Munch in his view of the centuries of Danish rule as the fallow period in Norway's history, although with Ernst Sars he held that the Norwegian peasantry had preserved intact much of the Old Norse heritage. He saw it as the mission of the new cultural elite, to which he proudly belonged, to recover the nation's identity and pride, and he saw ever more his rightful role as the tribune and moral conscience of his nation.

He nevertheless remained true to his Scandinavianist ideals in the belief, which he shared with like-minded Swedes and Danes, that the three peoples were of common stock and their ancient culture and traditions of common origin. Bjørnson therefore could not accept the exceptionalist theories of the more extreme nationalist Norwegian historians, and he became a resolute opponent of the *Landsmål* movement, both of which threatened not only to widen the social and cultural cleavages within Norway itself but to isolate the Norwegians from their fellow Scandinavians and the wider Western world. These views, in which nationalism, Scandinavianism, and cosmopolitanism formed concentric circles, remained widespread in Norway to the end of the union, not least through Bjørnson's powerful influence.[27]

Relatively few Swedes and Norwegians meanwhile had any firsthand experience in each others' countries during the first half-century of the union, in no small part due to poor communications that impeded travel in either direction. Lorenz Dietrichson later wrote of the "total unfamiliarity with Swedish conditions [in Norway] and *vice versa* that prevailed during the '40s and '50s" and claimed that before the coming of the railways travel to Sweden was "more or less like a journey to Honolulu or Japan."[28] The first rail connection between Christiania and Stockholm opened as late as 1871, well after Norway had become a popular destination for seaborne tourists from Britain and Germany.

During the early decades of the union, educated Swedes showed little interest in cultural developments in Norway. Their initial prejudices in this regard have been noted, and indeed the Norwegians as yet had little to offer in the cultural—as opposed to the political—sphere. The first striking manifestation to reach Sweden from across the Keel was surely Ole Bull's triumphal concert tour in 1843, the first of several. The violinist, who by then had already concertized widely in both Europe and the United States, took his Swedish audiences by storm not only through his virtuosity but with his fascinating rendering of old Norwegian folk melodies and motifs. A review from 1843 in *Aftonbladet* shows the resonance this aroused in Stockholm.

> One heard the melancholy tones of the thrush die away like a mild breeze in the Nordic summer night, but then its song rang forth again, as though aroused by an electric shock, echoing in the forest; one heard the herdsmen's horns of the children in the mountains and imagined the herds wending their way down into the valleys from the *sætre* [mountain pasture huts]. At times a storm welled forth from his strings and one heard the stouthearted Viking singing aboard his dragon-ship.[29]

At the Scandinavian student meeting in Uppsala in 1856, Norwegian song won great popularity. From this time, Jørgen Moe and Ole Bull's *Sæterjentens Søndag* (The sæter lass's Sunday) and other Norwegian vocal works became permanently incorporated into the repertory of *Allmänna Sången*, the Uppsala university chorus. Swedish composers such as August Söderman, Albert Rubenson, and Per Ulrik Stenhammar drew upon Swedish folk modes and motifs in the spirit of their Norwegian contemporaries. Söderman commenced writing his own incidental music for Henrik Ibsen's *Peer Gynt* even before Grieg. During the 1870s, he coedited the Scandinavian *Nordiske Musikblade* together with Grieg and the Dane C. F. E. Hornemann, and he set several of Bjørnstjerne Bjørnson's lyrics to music.[30]

In 1850, an exhibition of the works of the Norwegian Düsseldorf painters was held in Stockholm. The genre and landscape paintings of Tidemand, Gude, and their colleagues powerfully reinforced the picture of an archaic and idyllic Norwegian peasant life amid majestic natural surroundings with unmistakable allusions to the virtues and values of the heroic Viking age.

The Stockholm exhibition aroused widespread enthusiasm, especially among younger Swedish painters. King Carl XV, who was keenly interested in the arts and was himself a talented amateur painter, provided stipends for a number of young artists from Sweden to study in Düsseldorf throughout the 1850s and 1860s under, among others, Tidemand and Gude. Swedish artists now began to abandon classical Rome and turn to scenes from home—via Düsseldorf. The first to go, in 1850, was Carl Henrik D'Uncker, who was of Norwegian parentage. Bengt Nordenberg, Ferdinand Fagerlin, August Jernberg, and others followed, painting scenes from Swedish peasant life strongly reflecting the influence of their Norwegian masters. Doubtless the most talented, original—and eccentric—of the Swedish Düsseldorf painters was Marcus Larson, who concentrated on dramatic Nordic landscapes, including moonlit Norwegian fjords, as well as his masterwork, *Waterfall in Småland*. A later exhibition, in 1866, of the Norwegian Düsseldorf painters at the Scandinavian Exhibition of Arts and Industry in Stockholm further heightened Swedish enthusiasm.

Alongside genre painting in the Düsseldorf style, the Gothic-romantic school of art meanwhile continued to flourish throughout much of the nineteenth century. The painters Mårten Eskil Winge and August Malmström in particular distinguished themselves with scenes, both wistfully nostalgic and strenuously heroic, drawn from Nordic mythology, which likewise provided inspiration for the sculptors Carl Gustaf Qvarnström and Johan Peter Molin.[31]

The collection of folklore began earlier in both Denmark and Sweden than in Norway, where the first such collection did not appear until 1833. Asbjørnsen and Moe's collections of Norwegian folktales, the first of which came out in 1842, however, had a new freshness and verve that made contemporary Swedish collections, an inheritance from the Gothic League, seem stale and pedantic in comparison and provided a fresh impetus to Swedish studies. Ivar

Aasen's research into old Norwegian dialects, the basis for his *Landsmål*, stimulated interest in Swedish regional dialects. Swedish, like Norwegian, folklife studies were meanwhile enriched by the studies of Norwegian peasant crafts and traditional architecture by Eilert Sundt and his followers. Leonard Fredrik Rääf, a onetime member of the Gothic League, the artist Nils Månsson Mandelgren, Gunnar Hyltén-Cavallius, Nils Gabriel Djurklou, and others enthusiastically devoted themselves to field research in different areas of Sweden.[32]

The most ambitious undertaking of this kind was Artur Hazelius's Scandinavian Ethnographic Collection, established in Stockholm in 1873. Hazelius too had taken part in the great Scandinavian students' meeting in Uppsala in 1856 and was a steadfast Scandinavianist. He resigned his teaching position at a Stockholm secondary school to take up his true vocation, allegedly inspired by Eilert Sundt, whom he thereafter visited on his first trip to Norway in 1874. Although clear evidence is lacking, this impetus seems highly probable. From the start, Hazelius acquired items of Norwegian, as well as Swedish, material folk culture. In time, his Norwegian collection became so extensive, thanks largely to a dedicated peasant from Telemark, Torjus Leifsson, that it began to arouse the apprehensions of Norwegian nationalists. In 1880, Hazelius renamed his collection the Nordic Museum.[33]

While his Swedish colleagues rejected Peter Andreas Munch's Norwegian exceptionalism, his vast historical scholarship made its mark on them. His theory that the *Svear* of central Sweden were of separate Germanic origin from the *Götar* (Goths) of southern Sweden and closely akin to the Norwegians was in accord with the old Swedish tradition, reiterated by nineteenth-century Swedish scholars, that the nation came about when the *Svear* established their domination over the *Götar* in pre-Christian times. The latter were presumed to have given their name to the provinces of Östergötland (East Gothland) and Västergötland (West Gothland), as well as the island of Gotland.

Meanwhile, both philological and archaeological studies deepened knowledge of Nordic antiquity. Professorships in Nordic philology were established in Copenhagen in 1845, Uppsala in 1859, and Christiania in 1864, arousing a growing Scandinavian interest in Iceland, the "Saga Island." Archaeological excavation in the nineteenth-century North may be considered to have begun in 1844 at the three great grave mounds at Old Uppsala, traditionally believed to contain the remains of the first three Asa kings. Important finds followed: the Viking ships at Borre in Norway in 1852, the Iron-Age boats at Nydam in South Jutland in 1859–64, the Tune ship, the Gokstad ship, and the Oseberg ship in Norway in 1867, 1880, and 1904, respectively. The Nordic lands produced several outstanding archaeologists, including Oluf Rygh and Nicolay Nicolaysen in Norway and Hans Hildebrand and Oscar Montelius in Sweden. Growing familiarity with the old Nordic material and aesthetic culture was progressively reflected in art, for example in August Malmström's illustrations for successive editions of Tegnér's *Frithiofs saga*.[34]

In this area, Sweden initially lagged behind both Denmark and Norway, which could not but arouse some nagging self-doubts. The old Norse sagas, Pontus Leonard Holmström ruefully conceded in 1866, could not hold the same place in the Swedish historical imagination as in the Norwegian. "Since the most remote times," he wrote, "our history has been oriented toward the east, but unfortunately we know little about the deeds and accomplishments of our ancestors. The Baltic had no Iceland."[35]

Soon after, in 1873, the Swede Peter August Gödecke made a reverent pilgrimage to the ancient Urnes stave church with its celebrated portal ornamented with interwoven plant and animal motifs, said to be the oldest surviving examples in Norway. Sweden too had surely once had churches in the same style, he wrote, although due to differences in climate, they no longer existed.

> We nevertheless have runestones, buckles, and [metal] ornaments for drinking vessels, decorated with the most splendid intertwinings of the same kind, which prove that the creative imaginations of the old inhabitants of the North followed the same directions on both sides of the Keel. Indeed, we even have at Ramsundsberget in Södermanland as well as on the Rök runestone from the same province inscriptions from the same parts of Sigurd Fafnesbane's saga that in Norway are found in carved wood reliefs on the portal of Hyllestad [stave] church.[36]

Swedish morale was greatly improved by the discovery of the Ramsundsberget and the Rök inscriptions, which could be offered as proof that Sweden had indeed had its part in the *Norrøn* culture of the Eddas, thereby at last providing concrete evidence against the Keyser-Munch theory of Norway's essential monopoly of the heritage.

Sweden's pre-Christian antiquity was thereafter progressively illuminated by the discovery in 1881 of the impressive site at Vendel, near Uppsala. This would be followed in due course by the even more important finds at nearby Valsgärde in 1904, filling out the picture of the pre-Viking Vendel culture between the fifth and seventh centuries. Investigation meanwhile came to reveal that close to half of all the runic inscriptions to be found anywhere were located in Swedish Uppland, centering on Uppsala.[37]

Ultimately, it would be in the realm of literature that Norway would have the greatest cultural impact on Sweden. Here, too, awareness grew slowly at first. There was some interest in Wergeland and Welhaven, and in their rivalry, among a few of the literati. The first literary depiction of Norway to arouse a somewhat wider interest nevertheless came from a Swedish, rather than a Norwegian, pen. Fredrika Bremer, who spent much of the period from 1835 to 1840 near Christiania and who was well acquainted with both Wergeland and Welhaven, felt much sympathy for Norway, although she considered its upper class materialistic, banal, and generally lacking in aesthetic refinement. She was however greatly interested in Norwegian folklife, a basic theme of her *Strid och fred, eller några scener i Norge* (Strife and peace; or, scenes in Norway) from 1840, in which she saw the world of the Old Norse sagas mirrored · in contemporary peasant life.

The other important Swedish novelist from the "liberal era" of the 1830s to 1850s, Emilie Flygare-Carlén, who came from the border province of Bohuslän, an old Norwegian territory prior to 1658, also reveals Norwegian influences. It was more than coincidence that both Bremer and Flygare-Carlén were women, since by midcentury, women of the bourgeoisie formed the majority of the growing middle-class reading public, which was above all interested in accounts of the conditions and problems of domestic life in contemporary middle-class society.[38] This interest is well reflected in Bremer's widely read account of America, *The Homes of the New World*, from 1853–54.

The first great breakthrough for Norwegian literature in Sweden came with the publication of Bjørnstjerne Bjørnson's *Synnøve Solbakken* in 1857 — the year after the Scandinavian student meeting in Uppsala that had inspired his resolve to become a poet. This was the first of the immensely popular *fortællinger*, or tales of peasant life, that established his reputation as an author, and it was followed by *Arne* in 1859, *En glad Gutt* (A happy boy) in 1860, *Fiskerjenten* (The fisher maiden) in 1868, and *Brudeslaaten* (The bridal march) in 1872. *Synnøve Solbakken* reflected much of the idyllic atmosphere of the Norwegian Düsseldorf painters. Yet, its characters were much more than "Sunday peasants" in picturesque folk dress. There was a fresh breeze of down-to-earth realism, and its characters were convincingly true to type in both strengths and weaknesses. Family rivalries, drunkenness, and fighting played their part until the final, happy resolution was reached. Bjørnson, who grew up in a rural parsonage, was well acquainted with peasant life, which the field studies of Eilert Sundt and others were then further illuminating.

Bjørnson was at the time also writing plays on Old Norse themes, and the alternation of these with his peasant tales had its didactic purpose. Following the lead provided by both Wergeland and P. A. Munch, and anticipated in 1840 by Fredrika Bremer, Bjørnson sought to show the continuity of Norway's ancient national traditions through its peasantry. Fifty years after bringing out *Synnøve Solbakken*, he declared, "What I wrote was a plea on behalf of the peasant. . . . We had come to understand that the language of the sagas lived on in our peasants, and their way of life was close to that of the sagas. The life of our nation was to be built on our history; and now the peasants were to provide the foundations."[39]

The fresh realism and evocatively Nordic tone of *Synnøve Solbakken* and its successors called forth a powerful response in Sweden. Both the critics in the more liberal press and the reading public were enthralled. That these tales should create such a sensation was due to more than the interest in Norway aroused by its liberal constitution, the Düsseldorf painters, Ole Bull, Asbjørnsen and Moe, and cultural Scandinavianism in general. The upsurge of a vital and creative national romanticism in Norway by the 1840s and 1850s coincided with the waning of the golden age of Swedish romanticism, the era of Tegnér and Geijer and the Gothic League. An anonymous critic in *Aftonbladet* summed up the Swedish literary situation in 1862: "We have poets— but rather than cultivating the soil of our homeland, they offer us greenhouse plants, unsuited to our climate, the outpourings of borrowed expressions, foreign and without value to us. We have musicians—but instead of listening to the fabled and magnificently simple tones of our nature, they seek in foreign schools foreign models, and in that way a certain cosmopolitan vagabond character, which concerns no one."

Lorenz Dietrichson, who came to Sweden in 1869, offered a Norwegian perspective when he described in his memoirs the contemporary Swedish literary scene as characterized by "echoes of Tegnér, empty patriotic bombast, and great self-satisfaction." "I was altogether too spoiled when it came to hearing the words of writers of genius," he wrote, "accustomed to hearing Welhaven's finely formed, brilliant conversation or Bjørnson's rushing cascades of new ideas or Ibsen's fine sarcasms."[40]

The Swedish response to Bjørnson's *Synnøve Solbakken* is well illustrated by a letter to its author from the Swedish actress Thecla Hebbe in 1859:

> However much greatness and beauty we can always find in foreign literature, it moves our hearts in an entirely different way when we hear a voice that has gotten its tone from our own forests and mountains, that sings of our joys and sorrows as we know them, and the more seldom it is that such a voice is heard so much more is it longed for, and it is therefore dear to

all those who hold warm feelings for the North and its folklife when a new work by you appears in our midst.

Ellen Key, a lifelong devotee of Bjørnson, wrote this about him in 1902:

I recall from my childhood the enthusiasm with which *Synnøve* and *Arne* were received and how the Norwegian character and Norwegian nature became indissolubly associated with these novels and how through these novels they became a force. It was Bjørnson who led the band of young Norwegians who with song and play conquered Sweden at a time when our own great poets and composers from the first half of the century were ever more on the wane. Apart from the writers of the sagas, no Norwegian has impressed himself so deeply on our people as Bjørnson with his peasant tales.

To the end of his life, Bjørnson would have no more devoted friend than Key, who first met him when he was a guest in her parents' Stockholm home in 1873 and thereafter carried on an adoring correspondence with him. Her youthful diary is filled with him, much of it written in Norwegian — or, more exactly, a mixture of Norwegian and Swedish. "God bless you," she wrote to Bjørnson in 1875, "our own poet, the only one in the North who knows how to tell us the truth."[41]

The Norwegian Lorenz Dietrichson would prove to be the most important mediator between Norwegian and Swedish culture during the nineteenth century. Inspired to dedicate himself to this task at the Scandinavian students' meeting in Uppsala in 1856, he revisited Sweden in 1858 and 1859, making many friends in liberal circles before moving in late 1859 to Uppsala. Here, he managed to secure a university lectureship in aesthetics, concentrating on Danish and Norwegian literature. He proved a popular teacher and soon gathered around him a group of young poets. "All Swedes, at least in my time, were enthusiastic poets," he later recalled. "To fabricate verse formed a part of one's general education and every well-brought-up young man had this ability."[42]

It was evident to Dietrichson that these young literati hungered for fresh impulses and wider horizons, which he welcomed the opportunity to provide. He saw it as his mission to promote "a closer relationship between the young Sweden and the hitherto largely unknown literatures of the other Nordic lands. What Swedish youth sought, we back home in Norway possessed in abundance in our younger school of poets, Denmark in its older [school]." Dietrichson's students were particularly enthusiastic over Bjørnson, whose

Synnøve Solbakken had recently come out, and Henrik Ibsen, who up to that time had written historical dramas on medieval Norwegian themes.[43]

On Dietrichson's initiative, several of his young followers constituted the "Nameless Society" *(Namnlösa sällskapet)*, including, among others, Count Carl Snoilsky, Carl David af Wirsén, Pontus Wikner, Ernst Daniel Björck, and Peter August Gödecke, who together are best remembered in Swedish literature as the "Signatures" from their signing their poems with their initials (or pseudonyms) only. They sought to break out of the confines of traditional romantic idealism and find a new realism, yet in the event, these objectives left only modest traces in their work. Ultimately, only Snoilsky, who would become a close friend of Henrik Ibsen, and, to a degree, Wirsén would achieve any real literary prominence.

When August Strindberg later took the "Signature" poets ironically to task, accusing them of moral hypocrisy and lack of contact with reality, Dietrichson warmly defended them in his memoirs. "We recognized the claims of ideals and fantasy together with reality. . . . We believed in the ideals behind phenomena," he wrote. "*Modern* Realism, which actually is Naturalism, believes only in nature and nothing else." They professed, he continued, "art for life," rather than "art for art's sake." Their essential question for literature and art was "whether it has contributed to the development of the good and the true among us" by enriching aesthetic sense, intelligence, and ethical life.

Dietrichson, however, was at the time a good deal more radical than his Swedish followers. In reviewing a collection of their poems in 1872, he wrote wearily of the "virginal" quality of these young poets, their lack of contact with the struggles of their time, and their aestheticizing "poetry of small ideals," doubting that this truly reflected the character of a people who once had brought forth Geijer's *Vikingen* and Tegnér's *Frithiofs saga*.[44]

In 1862, Dietrichson held a public lecture in Stockholm in which he criticized what he called "Tegnérism," the reiteration of Tegnérian themes and rhetoric by the following generation of epigones, expressing his preference for the Swedish-Finnish poet Johan Ludvig Runeberg—as well as for the Dane Oehlenschläger and the Norwegian Wergeland. This was taken as an attack on the national poet himself, which was nothing less than heresy to the Swedish literary public, especially in the aftermath of the statholder controversy of 1859–60.[45]

Dietrichson left Uppsala and spent the next four years in Rome studying antique art. Back in Sweden in 1866, he soon won the favor of the artistically minded Carl XV and was given a post at the National Art Gallery in Stockholm. In 1868, he was appointed to the faculty of the Royal Academy of Art and was granted a professorship the following year. Here he remained until he departed in 1875 to become Norway's first professor of art history at the University of Christiania. In Sweden, he was highly active as a teacher, a lecturer, and a cultural journalist, seeking to make the arts accessible to a wider public and encouraging a growing interest in applied arts. He enjoyed many warm friendships and would later recall these years in Sweden as the happiest time of his life.[46]

While in Rome, Dietrichson had been closely associated with Henrik Ibsen, who was then living there, working on his drama *Brand*. Ibsen had left Norway in disgust over his compatriots' (and the Swedes') supine behavior in leaving their brother Scandinavians, the Danes, to face the German powers alone in the war of 1864. His *Brand*, the tragedy of an iron-willed pastor confronting human frailties in a west Norwegian parish, is a powerful denunciation of the "spirit of accord" *(Akkordens Aand)*, that is, the compromises and self-deceptions that undermine moral principle, determination, and resolve. *Brand* gave striking expression to the Danish philosopher Søren Kierkegaard's uncompromising principle of "either-or."[47]

Ibsen's *Brand* came out in 1866 and had an immense impact throughout the North, firmly establishing its author's reputation. In Sweden, it was the second great Norwegian literary sensation, following Bjørnson's *Synnøve Solbakken* seven years earlier. At heart, *Brand* amounted to nothing less than a challenge to traditional humanistic values, and it did not fail to draw much criticism on that account. However, for a generation yearning for ideals and commitment in a changing world—like Agnes in the play—*Brand* inspired the will to self-sacrifice for a higher cause. It meanwhile strongly reinforced the stereotype in Sweden of a stern, individualistic, and unbending Norwegian national character that could in turn be taken as a tacit criticism of a more flexible and less determined Swedish psyche. Arne Lidén, who studied the subject in greatest detail, claimed that of the Scandinavian lands, it was Sweden that was most profoundly influenced by *Brand*, as attested to by the numerous Swedish literary works over the following two decades at least that bear its unmistakable stamp. Gustaf af Geijerstam later recalled that no writer since had "anything close to the powerful grip Ibsen was able to gain on the intellectual and emotional world of the youth." According to Fredrik Böök, Ibsen was the most basic prerequisite for the Swedish literature of the 1880s, and *Brand* was the "catechism" *(andaktsbok)* for that whole generation.[48]

It was Ibsen who likewise provided the third great Norwegian literary sensation throughout Scandinavia with the publication in 1879 of his domestic drama *Et Dukkehjem* (A doll's house), in which a young wife comes to the understanding that her marriage is a trap preventing her free self-realization as an individual and thereupon resolutely leaves her husband and children to find herself. It fell like a bombshell, unmasking the genteel pretenses of bourgeois marriage and family life. To its numerous critics, it was an attack on the most sacred sanctuary, home and family. To idealistic cultural radicals, it heralded personal emancipation and moral integrity.

Bjørnson had already begun writing realistic contemporary drama with *En Fallit* (A bankruptcy) and *Redaktøren* (The editor), both from 1875. There followed a series of realistic dramas on contemporary social themes by both Ibsen and Bjørnson, which were avidly read and much debated in Sweden. These gave substance to the highly influential Danish critic Georg Brandes's *Hovedstrømninger i det 19. Aarhundres Litteratur* (Main currents in nineteenth-century literature), the first part of which was published in 1872, a ringing condemnation of romantic conservatism that declared it the essential purpose of literature to subject the social questions of the times to debate.[49]

Several of Ibsen's and Bjørnson's plays had their debuts in Stockholm. For a time during the 1870s, Norwegian dramas appeared more frequently than Swedish ones on the Stockholm stage, to the chagrin of August Strindberg, whose early dramas, most notably *Mäster Olof* (Master Olof), published in 1872, show the strong influence of Ibsen's *Brand* and who was still struggling to get his own work performed.[50]

The floodgates were now wide open to cultural impulses from Sweden's Nordic neighbors. Ibsen and Brandes became the canonical models for the young Swedish writers who embraced their combination of idealism and realism and rose to prominence as the "Generation of the '8os" or the "Young Sweden" group. They included most notably Anne Charlotte Leffler, Victoria Benedictsson, Gustaf af Geijerstam, Oscar Levertin, Tor Hedberg, Axel Lundegård, and—initially at least—August Strindberg. The literary center of gravity shifted from the quiet groves of academe in Uppsala and Lund to the bustling Stockholm scene.[51]

The characteristic Swedish literature of the 1880s was in notable degree written by and for women. The growing middle-class female public, educated in finishing schools, were avid readers, but perhaps because they lacked a background in classical idealism from the universities—which still remained out of bounds to them—they tended to find the great works of the past of little interest, compared with writing that dealt with the problems of real life, above all domestic matters. Flaubert's *Madame Bovary* struck closer to home than Plato's dialogues or Goethe's *Faust*. The "Woman Question" came to dominate Swedish social realist literature during the 1880s.

Inspired by Ibsen's *Doll's House* and by his compatriot Camilla Collett's *Fra de stummes lejr* (From the camp of the mute) from 1877—and more remotely, by Bremer's early feministic novel *Herta* from 1856—Leffler, Bene-dictsson (who wrote under the pseudonym Ernst Ahlgren), Alfhild Agrell, and others produced a "literature of indignation" decrying the moral hypocrisy and degradation imposed on their sex by conventional middle-class marriage and by insensitive, oppressive fathers and husbands. To Bjørnson, Leffler enthusiastically described her 1886 novel *En sommarsaga* (A summer tale), which, she wrote, "shall be my finest literary work," in which two idealistic searchers after truth and authenticity, she Swedish and he Norwegian, earnestly confront the problems of marriage. In it, she was proud to point out, the male protagonist spoke Norwegian throughout.[52]

Lorenz Dietrichson's reminiscences, especially from his second sojourn in Sweden between the mid-1860s and the mid-1870s, give a unique and color-ful picture of Norwegian-Swedish cultural relations at their height. He fondly recalled the wholehearted celebration, in both kingdoms, of the establishment of the union on 4 November 1864. "It was a delight to be a Norwegian in Swe-den in those days. . . . Simply to be Norwegian then served as a recommen-dation to the finest circles, and Norwegians enjoyed a consideration in Sweden from which I, too, benefited."[53]

And a distinguished company they were! Ole Bull "headed the parade" in 1860—following his earlier triumphs in Sweden—Peter Andreas Munch arrived in 1861, Camilla Collett in 1866, Bjørnstjerne Bjørnson in 1866, 1871, and 1873. Henrik Ibsen spent the summer of 1869 in Stockholm, Hans Gude visited the same year, Edvard Grieg with his "glorious songbird of a wife," Nina Hagerup, came in 1873, and the writer Kristofer Janson in 1874, while the painter Carl Hanson lived for several years in Stockholm. Numerous other Norwegian painters, actors, and authors likewise came to the Swedish capital. Dietrichson was in his element as their guide and mentor.

In other areas as well, Norway indeed sent its best men. The Norwegian ministerial residence, especially in [Georg] Sibbern's time but also later, was a place gladly frequented by the highest Swedish nobility and to which they appreciated being invited. The Norwegian Guards Regiment's officers and men were regarded as elite troops and quite simply the Stockholmers' favorites. Military committees, representatives of the army and navy, the

Norwegian commercial firms that were established in Stockholm, especially Astrup & Sørensen, all enjoyed a well-deserved respect. They were
indeed a group of countrymen who in all ways represented the best Norway could send forth from its bosom. And from these sympathetic personalities there fell for me an alluring light over my distant homeland. . . . That
was *Norway*, that was my fatherland, to which I was proud to belong and
which I yearned for.[54]

Bjørnson and Ibsen in particular were lionized in Stockholm and enjoyed
many close friendships in Sweden. Describing Bjørnson's visit to Stockholm
in 1871, Ellen Key recalled, "At the social gatherings between [his] lectures
as well as through the lectures themselves, Bjørnson exercised that strength
of spirit that can bring forth fresh springs even in the desert, which opens
closed hearts, fructifies receptive souls, and for a time raises everything up
into the world of essential principles." His resolute stand for full Norwegian
equality within the union was widely respected in Swedish liberal circles, with
which he had close contacts, even though here, too, he at times could give
offense with his more strident denunciations of Swedish policy. He was particularly close to the liberal politician Adolf Hedin and the influential editor
of the liberal *Göteborgs Handels- och Sjöfartstidning* in Göteborg, Sven Adolf
Hedlund.[55]

Ibsen had long held prejudices against Sweden, which were magnified by
the Dual Monarchy's ignominious conduct during the Danish-German war
in 1864. In his satirical *Peer Gynt* from 1867, Ibsen included a Swedish nobleman, "Trompeterstråle" (Trumpet-Blast), who embodied those delusions of
grandeur and fixation on his nation's past martial triumphs that Bjørnson
would later describe as characteristically *storsvensk* (Great-Swedish). Ibsen's
first visit to Stockholm, however, quickly changed his view. He was altogether
captivated by the city and the appreciation and generosity he there encountered. He also captivated Stockholm society. "One had expected," Dietrichson wrote, "to see in *Brand's* author an elderly, serious, strict ascetic, and there
appeared an elegant younger man in a tailcoat, refined, lively, and amiable."
During Ibsen's visit to Stockholm in 1887, Anne Charlotte Leffler wrote to a
friend that Ibsen had said, "Of all my fatherlands, Sweden is the one where
I have found most understanding."[56]

The aristocratic tone of Stockholm society appealed strongly to Ibsen's
patrician nature, as he candidly revealed in letters to Swedish friends. To Adolf
Hedin — "my friend who talks of revolutions" — he wrote in 1870 the celebrated lines: "You unleash the waters to make your mark. / I set a torpedo

under the Ark." The following year, he expressed his fundamental Olympian detachment to his Stockholm hostess:

> I pace my room, kid-gloved. . . . I shrink from the mob.
> I have no wish to be clasped to its hot bosom.
> I shall await whatever time may bring
> in a well-pressed morning coat.

He was on excellent terms with the literary monarch, Oscar II, and deeply gratified by the honorary doctorate conferred on him by Uppsala University in 1877.[57]

Before the opening of the Stockholm-Christiania rail connection in 1871 and the introduction of steam vessels in coastal traffic, cultivated Swedes seldom had, as has been seen, any direct experience of Norway. A few had earlier wandered there on foot, including the artists August Malmström and Egron Lundgren in the 1850s and in 1861, respectively, the Stockholm physician and Old Norse enthusiast Carl Curman in 1854 and 1858, and the writer Viktor Rydberg in 1858.

The wider reading public became acquainted with Norway largely thanks to the vivid accounts by Peter August Gödecke, an avid Scandinavianist and onetime member of the "Nameless Society" in Uppsala, of his wanderings in Norway published in 1873 and 1875, which give a good idea of what educated Swedes expected to find across the Keel. Norway, as Gödecke described it, was a fabled land of snow-capped peaks, lowering glaciers, plunging waterfalls, rickety bridges over yawning chasms, deep fjords with overhanging cliffs, and narrow valleys. Marveling at the majesty of the Jotunheimen massif, he exclaimed, "The great landscape I saw before me seemed to me like a temple in which God himself preached through his mighty work's vastness and beauty."[58]

Gödecke admired the Norwegians' lively intellect, feeling for nature, and warm attachment to their ancient farms and their constitution. Yet, he was not uncritical. He could appreciate the Norwegian peasants' hardiness and frugality yet questioned their economic sense. Such virtues consisted "more in their readiness to do without what they presently cannot produce than in their ability to acquire them through greater effort." Excessive thrift and rude simplicity could deprive life of any joy. Life in some of the more remote mountain valleys he found depressingly dull, dirty, sluggish, and deprived. Norway might become more prosperous than it was, although "never because neither

Per nor Pål make use of a tablecloth, but only if they work harder or plan more intelligently than father or grandfather did." It had been to Norway's disadvantage, he felt, that it had lacked a class of enlightened gentlemen landowners like those in Sweden who had led the way in agricultural innovation.[59]

Yet, Gödecke felt deeply ambivalent about traditional Norwegian rural life. Despite his utilitarian criticisms, he could not but deeply admire the Norwegian peasantry's staunch cultural conservatism in preserving the old values. Everywhere, he found stirring reminders of the saga age. He was fascinated by the mountain *sæter*—that well-recognized, central icon of midcentury Norwegian national romanticism—even if it often proved upon closer acquaintance to be not quite what he had been led to expect by numerous idyllic depictions in art, literature, and song. The sturdy milkmaids, he pointed out, were far too busy with their chores for them to "dream or sing away their days."

Life on the mountain pastures meanwhile vividly recalled to him the earliest pastoral existence of the Nordic peoples. "When our fathers, *Götar*, *Svear*, and Norse folk, moved into the virgin land to find their dwelling places, livestock was their main, indeed perhaps their only property." Millennia would pass before cultivation of the soil began. In northern Sweden, too, livestock raising was still more important than arable farming. "For us," he wrote, "the present system of farming in Norway should be of great interest as the mirror image of that stage of development through which we passed long ago."[60]

Gödecke was especially moved upon visiting Gudbrandsdalen's venerable farmsteads, which he described in loving detail. Through Norwegian art and literature, he had formed romantic impressions of what they must be like, but they nonetheless surpassed his fondest imaginings. Arriving at the impressive Bjølstad farmstead, he half-expected that "Jarl Skule or one of Norway's other old chieftains should come out that door!"

The great farms in Gudbrandsdalen still belonged to Norway's most distinguished peasant aristocracy, proud descendants of medieval kings and noblemen. This, too, prompted reflection on both past and present. The medieval nobility throughout the Nordic lands had originally arisen among the most outstanding families of freehold peasants, long before it had become a legal estate of society. "In those days the gulf did not exist that in privileges, culture, and attitudes separated the noble and non-noble sons of the cultivator," he wrote in 1873. "We too knew such a time and it is only unrecognizable to those who take as their point of departure all of a later period's aristocratic and democratic concepts." The great Norwegian peasant families strikingly reminded Gödecke—who at that time was engaged in translating the *Eddas*—of the old Icelandic family sagas. "In Gudbrandsdalen many family tragedies are still enacted that reflect the flaming passions and glowing emotions so powerfully described by the Icelandic skalds."[61]

Gödecke was fascinated by the archaic, sod-roofed "smoke-hole" houses in the Voss district, the interiors of which, when the sun shone down through the roof, created a "living picture by Tidemand, Norway's greatest painter." "Oft-sung" Sogne Fjord naturally recalled to him Tegnér's *Frithiofs saga*. One might easily imagine "with what emotions a Swede must look upon Balder's Meadow" by its shore. The Urnes stave church conjured up visions of the dawn of Christianity amidst the survivals of the Viking age.[62]

Hardanger Fjord was for Gödecke the glorious culmination of his wandering in both his accounts. He declared it the loveliest part of Norway, and it immediately evoked both Halfdan Kjerulf's well-known song *Peasant Wedding in Hardanger* as well as Tidemand and Gude's celebrated painting of the wedding party afloat that it had inspired. They all, in Gödecke's eyes, belonged to a cherished, common Scandinavian heritage.[63]

On a tourist boat in Hardanger Fjord, Gödecke heard English, German, French, Danish, and Russian spoken around him but noted that Swedish was still seldom heard in western Norway. Only a few years later, however, a returned traveler who identified himself as "E. K." wrote in *Ny illustrerad Tidning* in 1877 that Norway teemed with foreign visitors that summer, including "not a few Swedes."

> Ten years ago Norway's mountain tracts were still less familiar in Sweden than the peaks and valleys of the Alps. A changed political atmosphere, the scenes from Norwegian folklife and nature provided by Bjørnstjerne Bjørnson, Tidemand, Kjerulf, and others, whether in words, colors, or tones, together with the steadily growing stream of foreign visitors, have caused more venturesome Swedish travelers to discover that they can, closer than heretofore, observe magnificent nature and a remarkable folklife, and have aroused among them a more widespread desire to become acquainted with them.[64]

Among the most enthusiastic visitors of the time was Ellen Key, who together with three other young ladies wandered, mainly on foot, over much of southern Norway in the summer of 1876. Her main motive was, not surprisingly, to visit her revered Bjørnson at Aulestad, which proved a memorable experience. In the high mountains, she was constantly reminded of the world of Ibsen's austere *Brand* and his fantasy-filled *Peer Gynt*, and while descending to Hardanger Fjord, she wrote, "one has left Ibsen's ice-world and is once again in Bjørnson's peasant world. Both have their fascination."[65]

By the 1870 and 1880s, the Old Nordic vogue reached its height in Sweden, and in this respect, Norway at the time enjoyed undeniable advantages over Sweden. Everywhere, it was manifest in Swedish life: in fiction and rhetoric; in clubs and societies; in periodical articles on folklore and the Viking age—not least in their illustrations and vignettes; in decorative book bindings; in applied arts in wood, metal, glass, textiles, and even porcelain; in the names of streets, ships, and industrial enterprises and products; as well as in the ancient Nordic names given to so many of the children of that era, especially in cultivated middle-class families.

Beginning around 1870, numerous private villas were built in Sweden in the Old Norse style, replete with overhanging, arched, second-story breezeways, dragon-headed gables, carved reliefs with intertwining plant and animal motifs, and dim interiors richly adorned with solid, ornately carved furniture and woven wall-hangings in archaic patterns. Among the earlier and better-known examples was Lorenz Dietrichson's "Solhem" on Djurgården in Stockholm, a gathering point for enthusiasts for Nordic antiquity. The point of departure for such architecture was necessarily above all the still-existing examples of ancient Norwegian wood construction, including the farmsteads so meticulously described by Eilert Sundt in articles reprinted at the time in Swedish publications, and in particular Norway's medieval timbered stave churches. It should be noted that the earliest surviving Christian churches in Sweden, from the twelfth century on, were virtually all built with stone or later with brick, under the greater influence of the prevailing European international styles.[66]

If Swedes could regard Bjørnstjerne Bjørnson as their own poet, as well as the Norwegians', he in turned showed that he believed Swedes could be Norwegian in spirit. In 1874, he acquired the farm at Aulestad in Gausdal that is now a Norwegian national shrine. Here, he planned to build an imposing country home in the Old Norse style and engaged a Swedish architect, Victor von Gegerfelt. When a friend earnestly entreated Bjørnson to find a Norwegian instead, he replied that Gegerfelt was the father of the "new Nordic style" and that indeed he was more truly "Norwegian" in both language and design than the proposed Norwegian replacement. It was Gegerfelt, he wrote, who "has found *our style* in the Norwegian stave churches." Incidentally, Bjørnson wrote to S. A. Hedlund in 1876 that he hoped to employ Swedes on his farm, for they "work like devils!"[67]

The concept of the Scandinavian folk high school originated with Bishop Nicolai Frederik Severin Grundtvig in Denmark and was first realized with the *folkehøjskole* established at Rødding in South Jutland in 1844. In time, it came to Norway, where a similar school was established through private efforts at Sagatun, near Hamar, in 1864 and was soon followed by others.

Grundtvig's ideal was to raise the cultural level of the peasantry by inculcating familiarity with, and pride in, their nation's past and traditions. Learning was to take place essentially through the "living word" as conveyed by idealistic teachers who saw their work as a mission in life rather than through the dead letter of the written word, and it was not to lead to any academic degree, in contrast to the established secondary schools and universities with their emphasis on classical languages and formal requirements. Among the greatest Norwegian enthusiasts for Grundtvig's folk high school ideal by the 1870s was Bjørnson, who intended his lecture tour of Sweden in 1873 to be largely a crusade on its behalf. He aroused great enthusiasm among his Swedish friends and admirers, such as Adolf Hedin, S. A. Hedlund, the author Viktor Rydberg, and of course Ellen Key.

Disenchantment with traditional higher education was widespread in Sweden as well, as illustrated by Strindberg, who could not bring himself to complete his studies at Uppsala University.[68] The folk high schools offered an alternative education inculcating native Nordic rather than alien classical values and promoting the democratization of culture, society, and government. The first such schools in Sweden were established already in 1868 at Hvilan near Lund, Önnestad near Kristianstad, and Herrestad near Linköping, where Peter August Gödecke soon became the director as well as a leading theorist of the movement in Sweden. Inspiration for these schools derived, however, more directly from Denmark than indirectly from Norway. They were established on the initiative of local peasant farmers instead of by ideologically motivated young intellectuals, as in Denmark and Norway, and they placed greater emphasis on the written word and on practical subjects as opposed to patriotic inspiration and political indoctrination. The Grundtvigian ideal was not, however, without its critics in both Denmark and Norway. Lorenz Dietrichson, for instance, noted with approval that the Swedish folk high schools gave less emphasis to the "lyrical, emotional element, with folk ballads, patriotic songs, and poetic dilettantism," and were thus, in his view, "schools for the healthy, practical acquisition of knowledge, adapted to the needs of the peasantry."[69]

Throughout the period, the connections between enthusiasm for Nordic antiquity, Norwegian culture, and Scandinavianism, or at least unionism, on the one hand, and political liberalism and radicalism, on the other, are unmistakable. Everywhere, one encounters the same members of the Swedish liberal intelligentsia, including, for instance, the liberal politicians Adolf Hedin, Emil Key, and August Blanche; the newspaper editors August Sohlman of *Aftonbladet* and S. A. Hedlund of *Göteborgs Handels- och Sjöfartstidning*; the national librarian and editor of *Ny illustrerad Tidning*, Harald Wieselgren; the physician Carl Curman; the professor of physiology Frithiof Holmgren of Uppsala University and his wife, the author Ann-Margret Holmgren; the later polar explorer Adolf Erik Nordenskjöld; the folk high school rector P. A. Gödecke; the authors Anne Charlotte Leffler, Viktor Rydberg, and Ellen Key—staunch liberals and Scandinavianists all, and most of them eventually associated with the Nordic National Society *(Det Nordiska Nationalföreningen)*, established in 1865 to keep the Scandinavianist flame burning after the Danish-German war of the preceding year. It was surely not coincidental that at a later time the organ of the Socialist Youth Association was called *Brand* and that it carried a feature article on Henrik Ibsen early in 1905, the very year the Swedish-Norwegian union was dissolved, warning against the "spirit of accord"—in this case toward capitalists and militarists.

By the same token, the old aristocracy and political conservatives tended to be skeptical toward the Old Nordic heritage—as opposed to Greco-Roman classicism—to dismiss Norwegian culture as narrow, chauvinistic, and vulgar, to regard the democratic folk high school ideal with academic disdain, and to reject Scandinavianism as opposed to a traditional nationalism that looked back on Sweden's martial past.[70]

Nevertheless, the boundaries between political Right and Left became less distinct as Swedish society became more complex. Liberalism became more cautious after the tumults and revolutions of 1848–49. Although it had regained much of its fighting spirit during the early 1860s, it moved in an ever more socially conservative direction following the Riksdag Reform of 1866 and especially the frightening Paris Commune of 1871.

In the past, Swedish liberals had found inspiration in the fierce love of freedom they attributed to the Vikings of yore and their proud descendants in contemporary Norway. Their vision of the saga age carried its democratic message as well as its implied rebuke to existing Swedish government, society, and culture. It held out the vision of an Old Nordic world of free and equal peasant farmers, who gathered at the *Ting*, or assembly of freemen, to make their own laws and elect their own law-speakers and war leaders on the basis of their individual skill and prowess, and who could, if need be, freely depose and replace them. Foreign, European institutions inimical to the Nordic folk character had not yet corrupted the idyll: there was no hereditary monarch or nobility, no special corporate privileges, no appointed bureaucracy, no state church, no standing military establishment, no court, no social pretensions, and no enervating foreign luxuries or affectations.

The new icons of Swedish liberals became Torgny Lagman—the law-speaker—who, according to "Saint Olav's Saga" in the *Heimskringla*, bid defiance on behalf of the assembled freemen to King Olof Skötkonung when the latter sought to wage war against Norway around A.D. 1000, together with Engelbrekt Engelbrektsson, who in the 1430s rebelled against the Kalmar Union. Against such a background, Norway, both ancient and modern, appeared in a highly idealized light in which a Bjørnstjerne Bjørnson or a Johan Sverdrup could be seen in the guise of a latter-day chieftain or jarl.

Now, confronted with a new social and potentially political force—a growing, radical industrial proletariat—Swedish liberals came to place a new stress on the collective, stabilizing family values they could also seek out in old sagas and in an idealized Nordic peasant life increasingly threatened by the processes of modernization. The traditional household, where the patriarch sat enthroned on the high seat surrounded by his respectful family and retainers, now became the nostalgic ideal. "During the nineteenth century, [the Goths] settled down in the mountains of the North," Gunnar Broberg has written. "A little Viking expedition might be permitted in one's youth, but thereafter one should stand at the *Ting* and mumble assent to the lawman's speech." The old liberals now strove, as Bo Grandien has expressed it, "to ensnare the evils of the time in dragon coils."[71]

5

Norway and the Swedish Self-Image

Y THE EARLY 1880s, Norwegian cultural influence in Sweden was reaching its high-water mark. But a reaction was bound to come. To be sure, occasional discordant voices had been heard before. In 1861, for instance, one Jon Engström had written angrily in Kalmar's *Barometern* of how "the *Norwegian* Dietrichson" had sought to include "the Swedish king of skalds Tegnér" among "ordinary quasi-poetic scribblers." "Is it not true," he wrote ironically, "that *this is wonderful, since it is truly Norwegian?* Sweden must *not* have anything that can in the slightest compete with the ultra-Norwegian!"[1]

It was, however, August Strindberg who would lead the counteroffensive. His relationship with Norwegian culture had until this time been ambivalent. While at Uppsala University around 1870, he had founded the Runa Society, a student organization devoted to the Old Nordic past. His first play, *Mäster Olof* from 1872, showed influences from Ibsen's *Brand*.[2]

Yet, already as a young journalist in Stockholm, he had shown a certain skepticism toward Norwegian literature generally. In a review of a recently published anthology of Norwegian verse in *Dagens Nyheter* in 1874, he showed his antiromantic skepticism:

> There [in Norway] they are still young and write poetry. They are still discovering the 'shimmer from the glacier and the verdant hillside meadow,' they sing of their high peaks and Norwegian dales. It is lovely to read these lyrics, but have they then nothing else to think about? Norway will soon be sixty years old and that is no longer the time to remain a youth, especially as they have left so many hoary traditions untouched, so much national fanaticism that takes its toll on every new idea, no matter whether it comes from the great centers of experimental thought on the Continent or be ever

so revitalizing. This protectionism will hinder development and as long
as they venerate Harald Fairhair and Saint Olaf they will never move forward.

Three years later, in 1877, Strindberg had nonetheless revealed, in an unti-
tled and perhaps uncompleted poem, a reserved and grudging envy when
he briefly passed through Christiania on his way to the Continent for the first
time. In Norway, he wrote, mountains rose up like "angry wild boars," and
forests of firs "bristle against centuries of oppression." In Christiania, common folk took to the sidewalk while the gentleman walked in the street. Super-
stitious peasants cried "God forbid!" at the mention of their "expatriated great
men" — meaning above all such cultural luminaries as Ibsen, Bjørnson,
Grieg, or Ole Bull, who all spent extended periods abroad —

> men so great that they sufficed
> even for us awkward Swedes
> and do so still.

Yet, he ended with an encomium to Norway's proud peasantry:

> And I see thy gray walls,
> Storting House,
> Where great things are afoot,
> Weighty as a church on Dovre Fell,
> Where Nature's voices
> Speak a language unknown
> To cultivated weaklings
> Who have forgotten their native tongue.
> But I hear their voices
> As I heard them in my youth
> and when they call out from the Continent
> Clouds gather over the fjord.[3]

Strindberg would not thereafter return to Norway, but it would always remain
very much on his mind, both culturally and politically. While he would in
time do battle with certain of its "expatriated great men," he would always
remain a staunch supporter of its political aspirations.

From Paris, Strindberg described in a noted newspaper essay, "Nationalitet
och svenskhet" (Nationality and Swedishness) in 1883, how a "leading Norwegian poet" — clearly Bjørnstjerne Bjørnson — had pointed out to him the
remarkable extent to which the Swedes in recent years had fawned over things

Norwegian. They had bestowed their prizes upon Norwegians at the Stockholm Exposition of 1866, had filled their museums with Norwegian paintings, had given Lorenz Dietrichson appointments at their Royal Academy of Art and their new national art museum, and had opened their Royal Theater to Ibsen's "scandalous" plays, which could hardly be played in Christiania; Swedish student choruses had filled their repertories with Norwegian songs, and in every Swedish home Bjørnson and Kjerulf were regarded as virtually part of the household—while native Swedes were treated like stepchildren. "Let us therefore work toward [our own] national independence," he declared, "an independence that does not depend upon appropriating for ourselves the sagas of Norwegian kings or Iceland's Eddas, not upon boasting over the misdeeds of the past, but upon being ourselves—like [Ibsen's] Peer Gynt!"[4]

Three years later, in 1886, Strindberg wrote of how Sweden had received its new literature from outside, since it was too weak to create one for itself. Since 1865, this had consisted of "Bjørnson, Ibsen, and [Jonas] Lie!" The same year, in part 2 of his autobiographical novel *Tjänstekvinnans son* (The son of a servant), he launched a determined attack both upon Norwegian culture and especially upon his compatriots' idolatrous, uncritical love affair with it. "Rome conquered Greece, but Greece conquered Rome," he declared. "Sweden had taken Norway, but now Norway took Sweden." Swedes, he insisted, were not Norwegians. They had their own character and traditions. When they received "great new thoughts" from Norway, he declared, they should have "kept the wheat and left the Norwegian chaff."[5]

Strindberg's growing criticism of Norwegian cultural influence in Sweden had its personal aspect, as he developed strong antipathies during the 1880s first toward Ibsen and then toward Bjørnson—"*Dovregubbarne*," or "the Old Men of the Dovre [Mountains]," as he came to call them. Ibsen had, through his powerful literary persona, both fascinated and repelled Strindberg during his earlier years. He meanwhile could not but envy the Norwegian playwright for his success in Sweden at a time when he himself was still struggling for recognition. It was, however, the appearance of Ibsen's landmark play *Et Dukkehjem* (A doll's house) in 1879, which Strindberg saw as a tendentious feminist polemic, that decisively turned him against the Norwegian playwright.

Strindberg reacted strongly to what he saw as an alarming threat to a natural, loving, and sensual relationship between the sexes. While, initially at least, he held that women as well as men should be freed from the conventional constraints of bourgeois society, he regarded the woman's rightful role to be that of wife and mother within the home. At the same time, influenced by the Englishman George Drysdale and the German-Hungarian Max Nordau, he engaged himself in the contemporary morality debate, considering Bjørnson's demand, in his play *En Handske* (A gauntlet) from 1883, that men should observe the same sexual abstinence prior to marriage as women, to be harmful both physically and mentally.[6]

Whereas Strindberg had in 1874 dismissed the Norwegian poets for their dreamy national romanticism, he now confronted what he saw as their dogmatic and pedantic moralism. His response both to Ibsen's doll's house and Bjørnson's gauntlet was a collection of short stories, *Giftas* (Getting married), part 1, published in 1883. In an introduction, he chastised both Ibsen and the "Nora literature" of his Swedish imitators, accusing them of fomenting an artificial enmity between the "two halves of humanity." "The whole Swedish female literature," Strindberg wrote, "is Norse-Norwegian with its shameless ideal demand that men kowtow to spoiled women."

In particular, two key stories in *Giftas*, part 1, conveyed his message. In "Dygdens lön" (Virtue's reward) he described the ruinous consequences for a young man of artificially prolonged sexual abstinence. The concluding story, provocatively entitled "Ett dockhem" (A doll's house), showed how a normal, happy marriage came close to ruin when the young wife's head was turned by Ibsen's play. Thereafter, faced with the disapproval of his realist Swedish colleagues, he wrote defiantly to the Norwegian author Jonas Lie, "I know that my book is a great outcry from nature's bosom, that I am right, that my words come at the last minute to save us from a false turn, amid the monstrosities of an overrefined culture."[7]

His animosity toward Ibsen grew ever more implacable as his own marriage to the actress Siri von Essen was breaking up. She consorted with radical feminists and became in his eyes alarmingly like Ibsen's Nora. A second collection of short stories, *Giftas*, part 2, in 1885 bitterly accused women of being fundamentally false, manipulative, and power hungry, a view repeatedly expressed in his writings over the next several years.[8] This did not, however, deter him from two more, ultimately unsuccessful marriages, the last in 1901 to a young Norwegian actress in Stockholm, Harriet Bosse.

Ibsen, for his part, was rather more broad-minded toward Strindberg, whose work he could respect even if he could not accept his viewpoints. In 1893, he bought the Norwegian painter Christian Krohg's portrait of Strindberg, which he hung in his study. "He is my mortal enemy," Ibsen claimed, "and shall hang there and watch while I write." He liked to say that it stimulated him in his work to have "that madman staring down at me." Although on their Continental sojourns, they were often near each other, Ibsen and Strindberg never met.[9] Strindberg's relations with the other "Old Man of the Dovre," Bjørnstjerne Bjørnson, were no less stormy. In his autobiographical novel from 1886–87, Strindberg wrote of his fictional alter-ego "Johan":

> He had never seen Bjørnson. When he was in Stockholm and Uppsala, Johan had been afraid of him and had avoided him. He heard a rumble, as though a thunderstorm had swept over the land and he felt as though a magician had passed through with the power to cast a spell. He heard people come out stunned from his lectures as though they had witnessed a birth or death. Johan sensed that here was a powerful ego, stronger than his own, that might perhaps plant a seed in his soul. He sought to avoid this as if he feared a victor in the struggle and hid away. For the same reason he had not dared to read [Bjørnson's] *The Editor* or *A Bankruptcy*.[10]

Bjørnson meanwhile became increasingly interested in the young Strindberg. In October 1882, Bjørnson wrote to him, expressing his appreciation of Strindberg's *Det nya riket* (The new kingdom), a satirical attack on contemporary Swedish society that had just come out. "In its wake," Bjørnson prophesied, "a new, courageous literature will arise in Sweden—even if we must wait a while for it. . . . Unless a country's writers dare to speak out freely, national morality will not improve, for if these leaders fail, all will fail. I urge you to hold out until you feel that you have become strong enough in the attack for that which you did not dare attempt before." "I know of no skald in the North but you who follows me in staking your life on what we preach," Bjørnson wrote to Strindberg in April 1884. "That is what I have wished for in the new literary gospel. . . . You are to date the first modern Swede— entirely modern—I have known. With you there a new race begins to inhabit the land of Sweden."[11]

In December 1883, they at last met face to face. In Paris, Bjørnson and Jonas Lie sought out Strindberg, who had recently arrived there. Strindberg immediately succumbed to Bjørnson's charm. He became "my father confessor and soon my conscience," Strindberg later wrote. In a letter to the Norwegian painter Erik Werenskiold, Lie confided that Strindberg possessed a "concealed pietistic nature" and martyr complex, and that he and Bjørnson were seeking to "instill in him a bit of joyful, bright Nordic culture [and] belief in his own nation rather than dark doubts." For his part, Strindberg, in retrospect, at times perceived in Bjørnson "the Norwegian versus the

Swede; the conquered province against the enemy nation." He sometimes sensed "the stronger but less civilized race, which with both envy and contempt looks up to and down upon a race in decline."[12]

Strindberg's friendship with Bjørnson ended as abruptly as it had begun less than a year later. In the fall of 1884, Strindberg was arraigned in Sweden on charges of blasphemy for an irreverent reference to Holy Communion in his *Giftas*, part 1. He hesitated to return from France to face the charges. Bjørnson, who while sympathetic was inclined to preach moral lessons, wrote to him, sternly admonishing him to do so. Infuriated, Strindberg wrote a stinging reply and, although he ultimately did stand trial in Stockholm, he and Bjørnson thereafter remained personally unreconciled. Strindberg nonetheless wrote to Lie in December 1844 that he hoped to downplay his quarrel with Bjørnson, as they had too many interests in common. His friendship with Lie, who himself not long after fell out with Bjørnson, meanwhile lasted throughout his life.

There were, however, deeper, underlying aspects to this break. Strindberg later recalled that he came to realize that he had allowed himself to become "unfree" under the tutelage he had allowed the elder colleague to exercise over him, which became ever more intolerable. He departed for Switzerland to find himself once again. "The public man must renounce friendship, life's strongest spice," he concluded darkly, "for it weakens the free play of his thought."[13]

Strindberg's break with the Norwegian masters meanwhile expressed his growing weariness with the literary realism he himself had played so prominent a role in introducing in Sweden but that now increasingly seemed to him alien to Sweden's cultural character. In a passage later stricken from his 1887 play *Marodörer* (Marauders), a character pleads, "Give us back joy, you who preach the joy of life. Give us the cheerful little spirit of compromise, and send the Old Men of the Dovre back to their caves. They came from their misty peaks . . . and made life dark and fearsome. Now give us the sun again, just a little ray of sunshine. . . !"[14]

If friendship between Strindberg and Bjørnson was short-lived, there are indications that it was of lasting significance for Strindberg's life and work, and beyond that, for Sweden's cultural evolution. Ellen Key later recounted how Bjørnson, at the hundredth anniversary of Esaias Tegnér's birth in 1882, had declared in Göteborg that he looked forward to the appearance of Sweden's next truly great poet, who like Tegnér in his time would attack outmoded attitudes, direct the will of his people toward the future, and arouse in them the will to "make poetry of life itself."[15]

It is clear that Bjørnson envisioned this high vocation for the young Strindberg when they first met the following year, which calls to mind Lie's comment to Werenskiold that Bjørnson and he had sought to instill in Strindberg
"belief in his own nation." It may be recalled from the beginning of this chapter that Strindberg claimed it had been a "leading Norwegian poet" who
emphasized his compatriots' unseemly "norvegomania," and Bjørnson much
appreciated the essay, "Nationality and Swedishness," in which he had recounted this.

To Bjørnson, Sweden's cultural overdependence on Norway could be no
more desirable than Norway's political subservience to Sweden if an ideal
equality were to be established within the Dual Monarchy. For Norwegians
to find their own cultural profile, Swedes must hold fast to their own traditions, which he genuinely admired. This view of Sweden's rightful role he set
forth already in 1866, in a poem gratefully acknowledging his debt to Sweden's literature:

> Since I was a child thou won my heart
> For thou taught me what was great . . .
> Thou heart-folk, folk of fantasy,
> Of poetry, and of longing,
> O, fill thy heart, lift thy spirit:
> *Raise the banner of the North in Thy hand!*[16]

This hope for the emergence of a truly Swedish national culture would be
more than amply fulfilled during the 1890s and the first years of the new century. It is meanwhile evident that Bjørnson took very hard his break with
Strindberg and in future years would send him indirect greetings.[17]

In Switzerland, by the end of 1884, Strindberg became closely associated
with the aristocratic young Swedish dilettante Verner von Heidenstam, who
for a time became his enthusiastic disciple. Heidenstam, who for reasons of
health had spent most of his youth on the Continent and in the Near East,
undecided as to whether to become a painter or a writer, was doubtless influenced in his attitudes toward Norway and Norwegian culture by the older
Strindberg.

In June 1885, Heidenstam wrote to Strindberg of how strange it was that
in Sweden they accepted everything from the "neighboring land" while
rejecting Strindberg's true genius. Shortly before, he mourned in verse the
dilemma of the Swedish poet: "In others' poetic world he constantly seeks to
find his way / . . . if he is to write he must clothe his spirit in the threadbare
everyday garb from the neighboring land."

Unlike Strindberg, Heidenstam became well acquainted with Norway. His lively correspondence with his Norwegian friend and translator, Bolette Pavels Larsen, is revealing in this regard. In late 1888, he wrote her that "like almost all the youth in Sweden I felt the most lively sympathy toward Norway." Two years later, however, in 1890, his tone was cooler. "When I was in my early twenties, I was such a fanatical admirer of everything Norwegian." He had meanwhile abandoned his expatriate existence and returned to rediscover his own homeland, with a joy and an enthusiasm vividly portrayed in his first published collection of verse, *Vallfart och vandringsår* (Pilgrimage and wander-years), in 1888 and his semiautobiographical novel, *Hans Alienus*, in 1892.[18]

Heidenstam's reaction against Norwegian influence was above all aesthetic. With his vivid imagination and poetic bent, he turned against the literary realism of the 1880s, which in the Swedish context he associated primarily with France and—not least—with Norway. In 1889, he came out with a widely read polemical essay, *Renässans* (Renaissance), attacking the prevailing realist school and proclaiming that the time had come to return to a literature of fantasy, beauty, idealism, and national values. He held that while realism had been a healthy influence to begin with, it had now run its course. It was pedestrian, even if workmanlike, in prose, stifling for poetry, and dominated by an unrelieved "gray-weather" mood. "Naturalism," he wrote, "is the art of suppressing one's powers of imagination and emotions, of never saying anything in jest, of never using a brilliant metaphor." We should not, he went on, let ourselves be so burdened with guilty consciences over the ills of the world that we can find no joy in life.

The Swedes, Heidenstam claimed, must write from their own hearts rather than seeking to imitate the French—or the Norwegians. Had their attempts at realism not been inspired by Norway's great writers, their Swedish readers would never have been impressed by them. "Let us admit it, gentlemen, we are all of us most decidedly idealists. . . . we too can depict reality, but among us there shines forth something chivalrous and the inclination to magnify and to paint in brilliant colors." Drab "shoemaker realism" *(skomakarrealism)*, he held, "is particularly ill-suited to our nature, which is little inclined toward petty bourgeois fussiness."[19]

While his references to Norway in these writings were respectful and discreet, Heidenstam's poetry from this time clearly enough expresses his view of Sweden's sorrowful dependence on impulses from across the Keel. Thus, in *Den sovande system* (The sleeping sister) from 1889, he deplored Sweden's traditional backward-looking patriotism. "We sit in the house of sorrow / and our commemorations are graveside eulogies." Lifeless as Sweden now was, Norway's muse was youthful and vigorous:

> She greets the day, creates verse and is admired
> Her words go from the mouths of hundreds to hundreds
> Reverberating like an echo over wide distances.
> But she whom we love sleeps cold.

And in *Pingstnatten* (Whitsun's Eve) from the same year:

> Ever to mimic our neighbors
> Surely becomes a threadbare lesson
> Comrades! Have you tuned your lyre?
> The man shall from the child grow![20]

To Bolette Pavels Larsen, Heidenstam wrote in May 1889 that he hardly dared visit Norway for fear that he would become "more delighted than a Swede ought to allow himself" during that time of rising dissent within the union. That November, he wrote to Bjørnson:

> In Sweden I am myself now seeking to bring about a modest little literary revolt against the influence upon us of foreign examples, indeed even that from the Norwegians. This does not, however, mean that we should value Norway's or France's authors any the less, only it seems to me that we do not sufficiently take account of our own character, we sink to the level of imitators and thereby attain worse results than we should. What is more, you yourself expressed something similar when we [recently] first met in Stockholm and it immediately struck me that you, although a Norwegian, should make so insightful a reflection on our situation.

Again, Bjørnson's unobtrusive effort to promote a truly Swedish cultural renaissance becomes apparent.

In 1892, while he again assured Pavels Larsen of his admiration for much in Norway, Heidenstam expressed his growing reservations: "Everything in Norway is so youthful and so oppressively filled with optimism and self-assurance." Over time, he went on, Norway would outgrow these tendencies. "And when Norway becomes an old cultural nation, which like Sweden has seen its best summer days, it will better understand much in our character that it now looks down upon. And it will acquire more self-irony." This last was a theme to which he would later return.

By 1897, Heidenstam's opposition to Norwegian influence had reached its peak. "What suits the Norwegians is morphine to us—and vice versa," he proclaimed in a polemic article entitled "Om patriotism" (On patriotism) in the Stockholm newspaper *Svenska Dagbladet.* "Cultural intermarriage between two neighboring peoples is as unnatural an abomination and as sure a ruination as marriage between siblings. . . . Let us therefore not . . . be afraid to be patriots!"[21]

In 1890, the poet and critic Gustaf Fröding from the border province of Värmland, who knew Norway well, wrote from there, "It would not have hurt the Norwegian spirit, whose moral strength so easily runs to arrogance and narrow-minded moral dogmatism, if it had gotten an infusion of Bellman's all-forgiving humor, Tegnér's amiable wit and free — if not all too great — lust for life, of Viktor Rydberg's distinguished clarity and feeling for beauty, and Strindberg's daring, merciless attacks upon all tyrannical dogmas."

In an essay, "Om humor" (On humor), the same year, Fröding pled in the same vein. Who would at present dare to present the lovable ne'er-do-wells and lighthearted nymphs of past literature with sympathy and humor, he asked. Today, they would be "dissected" and found worthy only of the "button-molder's ladle" *(støbesleven)* — a clear reference to Ibsen's *Peer Gynt.* "Yes, our time is moralistic. But it tends toward fanaticism. Never has preaching been so much in vogue as these days, and although it is all in the name of noble ideals — love, brotherhood, altruism, etc. — it seems to me that rancor only increases. One preaches about love until one becomes heated and angry, people hit each other over the head with love and brotherhood."

According to Fröding, such humor as was to be found among the leading authors of the time, "for instance in Henrik Ibsen, is crowded into the background by moralistic considerations and acquires a tone of Mephistophelean irony." The search for truth, he held, must not become one-sided, for life itself was "endlessly variegated." Beauty and humor must be given free play, for in the "intensified struggle for existence," there was a greater need than ever for "an infusion of conciliation, which is one of the main ingredients of humor, together with the aesthetic."

In an essay from 1892, Fröding regretted that Bjørnson had become ever more determinedly moralistic, leaving behind the "marvelous treasure" of his youthful work with its "love for all that breathes, naively pleasant melodies with all the freshness of folklife in every note, the mighty saga tone, powerful symphonies in which the poet's soul is in harmony with the spirit of nature itself."[22]

The realist "New Sweden" movement quickly faded away. Strindberg, who was ever on the move intellectually, soon fell out with it, as has been seen. By the early 1890s, he went largely into eclipse in Paris, where for some years he devoted himself to quasi-scientific experimentation and occultism. Victoria Benedictsson (whose pen name was Ernst Ahlgren) died of her own hand in 1888 following an unhappy love affair with the Danish critic Georg Brandes, the paladin of realism in the North. Anne Charlotte Leffler dissolved her unhappy marriage in Sweden to marry a Neapolitan, the Duke of Cajanello, and moved to sunnier climes in the south, where she died soon after. Other members of the group, such as Oscar Levertin and Axel Lundegård, renounced their earlier literary ideals or, like Gustaf af Geijerstam, simply drifted along with the shifting literary current. By 1903, Strindberg himself was writing lyric verse. Increasingly, it appeared, realism had run its course, and although to some degree it carried over into the literature of the following decades, it had by now become formulaic, mechanistic, and aesthetically barren.[23]

In actuality, Swedish attacks on realism as a particularly Norwegian genre already lagged behind developments in Norway itself. Ibsen's later dramas can hardly be called realist, as they became increasingly concerned with individual psychology and symbolism. Moreover, Norway now had its own prophet of a new age, the young Knut Hamsun, whose role may in its way be compared with Heidenstam's in Sweden, despite his humble origins and early life, which stood in contrast to Heidenstam's aristocratic antecedents. In 1890, Hamsun's novel *Sult* (Hunger) and a series of polemical articles and lectures aimed particularly at Ibsen, Bjørnson, Lie, and Alexander Kielland set a new course in Norwegian literature toward fantasy, the unexplored realms of the unconscious mind, and the celebration of nature and of life.[24] During the 1890s, Swedish and Norwegian literature moved largely in the same direction, as part of a broader fin de siècle European neoromanticism.

It may seem curious that the term *national romanticism* is used in Sweden to describe the dominant cultural trend of the 1890s and the first years of the twentieth century, whereas in Norway it customarily denotes the period beginning a half century earlier, during the 1840s, and lasting into the early 1870s. The new era beginning around 1890 is referred to in Norway as *Nyromantikk*, or neoromanticism. Still, an underlying parallel emerges. National romanticism in Norway represented above all a reaction against Danish cultural hegemony. In Sweden, the reaction against what was seen to be Norwegian cultural dominance played a similarly crucial role.[25]

The national romantic movement ushered in a renewed period of great creativity in all areas, surely the richest in Sweden's past, comparable only to the high romantic era at the beginning of the century, and it has left its lasting stamp on Swedish cultural life down to the present. Not least, it provided the crucible for the forming of a strong and durable national self-image through its dedicated search for and revindication of the specifically *Swedish.*[26]

It is not our purpose here to describe Swedish national romanticism as such, other than to sketch out its main characteristics. The literature on the subject is vast and fascinating. The new trend was more varied in focus than the realism of the 1880s. While it appealed to national patriotism, its patriotism was in large degree local and provincial. Fredrik Böök has pointed out that whereas earlier nineteenth-century romanticism was centered mainly in the university towns of Uppsala and Lund, and the realist movement of the 1880s in Stockholm, national romanticism diffused the center of gravity out to the rural provinces.[27] The milieux described there were essentially those of the established and conservative elements: the manor houses, parsonages, and substantial peasant freehold farmsteads from which the writers came. Even the Stockholm-centered literature showed a certain fond localism.

Meanwhile, most of the writing of the era was of an intensely personal kind, the sensitive exploration of private emotions, the search to express the inexpressible. The obverse of its rhetorical patriotism was its aestheticism, which in some cases tended toward pure art for art's sake. Poetry once again flourished, following the 1880s during which the novel and drama had dominated. Debate over social issues subsided. The feminist "literature of indignation" fell silent—perhaps in part reflecting the substantial gains women had in fact made over the past decade—giving way to the celebration of love and sensuality. The new literature of the 1890s was filled with wonderment, beauty, and affirmation of life. "Courage and joy," Selma Lagerlöf wrote in 1891. "It is as though these were life's first commandments." Where the 1880s had regarded the past as the charnel house of past injustices, national romanticism looked back upon it with reverence as the treasury of the nation's magnificent heritage.[28]

Our focus here is on Sweden's search for its own historic and cultural uniqueness, most particularly in relation to Norway's. One side of this search was to invoke those aspects of Swedish history and culture for which Norway, during its long "lost centuries," could offer no real equivalents. There were Engelbrekt Engelbrektsson and the Stures, who in the fifteenth century had bid defiance to the Danish monarchs of the Kalmar Union, and Gustaf Vasa who at the head of his doughty Dalarna peasants had regained Sweden's independence and established his dynasty. There was Sweden's glorious seventeenth-century "age of greatness" beginning with Gustaf II Adolf's defense of the True Evangelical Faith at Breitenfelt and Lützen and ending with Carl XII's heroic defeat at Poltava and death at the siege of Fredriksten fortress in 1718.

During the eighteenth century, martial glory had given way to triumphs of the mind and spirit. There was the naturalist Carl von Linné (Linnæus), the "king of flowers," at Uppsala University and his young disciples who traveled to the far corners of the earth to reveal nature's secrets. There was the carefree poet and balladeer of wine, women, and song, Carl Michael Bellman, with his bacchic Movitz and winsome Ulla Winblad, in a Stockholm teeming with colorful life. There was the refined and sophisticated court of Gustaf III in Niccodemus Tessin the younger's magnificent royal palace in Stockholm and the idyllic rural retreats at Drottningholm, Ulriksdal, and Haga. Sweden possessed aristocrats of ancient lineage, manor houses, imposing castles, and the medieval towns at the center of Stockholm and in Visby on the island of Gotland.

A survey of the leading Swedish writers of the period and their work illustrates this celebration of the nation's proud heritage. The self-appointed, though by no means universally recognized, leader of the new movement was Verner von Heidenstam, who thirsted for such a role and filled it with bravado. His work, in both verse and prose, perhaps most fully exemplifies all sides of the era. His *Dikter* (Poems) from 1895, *Ett folk* (A folk) from 1902, and his polemical essays are filled with both high-flown national patriotism and warm attachment to his native Närke province, while also containing lyric poetry of an intensely personal nature. Among his most widely read and influential works were his panoramic historical novels: *Karolinerna* (The Charles men) from 1897–98, describing the heroism and sufferings of Carl XII's armies in facing their many foes during the Great Northern War, thereby achieving immortality in tragedy; his cycle *Folkungaträdet* (The tree of the Folkungs) from 1905–7, an epic of Shakespearean proportions about Sweden's Folkung dynasty in the thirteenth and fourteenth centuries; and his popular *Svenskarne och deras hövdingar* (The Swedes and their chieftains) from 1908–10. The ideal of a loyal people faithfully following their natural leaders was one that strongly appealed to his aristocratic nature.[29]

Heidenstam's closest associate was Oscar Levertin, the critic and author who was of Jewish origin and combined passionate Swedish patriotism with a broad and humane cosmopolitanism. He looked back with particular nostalgia to the aesthetic refinement of the Swedish rococo, seeing this trait as basic to the Swedish character, notably in his *Från Gustaf III:s dagar* (From the days of Gustaf III), published in 1896, with its warmly evocative essays on the "charmer-king" and on the carefree poet-balladeer Carl Michael Bellman, as well as in his *Rococonoveller* (Rococo novellas) from 1899. Levertin was highly influential as a contributor and a critic in the illustrated magazine *Ord och Bild* and the newspaper *Svenska Dagbladet*, the particular organs of national romanticism established during the 1890s. His prose fiction on Gustavian themes was widely imitated by numerous popular writers during the period and beyond. Selma Lagerlöf, who in 1909 would be the first woman to be awarded the Nobel Prize for literature, meanwhile evoked in luminous prose the romance of life in the manor houses of her beloved home province of Värmland, especially in her *Gösta Berlings saga* (Gösta Berling's saga) from 1891, an enduring classic. She also wrote on Swedish medieval themes.[30]

The other side of Swedish national romanticism was to revindicate Sweden's nature, early history, and folklife—the areas in which Norway enjoyed particular preeminence—as different yet in no way inferior to those of its western neighbor. The poet Gustaf Fröding, already encountered, who faced a long and ultimately losing struggle with mental illness, was devoted to his native Värmland. With warm sympathy and humor, he described the healthy love of life, earthy sensuality, and innate dignity of its peasantry, often in verse written in the pithy local dialect, which to this day remains among the best loved of the literary riches of the 1890s.[31] The other most celebrated regionalist of the era, Erik Axel Karlfeldt, celebrated in verse Dalarna and its strongly tradition-bound peasantry, from which he himself derived, in imagery drawn from its local folk culture.[32] Dalarna was likewise the setting for the first part of Lagerlöf's epic novel *Jerusalem* from 1901, which paints an unforgettable picture of the ancient peasant way of life confronted with new and disturbing currents from outside.[33]

National romantic regionalism both reflected and aroused fascination with traditional peasant folkways at a time when the peasantry throughout most of Sweden were abandoning them as a humiliating culture of social inferiority, seeking to emulate the ways of life of the town middle classes, or emigrating in large numbers to America.[34] In 1891, Artur Hazelius, who in 1873 had started the Scandinavian Ethnographic Collection that in 1880 became the Nordic Museum, established Skansen, the immensely popular open-air folk museum at Stockholm's Djurgården, which in time became the model for numerous similar places throughout the world. He moved old farmsteads and other buildings from throughout Sweden to Skansen, where they were occupied throughout the day by persons in folk dress practicing ancient crafts, celebrating traditional holidays, and performing folk music and dances to a delighted public.[35]

To visit Skansen became a veritable pilgrimage for city-dwellers of the upper and middle classes nostalgic for the old rural Sweden in a time of rapid and often unsettling urbanization and industrialization. It was here that the young aspiring writer Karl-Erik Forsslund, a national romanticist of the first water, came to the realization that he must escape the corrupting big city to find a more authentic way of life in his native Dalarna. Acquiring a venerable farmstead near Malung, he wrote an idyllic, fictionalized account of his way back to nature and his roots, *Storgården* (The great farm), which became a veritable cult book in its time. It was in character that Forsslund should be among the founders and the first rector of a folk high school, or *folkhögskola*, in Malung and the prophet of the movement for creating *hembygdsgårdar*, or local outdoor cultural museums—miniature versions of Skansen, as he envisioned them—throughout the country.

Dalarna had by now come to be regarded as the true heartland of the ancient peasant Sweden and was, as has been seen, extolled in verse and prose. Here, several of the leading cultural personalities of the period made their homes—the poet Karlfeldt, the composer Hugo Alfvén, and the artist Gustaf Ankarcrona in Leksand, the painters Anders Zorn in Mora and Carl Larsson in Sundborn—all of whom enhanced the image in the popular mind of Dalarna as the Swedish ideal.[36]

Typically, the cultural celebrities built and decorated their rural retreats in architectural styles reflecting local peasant traditions, above all those from Dalarna. Well-to-do middle-class people followed their lead in both summer homes and suburban residences. Old, half-forgotten crafts in wood, metal, glass, pottery, and textiles were enthusiastically revived, and local and national societies were established for their promotion. Middle-class persons now proudly wore folk dress on appropriate, including patriotic, occasions, and joined folk dance groups. The traditional Midsummer festivities with dancing around the maypole decorated with leaves and flowers, which had fallen into disuse in much of rural Sweden, were now revived in all their glory. The Lucia custom with its maiden crowned with burning candles on 13 December, which heretofore had been practiced only in parts of western Sweden, now spread to the rest of the country.

National romantic revival of interest in the old peasant Sweden nonetheless came at a time when much had already been lost and had therefore to be reinvented. Textile artists such as Ottilia Adelborg and Märtha Måås-

Fjetterström created new designs based on old peasant tradition. Where the complete festive folk dress could no longer be pieced together for particular parishes, the missing parts were imaginatively re-created. Where this could not be done, or where personal ties to ancestral parishes were no longer strong, there was a tendency toward the use of what came to be accepted as "provincial dress." Many chose meanwhile to adopt the blue and yellow national "Swedish dress" (sverigedräkten) designed by Carl Larsson and Gustaf Ankarcrona in 1903.

In addition to the collection, by August Bondesson and others, and revival of old folk melodies and dances, new "folk" music was composed, and dances or "dance-games" were artfully choreographed. A whole new children's culture based on an idyllic vision of an unspoiled rural Sweden came into being, created by such beloved writers and illustrators as Elsa Beskow, Alice Tegnér, Anna Maria Roos, and John Bauer. Alice Tegnér and others wrote children's songs, while Carl Larsson and Aina Stenberg created much of the imagery that has come to be associated with traditional Swedish Christmas.[37]

The revival of Swedish folk traditions was, to begin with, a markedly urban, middle-class phenomenon. Bankers built suburban villas in the style of old Dalarna farmsteads, and their daughters, clad in folk dress, sang artful arrangements of old folk songs at the pianoforte. In 1908, a visiting Swedish-American journalist noted, at a great national Midsummer fest in Delsbo, that it was the university students and city girls who joined in with gusto, while the local country folk tended to hang back and watch from the sidelines.[38] Gradually, however, the new national folk culture was enthusiastically promoted by various of the numerous "folk movements" (folkrörelser) of the period, in particular the folk high schools and the temperance lodges, and thus in time became the common property of the Swedish people as a whole, including the Swedish immigrant community in America.[39]

The situation was similar in Norway. Here, too, during the 1890s, there were dedicated efforts to preserve and revive the old folk culture, which likewise were initially supported most enthusiastically by the urban middle classes and which were reinforced by the growing conflicts with Sweden within the union. Oscar II had begun to collect old farm buildings, together with the Gol stave church, on the royal country estate at Bygdøy on the outskirts of Christiania already in 1881. Anders Sandvig's similar collection of rural buildings at Maihaugen in Lillehammer dated from 1887. Meanwhile, just as Artur Hazelius would seem to have been inspired by the aging Eilert Sundt in establishing his Scandinavian Ethnographic Collection in 1872, the founding of Norsk Folkemuseum, or the Norwegian Folk Museum, in Christiania in 1894 was encouraged by the concept and success of Hazelius's Skansen in Stockholm, which had opened its gates in 1891.[40]

Naturally, it is more difficult to trace direct influences in the fine arts, except where images are supplemented with words. The choice of motifs may be national—even though some of the most celebrated Scandinavian mythological, historical, and genre scenes were painted abroad using foreign models—but techniques are international common property.

The visual arts followed a somewhat different course than literature. There were always closer, more continuous, and congenial contacts between Scandinavian artists than there were among the writers, and the visual rediscovery of Sweden resulted in no ringing manifestos directed against Norwegian art. Norway, as the art historian Michelle Facos has succinctly put it, provided Sweden with "a template for the process of identity formation," while at the same time "it enabled Swedes to perceive with greater clarity the unique aspects of their own culture."[41] Moreover, the turn toward a truly national art began somewhat later in Sweden than the corresponding development in belles lettres.

The overall trend was nonetheless the same. Writers, artists, and musicians came from the same cultural milieu and shared a common, broadly humanistic upbringing. Many, furthermore, were involved in more than one field. Strindberg was a significant painter, and the composer Hugo Alfvén a gifted one. Artists like Carl Larsson, Richard Bergh, and Georg Pauli were also writers, as were, for instance, Christian Krohg, Christian Skredsvig, Kitty Kielland, and Edvard Grieg in Norway. The painter Ernst Josephson was a published poet, and his colleague Robert Thegerström composed music. The charmed circles of the intellectual and aesthetic elite in Stockholm and Christiania were small and intimate. Everyone knew everyone, and new cultural impulses spread freely.

Down to the late 1880s, developments in Nordic art took place largely outside of Scandinavia itself. Sweden had, to be sure, its Royal Academy of Art, which traced its origins back to 1735, and its National Museum of Art (*Nationalmuseum*), in Stockholm since 1866. But the Royal Academy's instruction was rigidly conservative, stressing mythological and historical painting and sculpture on the classical model. Norway, meanwhile, had no national academy. Aspiring Norwegians frequently received training in Copenhagen before moving on to the Continent, particularly to Düsseldorf from the 1830s to the 1870s, where after midcentury they were joined by growing numbers of Swedes.[42]

Scandinavia itself offered a severely restricted market for works of art. In Sweden, the Royal Academy served as gatekeeper to the National Museum's annual exhibitions, while in Norway the same function was played by the Art Society *(Kunstforeningen)* in Christiania, both of which staunchly upheld established canons of art. Nonetheless, while Scandinavian writers were limited to the relatively small public that knew their languages—except where their works might be selectively translated—the visual arts were immediately accessible everywhere. Scandinavian artists were able to find abroad a wider market for their work than existed at home.

By around 1870, the Düsseldorf school had lost its vitality, and there began a gradual exodus of Norwegian and Swedish students. Hans Gude had left already in 1861, and two years later, he became a professor at the Art Academy in Karlsruhe. During his later years, his landscapes and seascapes became increasingly realistic in tone. During the early 1870s, several Norwegians and Swedes studied at the Munich Academy, which championed historical painting on the heroic model, before drifting on to the new artistic mecca, Paris, beginning with the Swedes Alfred Wahlberg and Hugo Salmson, who arrived in the late 1860s.

Throughout the 1870s and 1880s, there was a numerous Scandinavian art colony in Paris, whose members regularly exhibited at the prestigious annual Salon, frequently won prizes, and found ready buyers. It was in Paris that a concerted revolt began against the entrenched art establishments in the homelands. Led by Ernst Josephson, the Swedish painters organized in 1885 as the "Opponents"—which in 1886 became the Artists' Union *(Konstnärsförbundet)*. Its best-known adherents included Karl Nordström, Carl Larsson, Anders Zorn, Nils Kreuger, Bruno Liljefors, Hugo Birger, Robert Thegerström, Oscar Björck, Georg Pauli and Hanna Hirsch Pauli, Jenny Nyström, and Richard Bergh, who served as their leading ideologue. In 1885, the Opponents organized their epochal exhibit, "From the Banks of the Seine," at the restaurateur Teodor Blanch's Salon in Stockholm. The following year, it was shown in Göteborg, where the wealthy merchant Pontus Fürstenberg was their steadfast patron. The way was cleared for a new era in Swedish art.

The Swedes in Paris were closely allied with the Norwegians Christian Skredsvig, Christian Krohg, Erik Werenskiold, Kitty Kielland, Harriet Backer, and others, as well Finns such as Albert Edfeldt, Eero Järnefelt, Akseli Gallen-Kallela, and Ville Vallgren, who during these years mounted their own, successful offensives against the restrictive institutions in their homelands.[43]

In Paris, the Scandinavians abandoned their academic and late-romantic traditions to become enthusiastic converts to realism and *plein air* painting.

Larsson described the new revelation in a letter to a friend in 1883: "For the first time in my life I saw nature. I cast all bizarre oddities onto the rubbish heap, and all my extraordinary idea combinations into the sea. There they will remain. I have taken nature to my heart, however simple it may be."[44] While they adopted a lighter, brighter palette and devoted themselves to an intense study of light, they remained on the whole relatively little affected by the more daring innovations of French impressionism during the period. In their realism, the Scandinavian artists drew inspiration from Gustave Courbet, François Millet, Jules Breton, and particularly Jules Bastien-Lepage, painters of everyday rural life.[45]

The Paris era in Scandinavian art reached its apogee by the early 1880s in the idyllic village of Grèz-sur-Loing near Fontainebleau, where several British and American artists were already established. The Norwegians Krohg and Skredsvig arrived there in the late 1870s and were soon joined by many of the Paris Swedes, who congregated in Grèz throughout the decade, together with several Finns. The Swedes included most notably Carl Larsson and his wife Karin—who soon became the colony's central figures—Nordström, Bergh, Georg Pauli, Liljefors, and Kreuger. Here, too, came August Strindberg and his wife Siri during an increasingly difficult time in their marriage.[46]

While the young Scandinavian artists professed sympathy for the common people, the social indignation that pervaded much of European realism at the time found relatively little resonance in their painting. The main exception was the Norwegian Christian Krohg. When his friend Hans Jæger was tried and imprisoned in 1885 for publication of his novel *Fra Christiania-Bohêmen* (From Christiania's Bohemia), which advocated free love, Krohg brought out a novel of his own, *Albertine*, and painted his celebrated *Albertine in the Police Doctor's Waiting Room* the following year, illustrating the evils of prostitution resulting from a hypocritical bourgeois morality. His later work during the decade showed the poverty and hunger of the poor in Christiania. Certain Danish and especially Finnish painters were also social realists, but there was little reflection of this aspect among the Swedes, who devoted themselves to celebrating nature and life in the here and now.

In reviewing a large exhibition of the new Scandinavian art in Copenhagen in 1888, Krohg complained that he found there nothing of the new direction that "was to make visual art something more than mere wall decoration in wealthy homes and galleries . . . a vital part in cultural evolution, so that it becomes gripping, rather than impressive." The Swedish artists in particular, he held, seemed to seek only "to make their work look as effortless and elegant as possible."[47]

Scandinavian artists in France frequently returned for varying periods of time to their own part of the world, and here the Danish artists' colony at Skagen, on the northern tip of Jutland, played a significant role as a kind of Nordic halfway house to the expatriates. Since the beginning of the century, the Danes had gone their own way, long remaining true to their close artistic ties with Italy and generally bypassing both Germany and France. From 1870, a number of them congregated at Skagen, where they were at times joined by certain Norwegians and Swedes, especially Krohg, Skredsvig, Eilif Peterssen, Oscar Björck, Wilhelm von Gegerfelt, Johan Krouthén, and the composer-painter Hugo Alfvén, who here applied the *plein air* realism they had acquired in France to everyday scenes among the local fisher folk.[48]

For the young Swedish and Norwegian artists, the chance to study and work in Paris had been a welcome liberation from the small and confining world at home. Richard Bergh recalled that the constant question among his friends at the time was "When can we leave?" And, he continued, "We departed. Away from the land of the barbarians. We became cosmopolites. The sound of bells from the snow-covered land up there in the North did not reach across the sea to disturb our cult of beauty. It was with melancholy contempt on our lips that we spoke of the land without motifs, the land of the red cottages, so impossible to paint." Contemplating a necessary sojourn back home, Carl Larsson wrote from Grèz during the early 1880s, "Well, now we will have to leave the glorious air of France to return to Sweden and try to get inspired by those damned wolves' teeth"—the jagged skyline of the Nordic coniferous forest.[49]

"When the younger generation has soberly sought artistic mastery and attained it," Ernst Josephson meanwhile prophesied, "then we will have a Swedish art in Sweden." By the turn of the decade, Swedish artists were following the example of Verner von Heidenstam and returning to their native soil.

To be sure, France during the Boulanger, Panama, and Dreyfus Affairs became a less hospitable environment for foreigners than before. But there were deeper reasons. France was not home. To Georg Pauli, then in Sweden, Bergh wrote from Normandy in June 1887: "Now it surely must be lovely in old Sweden too—at Midsummertime—one almost gets tears in one's eyes when one thinks of the long, light nights, the calm, clear water, in which the birch groves are reflected while the nightingale sings and the thrush twitters sentimentally in the forest. . . . We must be Swedes, we have been Frenchmen long enough!" "How often," Bergh later reflected, "have we ourselves, when we have looked with longing to the riches of the South, not become as

though petrified. Only in the North is there deliverance for the longing soul
·of the Nordic. May we in longing and love cultivate our own stony soil—
and it will gain life."[50]

The young Prince Eugen, youngest son of the reigning monarch, then
studying painting in France, wrote that in 1888, on the Riviera looking out
over the Mediterranean, he and a small group of Swedes read aloud from Heidenstam's *Vallfart och vandringsår* (Pilgrimage and wander-years) and were
seized by overpowering nostalgia for their homeland.[51]

Once again, Norway provided fresh sources of inspiration. It was there in
1872 that Josephson, too romantic a nature ever to become a full-fledged realist, was inspired by the old Nordic legend of the water sprite, symbol of the
primal forces of nature. This vision would preoccupy him until he completed
the final version of his *Strömkarlen* in 1884 by a rushing waterfall in Eggedal,
with a local Norwegian peasant lad for his nude model. Bergh would later
call this painting "a milestone in the development of Swedish art; during the
time ahead, the remains of naturalism's gray mists would dissolve and vanish
. . . for color and light and half-light belong together in painting; they are its
life, the signs of its vitality."[52]

The Norwegians, meanwhile, had never forsaken their native landscapes
to the same extent as the Swedes during the height of the cosmopolitan realist period. Already by the mid-1880s, most of their expatriate artists had
returned home for good. In 1886, a group of them—Skredsvig, Werenskiold,
Peterssen, Backer, Kielland, and Gerhard Munthe—spent the summer
together at Fleskum Farm, near Bærum in the Christiania area. Here
Skredsvig, Peterssen, and Kielland in particular painted twilight scenes
around the lake Dælivannet in an ineffably lyric and introspective vein evocative of the inner landscapes of the mind.[53]

The "Fleskum Summer" of 1886 is seen as the turning point toward a more
stylized and symbol-laden neoromanticism in Norwegian art, although there
had already begun to appear intimations of the new direction. By the early
1890s, the younger generation of Swedish artists returning from Paris were
likewise seeking to infuse their landscapes with *stämning*—that almost
untranslatable concept of mood and atmosphere. Having dedicated themselves in France to the intense study of light, they now turned *par préférence*
to the richly evocative Nordic summer twilight, which conveyed so much of
the new romantic ethos at the turn of the century: at once, the nostalgia of
sunset for a time now passing beyond recall and the hushed expectations at
dawn of a glorious new day to come.

To what extent the immensely creative national romantic era in Swedish art was directly inspired by new impulses from across the Keel is of course difficult to judge, for national romanticism—as well as the art nouveau that so strongly affected its language of form—were international movements throughout the Western world by the end of the century. But the similarities are unmistakable.

This influence is particularly evident in the case of Prince Eugen, who earlier had studied drawing with Hans Gude in Karlsruhe and who would prove himself one of the finest and most characteristic painters of his time, as well as a generous patron to his colleagues on both sides of the Keel. Together with other Swedish artists, he was deeply impressed by the works of the Norwegian Fleskum painters he saw at the 1889 Paris World Exhibition. They brought home to him, he wrote, the realization that "our Nordic landscape, with its clear air, its hard contours, and its strong colors is just as appropriate for artistic presentation as France's delicate gray landscape." He later recalled:

After the great Paris exhibition in 1889, where to be sure Swedish art enjoyed considerable success, several of our artists had the feeling that our Swedish exhibit lacked a particularly national tone, something that marked both the Norwegian and Danish exhibits, and they therefore decided quite spontaneously to settle down once again in our homeland. I myself got the strong impression at the Paris exhibition that our Swedish art there did not show the same freshness in color as the Norwegian exhibit showed in such high degree and which our nature surely should be able to afford. Fortunate circumstances resulted in my coming to Norway that summer. Through the natural impressions I received there, my painting came to show the same characteristics as Norwegian art and acquired a coloristic vigor that I later kept in [painting] Swedish nature.[54]

Prince Eugen spent that summer and the following one painting in and around the Valdres district in Norway, joined for a time by Richard Bergh, likewise a onetime pupil of Hans Gude and a warm admirer of his Norwegian colleagues. "Fir trees were considered by the [Swedish] 'Parisians' to be inartistic. But just for that very reason I was tempted to paint them," Prince Eugen later recounted. In August, he wrote to his close friend Helena Nyblom that "I who before never liked mountains am delighted with nature here. But Valdres is not western Norway [*Vestlandet*]!" He visited the Norwegian west coast the following summer, together with the Swedish artist Gunnar Gunnarsson Wennerberg, with whom he had studied in Paris. But he was glad soon to return to Valdres, which, he wrote his mother Queen Sophia, "offered much more of interest with its fields, houses, and forests than the West's overwhelming mountains." Valdres, in short, more closely resembled familiar and congenial Swedish landscapes such as those in Tyresö and Fjällskäfte in Södermanland to which he would soon devote himself and for which he is best remembered.[55]

Prince Eugen's paintings from the Valdres area in 1889 and 1890 bear an unmistakable likeness to those of the Fleskum group, not least Werenskiold's. It was in Norway that he developed his characteristic Nordic style as a landscapist over the next two decades. Throughout the 1890s, he was frequently in Christiania, where his private correspondence shows that he found an intellectual and artistic milieu both livelier and less constrained than in Stockholm. He formed close friendships with Norwegian artists, especially Werenskiold and Munthe, with whom he frequently corresponded in Norwegian. He remained warmly attached to Norway and to his Norwegian friends throughout his life.[56]

In 1994, Prince Eugen would be the sole Swedish artist represented in a great exhibition of Norwegian turn-of-the-century art held in Oslo. Its catalog justified this by explaining that until 1905 he was a Norwegian prince as well as a Swedish one, that he had such close ties with the Norwegian artistic world that up to that year he was regarded in Norway as "Norwegian," and that he played a vital role as an intermediary with the European and Swedish art worlds.[57] It may be recalled that in 1905 Bjørnstjerne Bjørnson and others in Norway seem to have considered him a likely candidate for their throne.

While Prince Eugen devoted himself before 1910 largely to Södermanland's landscape, his fellow artists in Sweden sought to bring forth the particular character and mood of other Swedish provinces: Karl Nordström focused on Bohuslän and Halland on the west coast; Nils Kreuger on Halland and on the island of Öland; Gustaf Fjæstad, whose name suggests his Norwegian descent, on Värmland; Anders Zorn and Carl Larsson on Dalarna; Eugène Jansson and Prince Eugen himself on Stockholm; and Helmer Osslund on the vast northern region, Norrland, as far afield as Lapland. Provincialism was no less marked in the art than in the literature of the day.

It would go well beyond the scope of this study to seek to characterize individually the leading artists of the Swedish national romantic pantheon. What gave an underlying unity to their work—as well as its unfailing appeal down to the present day—was their passionate love affair with the nature and landscapes of their native land. Criticizing classical academicism in art, Richard

Bergh wrote in 1896, "Norway has no academy of art at all—but *Norwegian art*. Do not believe that Swedish art should be like Norwegian art! Swedish art must be as unlike Norwegian art as the Swedish character is unlike the Norwegian."[58]

Like most of the intellectual elite of the 1880s and 1890s, the national romantic artists regarded themselves as political radicals. Bergh was a professed socialist. But Marxian Social Democracy in Sweden, under the leadership of Hjalmar Branting and August Palm, was by this time revisionist, no longer holding to the inevitability of violent revolution. It was possible to be at once a staunch socialist and an ardent patriot, as were Bergh and his friends, at least until the General Strike of 1909 led to a parting of the ways. The ideal of the radical intelligentsia was national unity and concord based on political equality and social justice.

Just as Verner von Heidenstam—like Bjørnstjerne Bjørnson—saw the poet as the true voice and conscience of his people, Bergh envisioned the artist as "a kind of high priest in a secularized cult of the fatherland," as Allan Elle-nius has expressed it. His true goal, in Bergh's view, was to foster a sense of national community that could rise above class conflict.

> The artist should bring old and young, rich and poor, town-dweller and country-dweller together before our Swedish nature, mother of our national character and silent creator of the forms of our culture. He should call us to meet and celebrate beneath the sparkling starry skies of winter and the summer night's quivering sea of light. He should teach us to understand our innermost being. . . . He should fill us with a great, common love and a common, hopeful longing. In this way he should also put steel into our character, through which we may defend ourselves from outside encroach-ment.[59]

The 1890s saw the high point of the Old Norse "dragon style" of orna-mentation in Norway. In painting and graphic arts, this led to a fascination with motifs from the sagas and from folktales. A particularly striking example was the classic 1899 edition of *Snorres Kongesagaer* (Snorri Sturlason's *Heim-skringla*, or Chronicle of the Norwegian kings), in Gustaf Storm's translation, with illustrations by Erik Werenskiold, Gerhard Munthe, Christian Krohg, Eilif Peterssen, Halfdan Egedius, and Wilhelm Wertlesen, a national treas-ure that since then has gone through new editions down to the present.

In architecture, Lorenz Dietrichson of Christiania University took the lead with his groundbreaking studies of old Norwegian woodcarving and stave churches that promoted a building style true to the nation's proud medieval heritage, although inspiration came in part from the Swedish archaeologist Oscar Montelius. Beginning in the 1880s, imposing tourist hotels were built in the dragon style amid spectacular surroundings on the western fjords and on the high ridge overlooking Christiania, most of which, unfortunately, have since burned down. The vogue likewise manifested itself in furniture design and in a wide range of decorative arts, expressing the same growing sense of national unity and purpose in the face of increasing conflict with Sweden over the union. By the turn of the century, meanwhile, a new, freer, and more creative phase in domestic architecture led by the artist Gerhard Munthe, with impulses from the exuberant later Norwegian peasant baroque and rococo traditions, arose in reaction to the academic archaeological dragon style espoused by Dietrichson and his disciples.[60]

In Sweden, the vogue that had flourished particularly during the 1870s for building and decorating in the old Norse fashion — in practice, based mainly on surviving medieval stave churches and old farm buildings in Norway — had meanwhile tended to lose its creative vitality during the 1880s. The most notable late example of the Old Norse style was the Biological Museum built for the Stockholm Exposition of 1897 and still standing.[61]

Urban architecture in Sweden remained highly eclectic through the 1890s, with a profusion of historicizing neorenaissance and neobaroque styles of Italian, French, central and northern European inspiration, as seen for instance in Stockholm's fashionable Östermalm district, as well as in the rebuilding of Sundsvall after its great fire in 1888. A trend is nevertheless discernible through the period toward greater simplicity and sincerity that by the second decade of the twentieth century would mature into a massive Northern neobaroque in native stone and brick, inspired above all by the great castles of the Vasa era in the sixteenth and seventeenth centuries at Kalmar, Gripsholm, Örebro, and especially Vadstena.

"Let us immerse ourselves in our good old architectural monuments," wrote the architect Torben Grut in 1903. The Vasa baroque — at times softened with elements of Continental *Jugendstil*, or art nouveau — came to be seen as the quintessential Swedish monumental style and to a high degree would set its stamp upon large urban commercial and residential buildings and public edifices up through the mid-1920s. Meanwhile, from around the turn of the century, there arose a new interest in the simple yet elegant neoclassical domestic architecture of the late eighteenth-century Gustavian period, when Swedish culture had achieved a new and unprecedented level of cultural refinement, setting a trend that would likewise culminate in the 1920s. In both cases, Swedish architecture unmistakably reasserted glorious epochs in the nation's past that Norway could not hope to match.[62]

It seems indicative that Elisabet Stavenow-Hidemark in her 1971 study of Swedish domestic architecture during the first decades of the twentieth century devoted sections to British, German, Austrian, American, and Danish influences—but not Norwegian. Private suburban villas came to be characteristically inspired by native provincial vernacular architecture, into which there merged what remained of the Old Norse elements. The homes that leading writers, artists, and musicians built for themselves in picturesque parts of the country offered widely emulated examples. In a book offering architectural plans for simpler rural dwellings, Adrian Molin would call in 1909 for buildings with *"a Swedish character . . .* Swedish homes like those our fathers built. For behind them lay *Swedish thoughts,* and it is Swedish thoughts we ought to be thinking."[63]

Styles in domestic furnishings and interior décor underwent a similar development, from somber and cluttered Victorian—or more properly, "Oscarian"—historical eclecticism toward a light, spare, yet tastefully eclectic, elegant, and harmonious simplicity, enthusiastically propagated by Carl Larsson in his immensely popular illustrated description of his home in Dalarna and by Ellen Key with her gospel of "beauty for all." The new aesthetic well matched the revival of a neoclassical architectural ideal beginning around the turn of the century. It would set its lasting stamp upon the Swedish home down to the present and even at the time was not without influence in Norway as well.[64]

Swedish musical composition during the romantic age, including the art songs of Erik Gustaf Geijer or Adolf Fredrik Lindblad and the symphonies and chamber music of Sweden's best-known composer, Franz Berwald, gave indeed some conscious indications of their national origin, although they are generally reminiscent of the work of Schubert, Mendelssohn, and Schumann. The music of August Söderman by the late 1850s revealed a more distinctly national character. Turn-of-the-century national romanticism created a renewed enthusiasm for collecting and studying old Swedish folk songs and dance melodies, which provided composers such as Emil Sjögren, Vilhelm Stenhammar, Vilhelm Peterson-Berger, and perhaps especially Hugo Alfvén with characteristic folk modes, harmonies, and meters, which they incorporated into their work. They also arranged—and in a sense domesticated—old folk songs and dances for concert performance.

Yet, here too, the influence of Norwegian national romantic composers from midcentury on, including Halfdan Kjerulf, Richard Nordraak, Johan Svendsen, Christian Sinding, and above all Edvard Grieg, who had found a Nordic voice based on a folk idiom widely shared across the peninsula, can only have been profound. This is in part borne out by the numerous Norwegian

poems set to music during this period by Swedish composers. The Norwegians again provided both inspiration and example.65

The search for a specifically Swedish landscape was a central concern for
Sweden's national romantic writers, artists, and composers. This search led
in two directions: to the discovery of heretofore little-known areas of wilderness in the north, on the one hand, and to efforts to capture the distinctiveness of the old settled regions of the center and the south, on the other.

The vast, landlocked interior of Norrland, the northern two-thirds of Sweden, much of which lay above the Arctic Circle, remained virtually terra
incognita to the great majority of Swedes, even of the educated classes, before
the building of railroads into the region, which was a relatively late development. Not until 1882 was the line completed from the Baltic coast through
Jämtland to Storlien on the Norwegian border near Trondheim. This brought
home to the Swedish public the existence of a magnificent mountain area
within their own borders that until then had been far less accessible than the
Norwegian mountains and fjords. The Storlien line stimulated the development of commercial tourism, both domestic and foreign, leading to the building of large tourist hotels with sweeping views of the mountains.

It has been said that mountains are the cradle of tourism. Thus it was in
Switzerland, thus too in Norway. Already in 1868, Den Norske Turistforening,
the Norwegian Tourist Society, was organized to encourage domestic tourism.
Now, following the opening of the Storlien line, Svenska Turistföreningen,
the Swedish Tourist Society, was established in 1885 on the initiative of a
group of young naturalists at Uppsala University, inspired by the Norwegian
society, to which several Swedes belonged. Its stated purpose was "to spread
knowledge of the land and its inhabitants . . . for the benefit of the fatherland."
The organizers declared that "citizens of means should no longer have to
spend money to travel to Norway or Italy, now that the northern trunk line
has made it possible to enter our own highland."

The activities of the Swedish society grew apace as railways advanced into
Lapland. A line from Luleå on the coast as far as Gällivare, where iron min-
ing was beginning on a large scale, was opened for public use in 1895. Its
extension to the border to connect with a Norwegian line to the port of Narvik
was open by 1903, making accessible to tourists an even larger and more spectacular region of subarctic mountains, which to this day comprises Western
Europe's largest wilderness area. "We seldom reflect on it," Fredrik Svenonius, editor of the society's yearbook, wrote in 1889, "but it is a fact that pre-
sumably no country in all of Europe can offer the nature-loving tourist a

greater wealth of shifting scenes and variety of interesting natural phenomena than our own fatherland."

At first, the Swedish Tourist Society promoted wandering on foot in the northern mountains, and they built huts at suitable distances for night lodging. This, to begin with, was an experience available only to the relatively well-to-do and well equipped. By the turn of the century, however, the society began to encourage tourism on a more modest level to a broader public throughout the country, now focusing on culture as well as nature. Like other manifestations of national romanticism, the society actively fostered patriotism and a sense of community. Its role in this regard, down to the present, has been inestimable.[66]

In the meantime, there was much earnest discussion among writers and artists regarding the aesthetic nature of the familiar landscapes of the Swedish heartland. A point of departure from an earlier time may be Carl Jonas Love Almqvist, who in 1838 rhetorically asked what the landscape painter could hope to find in Sweden.

> Sweden is on the whole low-lying, offers few picturesque views on the grand scale, shows nothing monumental as in Switzerland, fertile as in France, or magnificent as in Italy. A meager, confining landscape spreads out its modest canvas before our eyes, showing us a little lake, the pale green edge of a meadow, on the one side, a leafy thicket on the other, and perhaps some dark needle trees there, farthest away. So it looks almost everywhere, where it is not simply a common, unsightly heath, or nothing but forest.

Its appeal was, however, more subtle and not immediately apparent to the eye:

> Nature here is a quiet, withdrawn forest maiden, very modest, [who] does not enter the salon, and who would be ill received there. She whispers so slowly and speaks so softly, or more properly, not softly but like an Æolian harp out of the magical distance. The most sensitive ear is needed, one must have the tenderest, most sensitive spirit to become aware of beauties that seem as though intended as an eternal secret.[67]

Swedish visitors to Norway could not meanwhile but be impressed by its sheer natural splendor in comparison with their own homeland. Swedes were used to hearing their country described as "the land of mountains," Peter August Gödecke declared in 1863, but nothing could be less fitting. He who was accustomed to the pleasant central Swedish countryside could well appreciate the more impressive valleys of eastern Norway. "But we would not advise him to precede immediately to the west coast," where "he would feel overwhelmed by nature's astonishing and frightening grandeur." "Nature here truly possesses a majesty which we on our lowlands can scarcely conceive," he wrote from the Jotunheimen massif in 1863. "If our ploughlands are Nordic nature's prose and our mountains and forests her amiable little attempts at poetry, Norway's high peaks are her great, moving hymns to eternity."

Verner von Heidenstam pointed with wistful irony in 1896 to the incongruity between the Swede's "longing for the magnificent and the pretty [Swedish] landscape fragmented into countless details! Fantasy seeks in every way to conceal this discrepancy. Pines as depicted as sky-high. Precarious cliffs brood over thundering waterfalls, and offshore skerries, which the poet populates with dark Viking figures, become enchanted islands beyond the bounds of civilization."[68]

Richard Bergh later recalled how he and his colleagues asked themselves around 1880, "Where is the architectural and artistic unity that makes nature in the South, with its clear, harmonious lines, so attractive to the painter? Not here!" Still, by the end of the decade, they began to see their native landscape in a new and idealized light. Of a typical winter scene that before had seemed disorderly and banal, Bergh now wrote: "Open your eyes and see the transformation. The sky around the horizon is a sea of purest gold, so brilliant, so clear as only a winter day in the North can be. Consider what a banquet hall you wander in! What resonance, what healthfulness in this atmosphere!"

"The wild and widely changeable nature in the North does not accommodate the painter like the harmonious nature in France," Bergh wrote in 1896.

> The former does not, like the latter, offer the artist ready-made motifs like ripe fruits. To depict our nature it does not help simply to open our eyes to it; the painter must also know how at times to close them, he must be able to *dream* of what he has seen, he must understand how to listen with his *feelings* so that led by them he may find unity in this shifting multiplicity, in which extremes are often so juxtaposed. . . . In France a landscape painter may perhaps be an artist using only his eyes. . . . In the North the landscape painter must be a *poet*.[69]

This well describes Prince Eugen. In a letter to his mother from 1895, he described a train trip through "Småland's austere nature with the jagged silhouettes of firs and the glimmer of water here and there."

> It was so genuinely Swedish and I felt that it was something after all of that which we have within us. But also something of the warm, smiling, lovely nature with its meadows and fields, with blossoming buckthorn and bil-

lowing leaf-trees. Sweden combines *both* these kinds of nature, the severe and the beneficent. Of that Swedish mixture something good should come in many areas. In art it will surely be so if we only open our eyes to what our nature has to offer.[70]

To follow through with this thought, Carl Malmsten would write in 1916 of how modest the Swedish scene could appear to the traveler who had visited Norway or Switzerland.

His eye and mind are compelled to look closer, to their immediate surroundings. His whole psyche must adapt itself to receive other, less striking impressions. The inlet with the tall waving rushes and the sparkling reflections on the water, the slender birch trees that white and supple raise up their soft fans of leaves against the sky, the blueberry bushes that on the forest floor form a forest for small creatures and ants, all the little flowers of the meadow and roadside—all this emerges from the closed circle and it grows in depth. . . . Intimate contact with this Swedish nature compels the mind, in a way only comprehensible to us, toward an inner harmony.[71]

Erik Axel Karlfeldt in 1926 would once again reconfirm the concept of a uniquely Swedish ideal landscape, characterized by its human scale, balance, and subtle variety, the product of nature and culture alike.

Sweden is no tourist land in the usual sense and never can it be. Its nature is not formed to impress foreigners who demand wonders. . . . It has therefore always seemed to me unworthy to lure foreigners here with advertising and expectations. Once I traveled through Norway in the company of a couple of Frenchmen, who delightedly hung out the train window until the light of day faded away in mysterious Merakerdal. But when the following day they took up their observation posts, we were already far down into Jämtland and I felt a little ashamed that our country could hardly show them anything but mile after mile of rainy forest. No, Sweden is no showplace, and thank God for that! To appreciate our nature and our people one must be Swedish oneself, born to the feeling for all the varied riches that lie hidden amid all our plainness. One must have a Swedish eye to be able to travel in our country with pleasure and edification.[72]

The idea that the character of a people is determined by its physical environment can be traced back to antiquity. In the case of Scandinavia, a cold climate, long dark winters, and slender resources were commonly believed to have made its inhabitants hardy, bold, venturesome, and freedom loving.

This idea is, for instance, widely reflected in the travel writings of foreign visitors to the North during the eighteenth century, many of whom were surely familiar with Montesquieu's *L'Esprit des Lois* from 1748, which provided its *locus classicus*.[73]

By the nineteenth century, the Scandinavians themselves tended to see differing characteristics between themselves based on their natural settings. Swedes saw an evident link between Norway's more austere environment compared with Sweden's more varied and abundant nature and the effects of each upon their neighbors and themselves. They tended to regard the Norwegians as brave and patriotic, to be sure, yet hard, narrow-minded, self-centered, stubborn, and contentious, in comparison with themselves, whom they conceived to be generous, chivalrous, and cosmopolitan.

Anders Fredrik Skjöldebrand in the 1830s took the Norwegians to task for what he considered their absurd vanity and his own people for their excessive modesty. In opposing the Riksdag proposal for representational reform on the Norwegian model in 1840, Baron Mauritz Klingspor maintained in the Noble Estate that "the Norwegian is the inhabitant of the North, personifying its phlegm and frugality. The Swede has meanwhile acquired something of the Southern nature in his character, its passion, liveliness, and fickleness." K. A. Lindström essayed in 1860 a critical evaluation of the two nations in Stockholm's *Nya Dagligt Allehanda*:

> The one people is open, lighthearted, weak-willed, thoughtless, quick-tempered, easily taken in by [rhetorical] phrases, chivalrous, easily aroused, easily reconciled, often mistakes the cloud for Juno and fool's gold for real gold, always means what it says and not infrequently says more than it can live up to, is carried away with enthusiasm, is charmed by everything foreign, yet still loves its old native soil, even while constantly finding fault with it and is, sadly enough, weak in national feeling. . . . The other is closed within itself, calculating, mistrustful and suspicious in the highest degree, to the point of absurdity, never gets carried away, seldom loses its temper in acting but readily resorts to angry words with the idea of perhaps gaining something thereby and thus not having to act, never mistakes the cloud for Juno but gladly allows others to do so, despises and scoffs at everything foreign with genuine Yankee arrogance, is not burdened with courtesy, is callous in dealing with political adversaries, and is excessively strong in national feeling.[74]

August Strindberg specifically linked what he saw as the Norwegian temperament to the country's natural milieu in 1886:

In Norway's isolated valleys dwelt a people who through penury and a meager living found in Christianity's doctrine of renunciation a ready-made
philosophy of self-denial, which promised heaven in return for deprivation.
An oppressive, melancholy, and austere nature, a damp climate, long distances between settlements, loneliness, everything combined to preserve
Christianity in its medieval form. There is also something one could call
mentally unbalanced in the Norwegian spirit, of the same type as English
spleen. . . . The Norwegian character is the result of many centuries'
tyranny, of unjust treatment, of the hard struggle for bread, of lack of joy.
These national peculiarities should not have impressed themselves upon
the Swede, but they have Norwegianized him. Swedish literature is still
haunted by the Old Man of the Dovre [from Ibsen's *Peer Gynt*] and Brand
is there with his idealistic demands, which the Swede, with his Latin influences and lighter-hearted nature cannot really share. Therefore this foreign
garb fits him so poorly; therefore modern Swedish music sounds so dishar-
monious with echoes of the Hardanger fiddle, retuned by Grieg; therefore
the new local dialect movement is so inappropriate; and therefore there is
no end of talk of greater moral purity for the life-affirming Swede. He has
not been under long foreign oppression and does not need to search for
himself in the past; he has not become so gloomy in his broad, open countryside of lakes and rivers, and therefore a sour expression ill befits him.[75]

As always with Strindberg, his personal experience is not far beneath the
surface, and it is evident that his delineation of the Norwegian character
derived much from his enmity, by that time, toward Ibsen and Bjørnson. In
1877, he commented on the Swedish painter Julius Kronberg's just-completed
portrait of Ibsen: "The face is 'Brand's'; the high, broad brow of the fanatic,
the strong mouth . . . the cold, determined look that never wavered when it
stared 'the spirit of compromise' in the face." His first impression of Bjørnson
in Paris in 1883 was that of a "prehistoric hero, hewn from the bare rock, in
greater than human size. Head of stone, hair brushed back as though on a
helmet, bushy eyebrows . . . in a word, an Atlantean is town dress and with
gold-rimmed spectacles"—whom he soon came to regard as a colossus with
feet of clay.[76]

Such attitudes toward the Norwegians died hard. They would, for example,
be forcefully echoed in 1921 by the literary critic Fredrik Böök when he wrote
of the realism of the "Young Sweden" school of the 1880s:

In its querulousness and litigiousness there is a specifically Norwegian
element. The Norwegians during the union showed themselves to be

virtuosos in contentiousness. In Bjørnson there is no peace . . . and Ibsen invokes the Norwegian milieu in which irritability was nurtured: small constricted communities lacking breathing space or elbow room, where people look angrily at each other and behave in a particularly rude manner. Many of the problems and conflicts quite simply derive from the atmosphere of a small nation. In a larger society with freer conditions they would largely disappear. But the whole dissatisfied and critical atmosphere of the time found itself in predetermined harmony with this provincial environment reeking of whale oil. Thus the great popularity of the Norwegian literature. In the Swedish literature of the 1880s there is not only moral mountain air from Norway but also a large dose of this Norwegian spirit that lets everything turn to bickering and conflict: the generations and sexes stand opposed to each other as deadly enemies, father against son, man against wife.[77]

An outsider's perception of the attitudes of Norwegians and Swedes toward each other in a time of mounting conflict between them is provided by the British minister to the Dual Monarchy, Sir Spencer Buckingham St. John, in a report to the Foreign Office in February 1894: "[The Norwegians are] eminently a democratic people, hard working, and caring but little for anything which happens outside their frontiers, except insofar as it may affect their very considerable foreign trade. They have a contempt for the Swedes whom they look upon as indolent and luxurious, whilst the Swedes despise the Norwegians as a nation of rustics. The two peoples do not appear to have any feeling in common to bind them together."[78]

But apart from insidious comparisons with the Norwegians, how did the Swedes describe themselves? Again, Almqvist may provide a starting point. In his aforementioned essay from 1838, he regarded the Swedish temperament as the product of its environment and most specifically the basic poverty of the country, which, in his view, was a blessing in disguise. To be poor, he declared, meant to be compelled to rely upon one's own inner resources. The Swede was therefore basically unworldly, attaching little importance to earthly goods and spending them generously and often improvidently when he acquired them. Almqvist expounded the novel theory that people aged in relation to the number of months of warmth and growth during the year. By this calculus, a person of sixty years in southern Europe was much older in experience and world-weariness than one of the same age in the North, with its longer and colder winters. He thus rejoiced that the Swedes were still a young people, with a youthful outlook on life. "It is 10:00 o'clock in the morning in head and heart," he wrote, ". . . we struggle with the discontents and mistakes of youth, but enjoy its benefits."[79]

It was seen at the beginning of this chapter that Strindberg's first criticism of Norwegian cultural influences in Sweden appeared in an essay he wrote in 1883. Its essential message was that his compatriots lacked a secure and balanced sense of their own national character and identity. "For in a Swede there is a curious mixture of love and appreciation for what is his own and a depreciation of what is his! He loves his memories of greatness, but is hard toward his own children! He is so glad to be Swedish, yet at the same time he does not like to give its due to anything Swedish, unless it has previously gained recognition abroad. It is on this point that one must reckon with his much decried envy against his own: the 'Royal Swedish Jealousy.'"

Strindberg held that this attitude derived from fact that Sweden was practically unknown and of little interest to the wider world. In frustration, the Swedes tended to "drape themselves" in their past glories, to comfort themselves with the thought that "they had once amounted to something," which unfortunately hindered efforts to accomplish anything of importance in the present. Going to the other extreme, being romantic by nature, they tended to be uncritically enthusiastic over anything foreign. In this case, his implied focus was upon the vogue for things Norwegian. "The Swede," he concluded, "must give up some of his boastfulness but gain greater true self-confidence."[80]

Where Strindberg in 1883 criticized the Swedes' tendency to overvalue outside cultural impulses, Oscar Levertin, in an article first published in *Ord och Bild* during the fresh dawn of national romanticism in 1892, held aesthetic cosmopolitanism, together with the ability to adapt foreign innovations to their own conditions and temperament, to be quintessential Swedish qualities. For his ideal, he looked back to the refined and graceful era of Gustaf III, in which French and native Swedish traditions were felicitously combined. With the "charmer-king's" dramatic assassination in 1792, Levertin wrote, the Swedish "ancien régime" was crushed. "The Swedish rococo was dead, the last sunset gleam of the Age of Greatness was gone and our century's gray, bourgeois work-day began."

"If carefree, joyful frivolity can always be called Swedish and Stockholmian," Levertin wrote soon after, this was above all true during the rococo era. In his view, the poet and balladeer from Gustaf III's day, Carl Michael Bellman, represented the true embodiment of the Swedish psyche. Levertin marveled at the "immensely national, the remarkable Swedish character of his nature and work." There was no motif, however foreign its origin, that in his verse did not seem as though "sprung from native soil." This led Levertin to his overall appraisal of the Swedish character. While admitting to the difficulty of generalizing, he wrote:

> Our feeling immediately—as in perceiving a physical anomaly—rejects the idea that [Hans Christian] Andersen or Ibsen could be Swedes, or Bellman or Tegnér Norwegians or Danes. There is a definite Swedish disposition, which has set its stamp upon our whole literature: a youthful spirit, a musicality, and yearning for adventure, a martial and conquering spirit, exultant and melancholy, more easily moved than profound, more richly lyrical and sonorous than clearheaded and sharp-witted, flaming up in lovely, fast-burning bonfires, but seldom capable of producing a lasting fire and even warmth, invariably preferring holiday to workday, in need of the intoxication of festivity to feel the blood pulsing with life, extroverted and boisterous, and yet with a quiet undertone of anxiety and melancholy deep within, like a quaking aspen leaf.[81]

Verner von Heidenstam made the most ambitious attempt to define the Swedes' national traits. Already in his lighthearted essay "Hagdahls kokbok" (Hagdahl's cookbook) from 1890, he had written of "all the martial sumptuousness and love of pleasure in our nature, all the Renaissance-like, sun-filled joyfulness, the extravagant elegance, the exuberance, the aristocratic refinement and wit." In 1896, Heidenstam came out with a more serious, extended essay first published in *Ord och Bild*. This amounted to a criticism—albeit not lacking in sympathy and pride—of the Swedes' self-depreciation, uncritical admiration for everything foreign and novel, lack of pride in what was their own, stultifying bureaucratization, and adherence to matters of form.

> Our literature is filled with . . . attacks against ourselves, and they are always received with open or concealed delight. The Swedes fear nothing so much as being rapped across the knuckles for conceit. Nowhere in our time can a more dignified and appealing folk characteristic be found than this self-irony. How diffident, yet proud, does not such self-effacement appear beside the deification by other nations of all that is theirs! Such introspective insight only occurs in an old, high culture and during periods when a people's ability to see through their own faults and prejudices is sharpened to an extreme, indeed, tragic degree. The Swedish nation is like a widely traveled elderly man of the world who has experienced everything and tried everything. . . . he rubs his hands and bows and bows. Gentlemen, he says

to his neighbors, attach no importance to me. . . . I ask nothing, gentlemen, wish for nothing, and you should therefore ask nothing of me either.

"Such self-doubt, appealing as it may appear," Heidenstam declared, "unfailingly leads to decline." The Swede need only travel abroad to become aware of his country's true greatness. "Any young girl can play Grieg, while there are gifted Swedish composers whose names she scarcely knows." Despite a wealth of talent at home in all areas, Swedes were inclined to become enthusiastic only for what was foreign, not least for what came from their Scandinavian neighbors. In their restless search for modernity, they lacked that sound conservatism needed to cherish and protect their own heritage, in striking contrast to both Norway and Denmark. This deficiency derived, he held, from Sweden's long and close contacts with the rest of Europe. However, narrow cultural chauvinism could not long survive. "How quickly originality becomes diluted is most evident among the Norwegians," Heidenstam maintained, "who thanks to their conservatism and isolated location recently, during what until now was a favorable point in time, created a national literature, which nevertheless, following contact with other nations, has already begun to show evident decline and exhaustion." Norwegian writers themselves described the Christiania scene as dull and provincial, and both Bjørnson and Ibsen felt compelled to spend long periods abroad. Norway's cultural elite, he thus implied, was becoming culturally ever more like Sweden's.

The Swedish landscape was richly varied, Heidenstam wrote, reiterating a view that, as noted, was widely shared. "The character of the Swedes," he held,

> resembles their landscape in its fragmented mass of detail. While our neighboring peoples can often be described in a few words, the psychology of the Swedish character is so filled with contradictions and so variable that no one has yet succeeded in combining the colors into a complete picture. . . . Scarcely have you attributed a fault to the Swedes before you notice that it is a virtue, and hardly a virtue before you find it is a shortcoming. . . . Thus has the Swedish temperament been formed. It is Scandinavia's richest and most interesting—although undervalued by our neighboring nations and denied by its own tongue.[82]

Heidenstam's critique of the national character and his call for renewed national pride led to a debate revealing the intellectual Left's apprehensions of chauvinistic nationalism and the stirring up of anti-Norwegian sentiment during a time of mounting conflict over the union. In September 1897, Heidenstam responded to such criticism while justifying the need in Sweden for an elite leadership. "An old nation like ours . . . has, in contrast to the Norwegians, its natural, its only conceivable Left in the cultivated classes. It would be useless to seek for it elsewhere. Our peasant class is our consolidating and conservative force. [What is essential] is to foster within the educated classes the enlightened party that understands our history and makes itself the guardian of the cultural traditions of our fathers." Heidenstam went on to declare the need for his compatriots to unburden themselves of what he regarded as the incestuous bondage in which a vital Norwegian culture had too long held them. "A people cannot . . . maintain such an influence for more than ten to twenty years and the Norwegians are no exception to nature's law."[83]

Shortly thereafter, Ellen Key, one of Heidenstam's most faithful friends despite their ideological differences, weighed in with an open letter expressing her and her liberal friends' serious concerns over his appeal for a new patriotism. "Sweden for the Swedes," she wrote, "has been the patriotic slogan that has now joined together the currents of militarism, obscurantism, protectionism, and rising anti-Semitism. Sweden's honor has been the war cry by which our superpatriots have made the entire nation's honor dubious and brought about the most dangerous situation we have found ourselves in since 1814." She took Heidenstam to task for looking to Sweden's past greatness rather than to its future promise as the inspiration for a national spirit. The most important thing, she held, was simply to *be* Swedish rather than to consciously adopt certain prescribed attitudes. For her, true Swedish national sentiment was "the deep, shy, taciturn, modest love of [our] homeland, the earth-bound feeling for our own forest-scented home place, which—like any great love—is a passionate stillness, a humble pride, an aching bliss."

The Swedish character's most fundamental characteristic, Key declared, was its "love of the ideologically daring." Both Heidenstam and she were professed advocates of progressive reforms and were in agreement on the need for an "aristocracy of intelligence" to take the lead in bringing them about. But here she pointed to the fundamental difference in their philosophies. He based his hopes for a "national and political renaissance," she wrote, entirely upon the enlightened and historically minded elite. In contrast, she held with Almqvist that "the true Swedish character is presently to be found less among the upper classes than among the common folk." "It is from this element," she went on, "that I expect, within a generation or two, the cultivated party of the Left, the aristocratic radicals. In red-painted cottages and attic rooms the new

Swedish folk is growing up from which some day perhaps, when culture has refined natural vitality, this little nation within the nation will be formed." Sweden, indeed, already had its "peasant aristocrats." But these were at present all too inclined to seek wider horizons and greater challenges in America, resulting in a terrible waste of human potential.

Key had not failed to note that Heidenstam's characteristic Swede unmistakably reflected his own aristocratic values. Tegnér, she pointed out, was not "the whole Swedish nation," and that nation did not live only on Stockholm's exclusive Sturegatan and in a few country manors. Sweden's weakness was the gap between its social classes. The overriding concern of the Norwegian cultural leaders had been to create a strong sense of national solidarity. In Norway, she held, a lively interest was apparent among all classes in cultural questions and social reforms, "an optimistic faith in the future and in their own importance for it." She took this opportunity, moreover, to comment on Heidenstam's observations on the maturing of Norwegian culture:

> The self-criticism now occasionally becoming evident in Norway, which you see as an autumnal sign, is on the contrary the maturing man's insight that freedom is, to be sure, the precondition for cultural development, but that self-control is [the precondition for] beauty. A nation, like an individual, is seldom prouder and healthier than when it tells itself a truth. And the truth is that in the Norwegian people's personality there still remains much youthful coarseness, which is in need of culture, but also that when this culture ultimately matures, the Norwegians will then show us the essential traits of an aristocratic democracy. No less than Norway's political has its intellectual vigor reached its culmination.

The Swedes, Key maintained, need not fear too close a cultural interchange with Norway; such an exchange could be harmful only when one nation's culture threatened to be submerged by another's, as was true in Norway under Danish rule. "Indeed," she said, "it is often siblings who give each other the most vital lessons." From the Norwegians, Sweden's "aristocratic radicals" could learn how to lead opinion toward "the needs of modern times and awaken the practical idealism that seeks to meet such demands. . . . If culture is favored at the cost of political interests, the result will be as unhealthy as if political interests suffocated cultural [ones]." As her edifying example, she pointed to the widespread popularization of culture in Norway.

"Through overvaluing oneself, one becomes neither a good patriot nor a good citizen of the world," Key concluded. "That the Norwegians are beginning to abandon their self-satisfaction is, as I say, a healthy sign. That we Swedes, on the other hand, should cure what you call our *bloodless national pessimism* by becoming puffed up would be as tasteless as it would be useless."[84]

Heidenstam was not without a response. In an open letter to Key in *Dagens Nyheter* in January 1898, he stood his ground on the need for inspiration from the national past. She accused him of "cleaving the nation in two horizontally," he wrote, yet she herself sought for the national character only "under the dividing line."

> Peasant dress, the red cottages, forests of pine and fir, and the small, dark lakes—all that has grown to be so intimately a part of our life and our views that it is thus a not insignificant part of what is Swedish. . . . Nonetheless, it seems to me that just in this regard we have too shallow a concept of the national. We constantly look for the national in outward appearances, in the purely ethnographic, geographic, and botanical. Should we be driven out of our land like the Jews, our nationality would fall from our shoulders like an empty cape. . . . We are constantly being held to the idea that a worker floating timber on Norrland's rivers or a hunter who fells a bear is somehow more national than—let us say—Ellen Key by her lamp.

People of the working classes, he declared, were not so very different in different countries. Yet, how individually varied were the thinkers and writers of differing nationality! "It might perhaps not be impossible to place [Bjørnson's] Synnöve or Peer Gynt's mother in a Tyrolean landscape, but it would be vain to attempt to place under a flag other than the Norwegian the stern or extravagant ladies in Ibsen's latest dramas." He thus held to his conviction that true national leadership could only come from the educated elite. "The manor house is for us," Heidenstam wrote the following year, "what the farmstead is for Norway."[85]

Heidenstam's appeal for a new patriotism rode a wave of rising confidence in Sweden during the 1890s. Industrialization was at last proceeding at a dynamic rate, drawing upon the country's great reserves of timber, iron ore, and waterpower, opened up by the expanding rail network. Emigration was at last on the decline, at least until the end of the decade. The Norwegians had been forced to beat a humiliating retreat in the consular crisis of 1895. There was a building boom in Stockholm's opulent Östermalm district and in the fashionable new suburbs of the capital. The apogee was reached in 1897 with the great Stockholm Industrial Exposition on Djurgården, in connection with the twenty-five year jubilee of Oscar II's reign, which richly evoked

Sweden's past and the vision of its splendid future. National romantic writers, artists, and musicians celebrated the nation's nature, folklife, and history in a brilliant outburst of creativity. At that very time, Heidenstam was writing his novel *Karolinerna*, glorifying the heroism and endurance Carl XII's army during the Great Northern War, which would came out in two parts in 1897 and 1898 and enjoy immense popularity.[86]

The open debate between Heidenstam and his critics was followed by numerous contributions to the press on the nature of a true Swedish patriotism, of which a few examples may suffice. The Danish-born Helena Nyblom appealed for balance and moderation. The political scientist Rudolf Kjellén argued for a *Realpolitik* based upon what the Italian nationalist Vittorio d'Annunzio would later call "sacred egotism," not least vis-à-vis Norway. The historian Harald Hjärne's sharply attacked quasi-scientific theories of race and warned against the harmful consequences of chauvinism. Gustaf Fröding humorously dismissed "patriotism" as "patridiotism."[87]

Surely, the most widely read and influential attempt to analyze the Swedish psyche was an extended essay in 1911 by the liberal statistician Gustav Sundbärg, written in connection with the government's inquest on emigration, which he directed. The Swedes' lack of strong national feeling, skepticism toward their own accomplishments, and enthusiasm for things foreign he attributed to their freedom from foreign domination, in contrast to other European nations. Nationalism, the great intellectual current of the nineteenth century, had thus passed Sweden by, as Italy had been left untouched by the sixteenth-century Reformation. Traditional patriotism in Sweden had thus been backward-looking and conservative rather than liberal and popular. "Norway's history, as compared with Sweden's during the nineteenth century," he wrote, "is the history of a people filled with the most powerful national spirit, in contrast to a people lacking in any national instinct. . . . Here lies the most important explanation for Norway's *strength* throughout this entire period and for Sweden's *weakness*." All the Swedes had learned from "Norway's brilliant literature was to love—Norway." One is reminded of Bjørnstjerne Bjørnson's comment in Christiania's *Verdens Gang* in 1898, "The Swedes are an old people who doubt, and the Norwegians are a young people who believe."

Sundbärg stressed the Swedes' love and understanding of nature, and hence their scientific and technical bent, but maintained that they were deficient in psychological understanding and inept in interpersonal dealings. Naïveté and lack of business acumen caused them repeatedly to be outwitted by more sharp-witted and calculating nations, notably the Danes and the

Norwegians, in both diplomacy and commerce.[88] His criticisms—apart from his claim that his compatriots lacked psychological insight—amounted to a compendium of Swedish self-criticism throughout the period and even before, as Carl G. Laurin showed in a slender volume published the following year.[89]

That Sundbärg's indignant manifesto met with such an enormous response was proof, meanwhile, that the ground by this time was already well prepared by Swedish national romanticism and that the ideals of pride and self-assertion it propounded were widely accepted in a Sweden now no longer in union with Norway and moving on into a new era in its history.

Epilogue and Conclusions

NORWAY'S renunciation of the union on 7 June 1905 created great consternation and bitterness in Sweden. Even liberals who had consistently favored Norway and supported its demands were offended by the Storting's brusque actions. There was much indignation over what was seen as the deep humiliation inflicted upon the aging monarch. For Swedish patriots of the old school, dissolution crushed the last dreams of Sweden's imperial grandeur. It devastated faithful Scandinavianists' fondest hopes for the sister nations.

In a letter to his close friend Erik Werenskiold, Prince Eugen grieved in December 1905 over the way things had gone, though he had long accepted the idea that union in its existing form was doomed. Carl Curman, that dedicated Scandinavianist and Old Nordic enthusiast, wrote in March 1906 to Lorenz Dietrichson in Christiania, assuring him of his lasting friendship and respect. Curman's wife, Calla, meanwhile wrote to him more somberly, "For us, Carl and me, the year that has just passed has been an indescribably hard year—as it has been for thousands upon thousands of Swedish homes—yes, harder than I believe Norway imagines. These wounds will never heal so long as Swedish hearts still live that have been so deeply hurt." Three years later, in 1909, Bjørnstjerne Bjørnson's old friend Ann-Margret Holmgren invited him to participate in a planned world peace congress in Stockholm but cautioned him against saying anything whatsoever about 1905. Relations between Norway and Sweden, past or present, remained an extremely sensitive point for Swedes. "They are certainly prepared for friendship with Norwegians and with Norway," she wrote, "as long as one does not touch the wound, for it remains open and burns like fire."[1]

Yet, the regrets were not only on the Swedish side. As has been seen, only a tiny number of votes were cast in favor of preserving the existing union in the Norwegian plebiscite in 1905. Still, there were surely many in Norway who would have welcomed a more ideal union. Dietrichson, in the first three volumes of his memoirs, published between 1896 and 1901, evoked the bold dreams of the Scandinavianists of his generation and left a loving picture of his happy years in Uppsala and Stockholm around the middle of the century. The conservative historian Yngvar Nielsen, who had stoutly defended the union almost to the very end, retained his warm sympathy for Oscar II, which in 1912 he hoped posterity would come to share.[2]

Bjørnson himself wrote on 13 June 1905 to Henrik Hedlund in Göteborg that he was convinced many in Norway now realized that they had "behaved recklessly toward both Sweden and the king." To Verner von Heidenstam, he wrote an open letter printed in Stockholm's *Svenska Dagbladet* on 3 July holding that since dissolution had proved necessary, the manner in which it had taken place was not the principle issue. "Nevertheless," he added, "I shall regret it to my dying day. Already now it has had unfortunate consequences. My dear friend and colleague, let us work to diminish them." When in January 1906 he thanked a Swedish admirer for the only New Year's greeting he had thus far received from his country, Bjørnson declared that despite the dissolution, "Scandinavia must nonetheless stand together. Outwardly we must form an association *[forbund]* in which Sweden must take the lead. Therein more honor is to be won than in a union filled with strife."[3] For years, Bjørnson's political statements had made a consistent distinction between the unfortunate existing *union* and the need to replace it with a genuine *forbund*, a voluntary, yet firm association, or community, of Scandinavian nations.

In June 1906, flags flew in Christiania in celebration of King Oscar and Queen Sophia's golden wedding. In December of the following year, news of Oscar II's death called forth widespread mourning in Norway. The government decreed that flags be flown at half-mast, a steady stream of visitors offered their condolences at the Swedish legation, and Christiania's Trefaldighet Church was filled to overflowing for the late king's memorial service. The mourners were headed by the entire Norwegian cabinet led by Jørgen Løvland, one of the most ardent nationalists of the Pure Left, who at the Nobel Peace Prize ceremony in Christiania two days later offered a heartfelt impromptu tribute to the former monarch.

To Ernst Günther, Sweden's first minister to the new independent Norway, these manifestations gave "the most indisputable proof of the great affection that King Oscar actually enjoyed in Norway, and it must surely be unique in history that a people that has deposed its king shows such great feelings of sympathy and devotion for that same king as the Norwegian people did when

King Oscar died." Günther also emphasized that from the beginning he had been treated with the greatest courtesy and consideration in Norway, whereas the Norwegian minister in Stockholm complained to him of the colder reception that he had received in Sweden.[4] Overall, one gains the impression that the Norwegians made greater efforts at conciliation following the breakup of the union than did the Swedes.

In Norway, the end of the union ushered in a period of high hopes and national exhilaration, which would culminate with the grand centennial jubilee of the Eidsvoll constitution in 1914, on the eve of World War I. With the recent conflicts and anxieties over the union now behind them, the Norwegians could now turn their energies toward their nation's internal development and domestic questions.

In Sweden, the dissolution meanwhile aroused a long period of intensive soul-searching. Characteristic would be Carl G. Laurin's somber words in 1912: "At the beginning of the nineteenth century we lost Finland through lack of determination, carelessness, and treachery. At the beginning of the twentieth we lost the union with Norway through weakness, frivolity, and party strife. In that convenient way we got out from under both the Finnish and Norwegian questions. Now the question remains whether we want to keep Sweden."

Yet, at the same time, there was a new optimism in Sweden that what had been lost without must and could be regained within. To a Norwegian journalist, Richard Bergh's wife Gerda wrote already on 8 July 1905, "What a tremendous gain it has been for Sweden that this dissolution has come about. It is like a dawning hope that the time will now come when we can vigorously devote ourselves to our internal development. Now we should all be able to work toward great cultural goals and make Sweden strong." A petition signed by a large number of writers and artists published in *Svenska Dagbladet* on the same date, while declaring it would be unworthy to seek to force the Norwegians to remain within a union "that has never been able to bring together but only to drive apart the two nations," held that Sweden must now "enter upon the path of inner development," which alone could "lead a small people on to lasting greatness."

The voice seems that of Verner von Heidenstam, who at the same time issued his own, personal appeal to his compatriots for courage and determination in the face of "a new 1809." On 10 July 1907, two years later, Heidenstam wrote optimistically to Bjørnstjerne Bjørnson: "Yes, an awakening is now taking place here that reaches far down [into society] and which surely cannot die out entirely without bearing fruit. To arouse self-confidence, which was altogether extinguished twenty years ago, has been one of the most vital first steps."[5]

Here, Heidenstam alluded to his great preoccupation during the first years following the end of the union: his dream of assuming the role of a Swedish Bjørnson, his people's conscience and moral leader, the restorer of its belief in itself. Heidenstam had been fascinated by, and strongly drawn to, his older Norwegian colleague since their first contact in the 1880s as his own ambitions to arouse his nation's national spirit grew ever stronger. In 1897, *Dagens Nyheter* noted Heidenstam's evident desire to play the role of Bjørnson in Sweden, which Heidenstam answered by defending Bjørnson as "the embodiment of his people's whole instinctive life." He wrote, only half-jokingly, in 1903 that at Naddö, near Vadstena, he had found his own "Aulestad" — alluding to Bjørnson's celebrated rural retreat in Norway. To Bjørnson himself, he wrote in July 1907, "You are the personality in Scandinavia's cultural life that I have loved the most." During the last years of Bjørnson's life, before his death in Paris in 1910, when he had become, in Francis Bull's words, not only Norway's but "Europe's ever wakeful conscience," Heidenstam was his most faithful Swedish correspondent.[6]

Heidenstam found his ideal forum in the Youth Movement *(Ungdomsrörelsen)*, which itself followed an earlier development of the same kind across the Keel. The Swedish movement was directly inspired by a stirring speech given by the Norwegian Storting member and temperance leader Peder Svendsen at Hackås in Jämtland during the summer of 1898, and it spread rapidly, most notably in Dalarna. It was inspired by an exuberant optimism and a belief in the mission and the power of youth to sweep away the cobwebs of the old order and to bring about fervently desired, although somewhat vaguely conceived, reforms. At the same time, it was infused with a strongly rural and folkloric pathos. It inspired a generation, Gustaf Näsström later wrote, "that was going to make Sweden better and happier, however that was to be brought about."[7]

The height of Heidenstam's effort to make himself the nation's moral leader came with his stirring speeches at the great youth rallies held at Mösseberg and Ransäter in the summer of 1907, at which over ten thousand enthusiastic young listeners heeded to his dramatic and optimistic depictions of their country's glorious future, which ended with an invocation to "the new youthful age, which is beginning to shine forth like the daybreak after a short summer night." "Consecrate the band of youth gathered here to a people's army," he declared, "that with courage and song marches out into life to raise its own fatherland to that place in the North that is natural and predetermined for it!"[8]

Heidenstam, however, in the long run could hardly equal his ideal, Bjørnson, as a popular leader. His personality was too aloof, his values too aristocratic and aesthetic. While he could powerfully stir the imagination, he had no concrete program of reform to offer. He became increasingly conservative in the face of the rising socialist and labor movements, most definitively after the great General Strike of 1909, ironically the very year in which he was ceremoniously proclaimed the national poet.[9] More radical and determined prophets of a new age were beginning to take the stage, and Heidenstam withdrew ever more into Olympian isolation.

It was, however, entirely fitting that Heidenstam in 1910 should represent Sweden at Bjørnstjerne Bjørnson's funeral in Christiania. In a moving tribute, he declared: "Almost as long as I can remember, your verse has come to us as a fresh and invigorating wind. When we Swedes have thought of Norway, we have thought of you. When we have been indignant, we have been indignant with you. Now the two peoples are going their separate ways. Yet there are places where our paths cross! That is at the graves of the great. The cultural, the best, we share in common. It is the witness of sister languages, of the same blood, of the same future." Sweden, he declared, mourned for the departed chieftain, "as though one of our own." This was, it has been held, the first public sign of conciliation Norway received following the dissolution of the union five years earlier.[10]

In 1856, the Swede J. E. Ekström regretfully concluded his account of travels in the sister kingdom the previous summer: "In short, everywhere in Norway a Swede is treated in stepmotherly fashion, while on the other hand, Norwegians in Sweden everywhere encounter courtesy and good-will." While other Swedish visitors left more positive descriptions, Ekström had put his finger on a sensitive point. It was as Bjørnson's devoted friend Ann-Margret Holmgren wrote to him in April 1899, "Alas, my boundless love for Norway is at once my greatest joy and my greatest sorrow." Sigurd Ibsen is reported to have commented ironically around the same time that "the undertone in Sweden's relationship with Norway is unrequited love."[11]

The bitterness of love rejected and spurned fills a lengthy open letter from Calla Curman to "her Norwegian lady friend" in May 1906. Most Swedes, she declared, had felt no sympathy for the "Great-Swedish" chauvinists and sincerely desired Norway's equality within a union that assured a strong and independent North, a nobler dream than the Norwegians' self-centered separatism. While the Swedes had admired Norway, the Norwegians had shown little appreciation of, or understanding for, Sweden.

> How happily did we not visit your country, how trustfully did we not form bonds of friendship there, how natural did it not seem to regard you as our brothers and sisters! We read your books, we sang your songs, yes, even your patriotic songs! At our private gatherings and at festivities and public meetings they were always sung together with our own patriotic songs! Every inch of Norway's soil was dear to us, for it was a glorious part of the North! . . . We Swedish mothers loved to gather our children around us to tell of all we knew that was proud and beautiful about Norway, and when the children grew older we took them with us to that land that we had taught them to love and respect together with their own. These were the feelings in our Swedish homes, the thousands upon thousands of homes in town and countryside! . . . Can you not understand that when one has felt a boundless trust—and is then betrayed—a terrible change in one's feelings must follow?[12]

At a deeper level, their visions of Norway reflected differing ideals among Swedes as to what those visions could and ought to be. One vision was that of the union as living testimony to Sweden's rightful and continuing role as a European power, the last vestige of its proud "Age of Grandeur"—as still expressed in the national anthem: "I know that thou art and shalt be what thou wert."[13] Another vision was that of a Sweden that followed Norway's sound example in cherishing and reclaiming its ancient Nordic social structure, form of government, way of life, and folk culture, in essence seeking back to its lost innocence. Yet another was the Scandinavianist dream of the essential unity of the Nordic lands and the artificiality of formal barriers between them. All these visions could in various ways be intertwined. Dissolution of the union could not but bring grief and disillusion to them all.

This result notwithstanding, the sequel would prove Bjørnson's prescience in consistently maintaining, from the 1860s onward, that the union in its existing form was a hindrance to a closer and more wholehearted association between the two nations. Scandinavianism, he declared in 1896, was "the greatest political idea the North had ever had"—provided it built upon a "popular foundation." And in 1899, he added, "Under one king, under two, under a republic, through good days and bad, [our] association must endure." Bjørnson's ultimate ideal for the future, as he expressed it in 1902, was *"large alliances between peoples;* within these: *cultural nationality groups;* within these: *an endless variety of small communities."*[14]

The American historian Raymond E. Lindgren (a Swedish descendant) aptly summarized the course of Swedish-Norwegian relations to the mid–twentieth century in the subtitle to his valuable study from 1959 as "union, disunion, and Scandinavian integration."[15] Norway's complete independence in 1905 would lead, down to the present, to a far closer de facto coordination between the internal policies of the two nations in a wide variety of fields than ever was, or could have been, possible under the union constructed in 1814. Moreover, it cleared away the political obstacles to fully integrating Denmark and eventually—after their full national sovereignty in 1917 and 1944, respectively—Finland and Iceland into the evolving structure of Nordic cooperation, which has been presided over since 1952 by a common Nordic Council. Furthermore, from at least the 1920s onward, a vast network of close inter-Nordic ties has developed at the grassroots level between businesses, private organizations, families, and individuals, while travel between the neighboring lands has never been greater.[16]

The Swedish-Norwegian union has commonly been judged a failure by historians of both nationalities on the basis that it failed to last. Its origins, conflicts, and ultimate collapse have provided the focus for a voluminous literature, much of it polemical from predetermined national standpoints. There is little to be added here to this controversy. Above and beyond what has been discussed in previous chapters, a few general observations may suffice.

The union lacked—and indeed did not have time to develop—the same strong historic and sentimental bonds that still existed between Sweden and Finland, on the one hand, and Norway and Denmark, on the other. Even those cultivated Swedes best disposed toward Norway were most often only familiar with it through its literature and art rather than from any very direct experience or acquaintance with Norwegians, as Gurli Linder recalled, and the reverse was no doubt true as well.[17] The union created no real economic interdependence. Outside the political and cultural elites, the great majority of Swedes and Norwegians felt themselves little affected by what happened across the Keel. The terms of union in 1814 were vaguely and ambiguously formulated, leaving ample room in the future for conflicting interpretations. Historic traditions and profound differences in social structure meanwhile ruled out any political amalgamation between the two realms. Far fewer deeply embedded vestiges of the past inhibited the free development of a new society in Norway than in Sweden.

Norwegian nationalism became allied, for internal political reasons, with the vital forces of liberalism and radicalism, whereas in Sweden a backward-looking chauvinist patriotism was associated with hard-line conservatism, while liberals professed broadly cosmopolitan ideals. Norwegian preoccupation with legal principle confronted Swedish pragmatic concern over practical problems, above all the security of the peninsula against the Russian colossus to the east. Increasingly, the leaders of Swedish and Norwegian opinions and politics were talking past each other. In a wider sense, binational unions have always proved fragile, especially those between a stronger and a weaker nation, as Per Fuglum has pointed out and as recent experience in Europe and elsewhere has borne out.

In the final crisis, the Swedish government unquestionably played its cards badly. In part, this would seem to have resulted, as Prince Eugen later reminisced, from the deadlock within the Riksdag. "The First Chamber's policy of force fell before the Second Chamber's opposition," he wrote. "And the Second Chamber's reform proposals could not be realized because of the First Chamber's resistance. The outcome was always half-measures that satisfied no one."[18]

Yet, there is a constant tendency to read history backwards, starting from the final outcome of a historical process. To be aware of this raises the question whether the union really was a "failure," and if so, in what respects and to what extent. Might it not with at least equal justification be regarded as a reasonable solution that in time outlived its usefulness? Norway had no real choice in 1814 but to accept some kind of union with Sweden. Yet, the terms of the union were such as to create a favorable environment in which Norway could freely develop its own political institutions and traditions and its own sense of national identity until the point was reached at which union was no longer feasible. Prince Eugen understood this well enough when he wrote to a Swedish confidant in March 1905:

> In my view—which you have often heard from me—it was a mistake that Sweden right from the beginning of the union did not conceive its mission to be to guide the union forward toward ever decreasing interdependency, to give form to new conditions until the union fell like a ripe fruit. At our side would then stand a land with entirely different means and possibilities to manage its own affairs than the Norway of 1814. One can take the whole

thing more philosophically if one can see in this development the working-out of a law of nature, which ought to have been promoted.[19]

It might be argued, as Göran B. Nilsson has done, that the causes of conflict between the two kingdoms were more symbolic than substantive in nature. "If we did not have Norway," Sven Adolf Hedlund wrote only half humorously to Bjørnstjerne Bjørnson in 1883, "we would suffocate in sultry stillness. But fortunately you cause us now and then to arouse ourselves."

Nonetheless, symbols are important. During the repeated crises within the union, political factions on both sides manipulated them against their domestic rivals. Nilsson has provocatively described the Swedish-Norwegian conflict over the union as largely a "grand play of illusions" *(ett illusionsnummer i stor stil)*, in which Swedish conservatives raised exaggerated fears of Russian aggression to justify upholding the union while Norwegian radicals similarly played upon the specter of Swedish domination to justify ending it. In the end, he points out, 1905 brought about no basic changes in either country, other than that Norway now had its own king and its own foreign minister. In actuality, far more was gained through dissolution. Fresh energies were released—on both sides—by the events of 1905.[20]

Norway's union with Sweden meanwhile at last removed the apple of discord that had led to centuries of warfare between Swedes and Finns, on the one side, and Danes and Norwegians, on the other. To what extent it secured the long *Pax Scandinavica* that was in fact only broken by the German invasion of Norway and Denmark in 1940 would be difficult to determine, since the Dual Monarchy was never directly threatened by invasion. Nonetheless, the union undoubtedly strengthened its strategic security during a period of extensive territorial reshuffling in Europe.

The basic concern of this study has been to explore the positive results of the union from the Swedish perspective, most specifically in the intertwined areas of politics and culture. While much scholarly attention has been devoted to its negative aspects and ultimate demise, relatively little and only sporadic attention has thus far been given to the credit side of the ledger.

In the cultural sphere, Swedish scholars gave almost no attention to Norwegian influences upon their literature before the 1920s. Volume 4 of the second edition in 1916 of Henrik Schück and Karl Warburg's encyclopedic standard history of Swedish literature, for instance, devoted only ten pages specifically to Norwegian literature as part of a wider survey of the contemporary European literary scene and provided no overall discussion of its influence in Sweden. The question was first seriously raised by Fredrik Böök in 1921, with particular emphasis on Ibsen's significance. Five years later, Arne Lidén brought out his groundbreaking and invaluable doctoral dissertation at Uppsala University on Norwegian currents in Swedish literature, covering the period from 1814 down to the end of the 1870s. His study was intended as the first part of a two-volume work, but unfortunately it was never followed by its intended sequel. In 1946, Staffan Björck, in his now classic study of Verner von Heidenstam and turn-of-the-century Sweden, cast valuable light on Heidenstam's role in the national romantic reaction against Norwegian literary influences. While in 1961 the American literary historian Alrik Gustafson, in his valuable volume on Swedish literature, recognized important Norwegian influences during the later nineteenth century, the most recent surveys largely ignore them.[21]

Even less attention was devoted to Norwegian influences on art and architecture in Sweden before Bo Grandien's broad and thought-provoking survey in 1987 of the neo-Gothicist cult of Nordic antiquity in Sweden, which, like Lidén's literary study from 1926, does not go much beyond 1880. More recently, the American art historian Michelle Facos has given some consideration to Norwegian-Swedish artistic relations in the 1880s and 1890s.[22]

Remarkably, it would seem, least of all has been written about Norwegian influences upon Swedish internal politics and administration. Gunnar Rexius's stout volume from 1915 on the political ideas leading up to the Swedish Riksdag and suffrage reform of 1866 gives scant attention to Norwegian precedents in comparison with British, French, and American influences. In his 1926 literary study, Lidén provided some useful material regarding political thought. The Norwegian historian Halvdan Koht in 1947 brought out a brief but suggestive article entitled "Norwegian Help to Swedish Democracy" that examined Norwegian inspiration to Swedish liberals between the 1830s and the 1850s, based on contemporary American diplomatic reports. In 1948, Berit Borell gave Norwegian impulses a prominent place in her work on the Swedish liberals and the representation question during the 1840s. After a long interval, Jan Christensen's more recent study of the Peasant Estate in the debate on representational reform during the 1840s, which came out in 1997, has added further insights into the subject. Johan Norberg's survey of the history of Swedish liberalism from the following year, however, mentions Norwegian influences only briefly and in passing.[23]

Much remains to be done on the substantive results of the union on both sides. A promising new beginning in this direction was undertaken by Grete Værnø, a member of the Storting and at the time the wife of the Norwegian ambassador to Sweden. In 1987, she organized "Dialogue: Norway-Sweden," a series of eight symposia that continued over the next three years, involving both Swedish and Norwegian scholars and covering both the union and the twentieth century after its dissolution. Some of the symposia papers, on political and economic aspects of Norwegian-Swedish relations, were published in 1990.[24]

The work of the "Værnø group" may be taken as the harbinger of a promising new era of research that will explore in detail all aspects of the relationship, both during and after the union. Already in anticipation of the centennial jubilee of the end of the union in 2005, ambitious research projects are afoot in this area.[25]

In seeking to evaluate the overall impact of the union with Norway upon Sweden's political development between 1814 and 1905, it is evident that there was powerful "Norwegian help for Swedish democracy," as Halvdan Koht put it in 1947. One thinks most notably of the immediate inspiration provided by the Norwegian constitution of 1814 and by the political rise of the peasantry in Norway during the 1830s and 1840s to Swedish liberals and radicals, both inside and outside the Peasant Estate, in their struggle to reform representation in the Riksdag during those same decades.

It will be noted, meanwhile, that the modest bibliography of Norwegian political influences in Sweden concentrated particularly on the period between roughly 1830 and 1850, leaving a relative void for the last half century of the union's existence. Göran B. Nilsson in particular has more recently pointed, without detailed elaboration, to some significant questions that to date have remained largely untouched. These include the close relations between the Norwegian Left *(Venstre)* and the Swedish Farmers' Party *(Lantmannaparti)* during the 1870s and 1880s, and in particular, practical administrative reforms in Sweden based on Norwegian models.[26] One should add to this list, for instance, the impulse toward parliamentarianism in Sweden from the de facto establishment of that principle in Norway in 1884, and inspiration for franchise reform, especially after 1898, when Norway legislated universal manhood suffrage.

These impulses would continue to operate after the dissolution of the union, until by 1920 both countries had not only fully parliamentary systems but universal suffrage for citizens of both sexes over the age of twenty-one. Yet, it must also be recognized that at times, particularly during the 1890s, hostility toward Norwegian democracy and demands within the union stiffened the resistance to reform of the conservative-dominated First Chamber of the

Riksdag and government establishment, thereby slowing its pace at the very time it was gaining momentum in Norway. By the turn of the century, however, there arose a "Young Right" movement in Sweden led by Rudolf Kjellén, Adrian Molin, and others, which strove to supplant the old conservatism with a new, progressive, and popular version that could rally patriotism against the perils of socialism, the labor movement, and emigration. Just as the Norwegian Right *(Høyre)* was prepared to abandon support for the union to ensure its political survival during the final union crisis, the Swedish Young Right conceded the need for electoral reform, finally enacted in 1907, as the price for political rejuvenation and military reforms in 1901 when the union seemed close to shipwreck and the menace of Russification loomed in Finland.[27]

In Norway, the very fact of its notably democratic regime derived above all from the union.[28] Here, there is good reason to reverse Koht's formulation and speak of "Swedish help for Norwegian democracy." It is generally agreed that Norway's elite, in the new constitution framed at Eidsvoll in 1814, established a far more democratic legislative body and popular franchise than it conceivably would have done had it not felt the imperative need to rally the whole nation against the threat of Swedish annexation following the Treaty of Kiel. It was in large part due to the popular backing thus gained that Norway succeeded in preserving its constitution under the union with Sweden confirmed that fall and in standing fast against any attempts thereafter, from Carl XIV Johan's time onward, to amend it.

Yet, the form of government instituted by the official elite in 1814 could be—and was—turned against it. Its political dominance was shaken by the peasant movement in the 1830s and 1840s and at last decisively broken with the establishment of ministerial responsibility after the crisis of 1884. As the Norwegian Left succeeded brilliantly in harnessing the forces of nationalism from the 1870s down to the end of the union in 1905, it was able largely to disarm its opponents on the Right. It was under the nationalist banner, for instance, that the Left succeeded in passing universal manhood suffrage in 1898.[29] Moreover, during the parliamentary crisis of 1884, and again in 1891–95 and in 1905, the Swedish Left forestalled any possibilities of intervention by force against Norway, a question that has thus far drawn relatively little attention from historians. While the later conflicts over the union ultimately united the Norwegians, they tended ever more to divide the Swedes.

The dissolution of the union meanwhile permitted purely internal questions that had long been held in abeyance during the union conflict once again to come to the fore in both Swedish and Norwegian politics. Following the suffrage reform of 1907, the Social Democrats would quickly emerge as Sweden's largest political party. As for Norway, "now things were set straight, it was felt," Alf Kaartvedt has written, "for a reshuffling of the party structure along normal socioeconomic lines and for an overdue domestic liberal-conservative policy against bourgeois Left radicalism and socialism." To Erik Werenskiold, Prince Eugen—who was by then known as the "Red Prince" as well as the "Painter Prince"—wrote in December 1905:

> You are so right that it is the social questions that are now coming to the fore and that the [Norwegian] liberal party which does not understand that and does not dare to be accused of "dissolving society" has been passed by—it will be conservative within a few years. Things move quickly nowadays. I am so far from being fearful of social change that I believe it will bring many benefits. There is something splendid about the sense of community that forms the foundation of the labor movement, from which *much good* can result. . . . It will be a delight to be there when that time comes.[30]

In Sweden, from the middle of the nineteenth century, strong Norwegian influences revealed themselves in the realm of culture, beginning with the concerts of Ole Bull and the exhibitions of the Norwegian Düsseldorf painters, continuing with Bjørnson's immensely popular peasant tales, and followed by Ibsen's powerful *Brand* and provocative *Doll's House*. The Norwegian vogue reached its height by the mid-1880s in conjunction with the realist phase in Swedish literature and art. Only thereafter did a reaction against the uncritical acceptance of all things Norwegian begin to set in by the late 1880s.

In both politics and culture, the same dialectical process seems apparent, albeit in different periods. Swedish liberal enthusiasm for Norway's form of government reached its peak in the mid-1840s, but thereafter it was increasingly tempered by the sober realization that constitutional reform in Sweden would have to take account of the nation's older and more deeply rooted historical traditions and its more complex social structure. Henceforward, Norway's greatest influence on Sweden became cultural, but after culminating in the mid-1880s, the national historical and cultural differences likewise began to reassert themselves in the Swedish national romanticism of the 1890s and the early twentieth century.

It is meanwhile obvious that the Swedish cultural reaction was closely related to the gradual breakdown of the union, for Swedish enthusiasm for Norway and the Norwegians was predicated on optimism toward its future.

The union was seen not only as the natural and proper relationship between them but widely as the ultimate guarantee for the development of a more just and democratic Sweden. As it became increasingly evident that opinion in Norway was turning against the union, the political underpinnings of Swedish "norvegomania" gave way, and it became ever more apparent that Sweden must develop a strong national sense of its own if it were to survive alone in an increasingly belligerent world.

The intimate association between culture and politics has been repeatedly noted in this study. In sum, those in Sweden who most warmly responded to Norwegian folklife, literature, art, architecture, and music were likewise those most inspired by Norway's more liberal constitution and democratic movement. To them, Norway embodied in the purest form indigenous Old Nordic political and cultural values, as opposed to cosmopolitan European, mainly French, influences that had long prevailed in Sweden. It provided a reassertion of the unique character and innate strength of the Scandinavian North.

Yet, there was likewise a notable *disassociation* of culture from politics. Prince Eugen wrote to a Danish friend in 1902 that "here cultural interests stand altogether isolated and unaffected by politics. That is perhaps a weakness, but I am beginning to believe it is a [sign of] strength for it to stand for itself." Even during the fiercest conflicts over the union around the turn of the century, Norwegian culture did not lose its popularity in Sweden. National romantic pride in Sweden's own cultural riches by no means ruled out a continued appreciation for Norway's. "Surely never have Norwegians and Swedes . . . felt more strongly drawn together," August Strindberg wrote already in 1883, "as they do just now in these sorrowful days of strife." Verner von Heidenstam reiterated the same thought when he wrote in 1897, "two peoples, despite the many reckless words, have seldom opposed each other in a feud with so much mutual respect and so clean a shield."[31]

It was during these very years, in 1898, that Oscar II conferred the Swedish Grand Cross of the Order of the Northern Star on Henrik Ibsen, referring to "we two kings" at a splendid banquet. No less than previously, Ibsen was feted by Sweden's social and cultural elite and, not least, idolized by the ladies. The letters Bjørnstjerne Bjørnson steadily received from numerous Swedish correspondents, including some who forthrightly took issue with his political stance, were filled with warm admiration for Norway and its culture, as well as for the skald himself. Swedish admirers showered Bjørnson with congratulations on his seventieth birthday in 1902. The following year, he became the first Scandinavian to be awarded the Nobel Prize for Literature in Stockholm, where he was warmly welcomed by his old adversary Oscar II.[32]

Edvard Grieg gave testimony on the strong cultural bonds he found on his later visits to Stockholm in 1896, 1899, and 1904. As a devoted Norwegian patriot and supporter of the Left, he felt apprehensive on these occasions over the reception he might encounter in the Swedish capital. But each time he met with an enthusiastic response and warm welcome, including from the royal family itself. In November 1896, Grieg wrote a friend at home of how those assembled at a banquet lustily sang *Ja vi elsker dette landet* (Yes we love this land), Norway's national song. "It was a remarkable moment," he continued, "to hear these words from those throats! But this I say, that no one will make me believe any longer in hatred between peoples, for the desire of the people is for good understanding; that is the idea that strongly impressed itself on me." A poem by Carl Snoilsky, *Då tvenne barn förirrat sig i fjällen* (When two children had gone astray in the mountains), had brought tears to his eyes, for it put into words "exactly the thought that deepest down brought me to Stockholm."

In 1899, Grieg expressed wonderment that Sweden, the Scandinavian country where he had spent the least time, should be the one where he was best known. And in March 1904, he described how among his listeners he had seen nothing but "signs of the warmest sympathy—and that has done good. . . . Musical life here at present is much influenced by Norway. And it is remarkable how they here allow themselves to be electrified by *Norwegian* art. Imagine, before I came here, three concerts were sold out! At home such a thing would be impossible. Perhaps three sports events! But three concerts—never!"[33]

To be sure, Grieg was indignant to hear that at a concert in Sweden right after Norway's dissolution of the union in June 1905 his music was interrupted with jeers and catcalls. It nonetheless seems remarkable that his music was performed at all in Sweden during that time of crisis, and such reactions quickly passed. The cultural ties between Sweden and Norway proved far stronger than the political conflict that brought the union between them to an end. Nor did Norwegian cultural currents—by now balanced by a healthy appreciation for the uniquely Swedish—cease to be felt in Sweden after 1905.[34]

The Roman poet Horace in the first century B.C. wrote the oft-quoted passage "Græcia capta ferum victorem cepit" (Captive Greece conquered its rude conquerors). August Strindberg evoked this dictum when, as has been seen, he wrote in 1886, "Sweden had taken Norway, but now Norway took Sweden."[35]

In actuality, however, Horace and Strindberg referred to opposed cultural phenomena. Horace had described the experience, repeated since the dawn of history, of fierce barbarians who conquered more civilized peoples and in turn absorbed their higher cultures. In Scandinavia during the nineteenth century, the process was reversed. Sweden, with its greater population and resources and long traditions of independent statehood and cultural life, possessed in 1814 far more of the attributes of cosmopolitan European civilization than did Norway, just then setting its course as a new nation. Yet, under their union, it was Sweden that was more directly influenced by Norway in politics and culture than the reverse. Herein lies the key question underlying the present study.

How is this development to be explained? Norway was during that period at once more archaic *and* more modern than Sweden. Reactions to the ongoing processes of modernization in the world—following upon the great political and economic revolutions of the late eighteenth and early nineteenth centuries—could be either backward- or forward-looking or various combinations of both. One could seek refuge in a nostalgic Arcadian primitivism—in the romantic tradition of Jean Jacques Rousseau and Johann Gottfried von Herder—looking back, in Scandinavia, to an idealized Viking age and its hardy survivals among the peasantry. Or conversely, one could seek to accommodate and advance the course of modernization—political, social, and economic—to create a more just and more abundant society for tomorrow.

On both counts, Norway seemed in Sweden to have more to offer than the time-honored model, France in the classic, prerevolutionary age. As of 1814, Norway already possessed a more democratic social structure and form of government than anywhere in the Western world outside the United States, with which it was frequently compared. As Samuel Laing had put it in 1839, Norway "had started with the freshness of youth—a new nation, as it were, called suddenly into life."[36] Modernization could proceed there against fewer obstacles than in Sweden, which remained burdened with the social and institutional survivals of the early modern era. Yet, at the same time, the contrasts in Norway were starker and more dramatic between the new ways and the old. Somewhat paradoxically, it might seem, those in Sweden most enamored with Norway combined *both* the backward- and the forward-looking views as at once liberals or radicals, Scandinavianists, and enthusiasts for the Old Norse past and peasant life. Peter August Gödecke's travel accounts from Norway in the early 1870s, discussed in chapter 4, are perhaps especially revealing in this regard.

How then may Norway's overall impact on Sweden during the union be evaluated? Arne Lidén summarized it in 1926:

> The Norwegian current . . . reveals in all its aspects a distinct and consistent character. It represents the democratic and the national, assertion of the unique folk character, emphasis upon the indigenous and original. Everywhere Norwegian sympathies are engaged against the aristocratic, Romanizing tendencies in Swedish social and cultural life. In politics the Norwegian peasant society stood fast against the Swedish noble aristocracy and gave support to Swedish strivings toward popular and national goals. The relationship is the same in the various areas of cultural life. Norwegian national romanticism's successful striving to express in literature, art, and music the distinctively national showed the way toward emancipation from Romanizing aristocratic culture and the assertion of Sweden's own national culture in a deeper sense.[37]

There is another aspect of the question having to do with contrasting cycles of cultural creativity in the two countries. Carl G. Laurin addressed this matter in 1912:

> Was it not natural that Grieg's melodies, Ibsen's brazen tones, and Björnson's pathos as the passionate prophet of the peasantry should ring forth more loudly than Norwegian political wrangling? Their quarrel was, moreover, only with Swedish kings, Swedish ministers, governors, generals, and other bad types, which many Swedes also heartily wished would fail in all they undertook. . . . It had been as though the whole spirit of initiative, the idea that the Swedes through their own actions could accomplish anything, had died out. . . . But if one may smile at the rather artificial and exaggerated enthusiasm for Norway, where everything was better than what we had . . . it cannot meanwhile be denied that we were unmistakably right in taking unto ourselves [the Norwegians'] literature, which at that time far surpassed our own, whether one thinks of Ibsen's analytical acuity, Björnson's genuine and broadly conceived nationalism, or Jonas Lie's soulful psychological novels.

It was not surprising, Laurin went on, that the Swedes, "one of the world's few ancient and pure Germanic peoples," living in an isolated region, should be threatened with "inbreeding and sterility in many areas." Thus, the enthusiasm with which they took to outside influences during the 1880s perhaps revealed "an instinctive feeling that the machine was beginning to run dry and that we had consumed much of our cultural capital." But they thereafter proved that what they had acquired from outside they were soon able to make "national in the highest sense."

"In Norway," Fredrika Bremer wrote in 1847, "I learned all the better to understand Sweden, and all of the North." The French historian Erica Simon alluded to the same cultural dialectic in 1960, when she spoke of the Swedes' seeking a "Norwegian detour" to their "Swedishness *[suédité]*." In 1997, the American art historian Michelle Facos took up the same idea:

> Sweden's National Romantic artists and intellectuals played a major role at the turn of the century in defining a modern Swedish national identity. They did this dialectically, first by comparing Sweden to France (and Paris in particular), and later to Norway. This transition created an entirely new context for understanding Swedish culture, tradition, and geography, and was accompanied by a rise in national pride, which replaced the previous self-image of provincial inferiority. For Swedish National Romantics, Norway served two important functions. Firstly, it furnished a template for the process of national identity formation. Secondly, it enabled Swedes to perceive with greater clarity the unique aspects of their own culture. What Swedish National Romantics admired most about Norway was its provincialism, its independence, and its egalitarianism.[38]

The task was not easy, for national character seemed a more complex and diffuse concept in Sweden than in the neighboring Nordic lands. This was surely due largely to the fact that Swedes had long been freed from threats or apprehensions of foreign oppression, such as was the case, in varying degree, with the Danes, Finns, Icelanders, and Norwegians. Swedes tended to be more open to outside ideas and influences. But this in itself could arouse anxieties, since it appeared to blur the clear contours of national identity.

Throughout the nineteenth century, Norwegians had struggled with the difficult question of what was truly Norwegian, beginning with the rivalry between the "Patriot" and "Intelligence" parties of Wergeland and Welhaven. It was, as Anne-Lise Seip has expressed it, a question of "tradition" versus "civilization" — Scandinavian and European cosmopolitanism as opposed to the ancient, indigenous heritage. But Swedes too faced the same perplexing dilemma, with the added complication of how to relate the *Norwegian* to the purely *Swedish*. If Swedish culture was not "Scandinavian," including Norwegian elements, what was left? Strindberg struggled with this fundamental question already in the 1870s and the 1880s.

How cosmopolitan could the Swedes be and still remain fundamentally Swedish? Any outsider who has spent any length of time in Sweden cannot but be impressed with how well, on the whole, they have managed to achieve a balance. One recalls how Oscar Levertin, in his essay on Carl Michael Bellman from 1892, indeed regarded the ability to assimilate outside ideas and make them Swedish as a fundamental national trait. Yet, Verner von Heidenstam's view that the Swedish character was as varied as Sweden's varying landscape also comes to mind.[39]

The Scandinavian peninsula is large geographically. But the human arena was small and intimate, and thus the roles of individuals in shaping the course of developments seemingly emerge with greater clarity than in the greater European powers. One need only think in this regard of Carl XIV Johan and his successors on the Swedish and Norwegian thrones, particularly Oscar II, and of Carl Henrik Anckarsvärd, Henrik Wergeland and his opponent Johan Sebastian Welhaven, Lorenz Dietrichson, Johan Sverdrup, Adolf Hedin, Henrik Ibsen, August Strindberg, Verner von Heidenstam, and perhaps above all Bjørnstjerne Bjørnson.

Many others in various positions of power and influence likewise played their parts, as has been seen. One should meanwhile not leave out of account the sizable number of Swedes living in Norway and of Norwegians in Sweden, especially toward the end of this period. In a brief study published in 1964, the Swedish historian Sten Carlsson addressed this matter. On the whole, he found that relatively few from either country settled permanently across the Keel, despite long-recognized similarities in background, language, culture, and economic interests. There were, however, significant differences between the migrating groups. Down to 1903, there was heavier migration from Sweden to Norway than the reverse, reaching a peak of some ten thousand persons during the 1860s, at the same time that large-scale Swedish emigration to America began. By 1900, there were some fifty thousand Swedes in Norway, mostly from the border provinces. That same year, some eight thousand Norwegians were resident in Sweden. In 1905, Ernst Günther reported that some ten to twelve thousand Swedes were living in Christiania alone.

Moreover, while the great majority of the Swedes in Norway were laborers, reflecting the relatively early industrialization particularly around Oslo Fjord, many of the Norwegians in Sweden achieved prominence in various walks of life, including, according to Günther, "ladies at court, opera singers, and timber merchants," as well as a couple of members of the Riksdag. In time, there were a number of distinguished Swedes who had Norwegian mothers. Interestingly enough, Norwegian migration to Sweden at last surpassed movement in the opposite direction in 1903, which would seem to indicate that neither the existence of the union nor its problems had much to do with the process.[40] The topic merits further study.

The basic focus of this study has been the Norwegian impact on Sweden during the union. Swedish influences in Norway have been touched on only in passing, but in conclusion, the question deserves some further examination. In the political sphere, as has been seen, the union affected Norway primarily in a negative sense, stimulating developments in reaction to Swedish policies or the fears they aroused.

But meanwhile, what of cultural influences? Gustav Sundbärg concluded glumly in 1911 that "in literature and art, Sweden's influence upon Norway during the nineteenth century was as good as nil, which may surely be explained by the fact that with us, both had so little national character."[41] More recently, however, the Norwegian scholar Kristian Magnus Kommandantvold, in a detailed study of Swedish influences in Norwegian literature published in 1958, proved that this was far from true. He showed that virtually all the leading Norwegian writers, with the evident exception of Alexander Kielland, had a sincere appreciation for Swedish culture, regardless of their attitudes toward the existing union. In this respect, Bjørnstjerne Bjørnson took his countryman Kristofer Janson to task in 1874: "You are too hard on the Swedes, you see only the one side: the Swede is so humane [mænniskelig], he is greater [in that regard] than we, and let him only complete his material foundation and he will quickly reveal an idealism that will push all of us aside, for we are far from as lyrical, open, and natural in manner as the Swede. We are more correct, 'more moral,' but what does that mean when it is so often at the expense of humaneness?" In 1897, during troubled times, he wrote of the Swedes in the Christiania newspaper Dagbladet, "It seems to me that there is more of what one calls true civilization in that old nation than in ours. . . . Sweden could, best among all of the smaller nations, become the standard-bearer for freedom and the tasks of the future." Other Norwegian writers too expressed warm admiration for their eastern neighbors' greater sophistication and urbanity, for their tolerance, chivalrous generosity, and tact, and for their romantic fantasy and festivitas, the capacity to enjoy life to the full.[42] Norwegians as well as Swedes thus found admirable qualities in each other that, they felt, were complementary to their own and that they themselves ought to possess in greater degree.

While Swedish types were on occasion parodied by Norwegian writers, for instance the aristocratic "Trompeterstråle" in Ibsen's *Peer Gynt*, the Swedish character as such seems never to have been as bitterly criticized by the more prominent Norwegian writers as the Norwegian character was by prominent Swedes. The exception was, of course, that clique of highly placed ultraconservatives that Bjørnson labeled the *storsvensker*, or "Great-Swedes," and whom liberals in Sweden as well as in Norway blamed for the ills of both nations. One notes too that Ibsen in his *Brand* and *Peer Gynt* and Bjørnson in his polemic writings accused their compatriots of lacking belief and true pride in their own land—the same complaint that such writers as Strindberg, Heidenstam, Sundbärg, and Laurin made against their compatriots.

Kommandantvold has revealed that both during the union and after its dissolution there was widespread admiration for, and no small influence in Norway from, the Swedish national romantic writers, including most particularly Gustaf Fröding and Selma Lagerlöf. Strindberg, Heidenstam, and Levertin too had their Norwegian followings. Swedish song enjoyed—and still enjoys—widespread popularity there, not least the ballads of Carl Michael Bellman. In Kommandantvold's view, after decades of Norwegian influence in Sweden, the cultural current began indeed to flow in the opposite direction by the 1890s.

Norwegian writers frequently praised the subtle beauties of the Swedish landscape. In the 1840s, Jørgen Moe wrote in his poem *Hilsen til Sverige* (Greeting to Sweden):

> Land with the broad, sparkling lakes
> Gleaming beneath the bright heaven of springtime
> Sweet as the glance of a Nordic maiden
> Land, thou captivateth our eyes and minds.

"What a land, this Sweden!" wrote Eilert Sundt in 1862. "It unites something of Norway's majestic with Denmark's gentle nature; here are forests and mountains, tracts where conditions are meager, indeed hard, and there broad plains whose fertility blossoms forth on manors." Sweden's proud history, with its great deeds of yore, was likewise much admired by Norwegian writers.[43]

What is perhaps most notable is that appreciation for Swedish culture appears to have grown at the very time it became most quintessentially Swedish, as the union was facing its greatest trials around the turn of the

century. A new, younger generation of Norwegian writers, including such figures as Nils Collett Vogt, Vilhelm Krag, Sigbjørn Obstfelder, and Nils Kjær,
who, like the painter Edvard Munch, were influenced by European symbolism, were turning away from the determined assertion of Norwegian
uniqueness toward more subtle, universal themes. Verner von Heidenstam's
prognosis during the 1890s that Norwegian culture was maturing to the point
where Norwegians would better be able to understand and appreciate
Swedish culture seems indeed to have been borne out. Especially after 1905,
cultural currents in Norway and Sweden have tended ever more in the same
cosmopolitan directions.[44]

Nils Collett Vogt, whose wife was Swedish and who spent much time in
Sweden, wrote dejectedly in 1922, "In Sweden a new national life has blos-
somed forth since 1905. Can we say the same here?" Many Norwegians, he
claimed, now felt that their national energies had declined since then and
that "we instead are marking time or—imagine if that were so?—a nation in
decline? . . . A ninety-year period of weakness has passed and now, with awakened national instincts Sweden goes forth to meet its future. Let us learn from
the Swedes. . . . It is shameful to imitate, not to learn." The trials that lay ahead
for Norway after 1922 would of course amply prove that it was hardly "a nation
in decline."[45]

In concentrating upon Norwegian influences in Sweden during the period
dealt with here, one must ever be aware of the limitations of a study such as
this. In the first place, to single out this particular aspect of the period may
give the impression that it played a greater role in the internal life of the two
kingdoms than it did. It was only one of many concerns for Swedes and Norwegians throughout these years and by no means always the most important.

In the wider Scandinavian context, Denmark naturally figures prominently, as to a lesser degree does Finland as well as Iceland, the treasury of
the Old Norse literary heritage. Norway's constitution was an inspiration to
Danish as well as Swedish liberals, until Denmark at last acquired a constitution in 1849, which at least until 1866 rivaled Norway's in its democratic
franchise. Hopes of including Denmark in a wider union with Norway and
Sweden at times fueled enthusiasm for the Scandinavianist movement, while
the dangers inherent in the Schleswig-Holstein question and the final debacle in 1864 prevented its realization, even though this did not prevent ongoing Nordic cooperation on the practical level.

Culturally, even if not politically, Denmark too played its part within the
union, as the powerful influences of such figures as Adam Oehlenschläger,

Nicolai Frederik Severin Grundtvig, Søren Kierkegaard, and Georg Brandes attest. Nor should one overlook the role of Frederik Hegel, head of the Danish Gyldendal publishing house, who brought out virtually all of the major works of Ibsen, Bjørnson, and most of the other leading Norwegian writers in the essentially common Dano-Norwegian literary language. Throughout, Copenhagen held its place as the metropolis and cultural forum of the North.

Denmark was thus at all times very much a part of the equation. To have fully integrated it into this study, however, would have shifted attention away from its intended focus on the two kingdoms joined together in dynastic union in 1814. Yet clearly, Denmark must always be kept in mind.

At the same time, it is also clear that both the political and the cultural currents examined here in the Dual Kingdoms were international in scope, however much local coloration they showed in the Scandinavian setting. This was as true of liberalism, democracy, socialism, nationalism, and pan-nationalism in the realm of politics as it was of high romanticism, realism, naturalism, and neoromanticism in the cultural sphere. Developments in Sweden and Norway call to mind constant parallels and comparisons in the wider Western world.

These developments likewise were reflected at the time among the large Swedish and Norwegian immigrant communities across the Atlantic in America. Scandinavian Americans put their own interpretation on the Old Nordic past, stressing the proud Viking spirit of adventure as the moving force behind their pioneering in the new land, in opposition to critics of emigration in their homelands. Historiographic conflicts in Scandinavia itself over the true locus of the Viking heritage had reverberations in a lively dispute between Norwegian American and Swedish American cultural leaders as to whether Leif Ericson and his men from Greenland, the first Europeans to reach North America in A.D. 1000, were "Norwegians" or "Northmen"—which could include other Scandinavians.[46]

The Swedish liberal Riksdag member Paul Peter Waldenström, traveling in the United States in 1901, was indignant to find that the Norwegians there were "more Norwegian than the Swedes were Swedish." It also irked him that the American press seemed more positively disposed toward Norway than toward Sweden. Yet, in 1900, his compatriot Carl Sundbeck still optimistically hoped that in North America Swedes and Norwegians, removed from the political strife between their homelands, could at last amalgamate into "*one* people" to form a "New Sweden" in the New World. Norwegian American and Swedish American publications as well as private letters from the time show how passions could be aroused on both sides. Yet, on the whole, both groups proved to be good neighbors throughout the period where, as they often did, they lived in close contact with each other.[47]

Although the broader trends of the period were international is scope, one is still hard put to find any real parallel to the greater influence that Norway, the smaller nation initially lacking a truly national, recent history or a developed national culture, exercised over Sweden, the larger partner, with its long, unbroken national history and cultural life. Therein lies its special fascination.

In 1880, Bjørnstjerne Bjørnson wrote his friend Sven Adolf Hedlund in Göteborg of his determined opposition to the idea that Sweden-Norway should evolve into a kind of "England-Scotland." To be sure, Scotland in the nineteenth century, as Øystein Sørensen has written, "had, in contrast to Norway, not reestablished a state of its own. But Scotland had Walter Scott." And Scotland, as Kenneth Clark pointed out, was—like Norway—"a country that still had the energy of newness." Not incidentally, Scott, together with Henrik Wergeland, was a particular inspiration to Bjørnson in his efforts at cultural nation-building. The English infatuation with wild and romantic Scotland since Scott's day offers perhaps the closest parallel to Swedish visions of Norway during the union, as do the mingled feelings of the English—admiration tinged with envy, tolerant amusement, and aggravation—toward their dour, hardy, yet canny, and energetic northern neighbors.[48]

In a world of tensions between nationalism and internationalism, regionalism and localism, the Swedish-Norwegian union in its time provides us with a prime reminder that each case is unique, yet it offers its particular insights into complex relations between governments, nationalities, and cultures. It furthermore illustrates how views of the past all too easily become one-sided and stereotyped by reading history backwards, starting from what in retrospect appear to have been the inevitable end results. It reminds us that if history is written by the winners ex post facto, we need to go back and examine it as contemporaries lived it at the time, when ultimate outcomes still lay hidden in the future.

Notes

1. The Road to Union

1. See, e.g., W. R. Mead, *An Economic Geography of Scandinavia and Finland* (London, 1958).

2. See Michael Roberts, "On Aristocratic Constitutionalism in Swedish History," in *Essays in Swedish History* (Minneapolis, 1967), 14–55.

3. The remainder of this chapter is based primarily on my *Scandinavia in the Revolutionary Era, 1760–1815* (Minneapolis, 1986). See also B. J. Hovde, *The Scandinavian Countries, 1720–1865: The Rise of the Middle Classes,* 2 vols. (Boston, 1943).

4. Axel Lindvald, *Oplysningens Tidsalder,* Schultz Danmarkshistorie, ed. Aage Friis et al., vol. 6, part 1 (Copenhagen, 1943), 191.

5. Barton, *Scandinavia,* 19.

6. See Sten Carlsson, "Bondeståndet i Norden under senare delen av 1700-talet," *Scandia* 19 (1948–49): 574–624; Kåre D. Tønnesson, "Problèmes de la féodalité dans les pays scandinaves," *Annales historiques de la Révolution française* (1969): 331–42.

7. Note esp. Andreas Elviken, "The Genesis of Norwegian Nationalism," *Journal of Modern History* 3 (1931): 365–91, and *Die Entwicklung der norwegischen Nationalismus* (Berlin, 1939); Øystein Sørensen, ed., *Jakten på det norske. Perspektiver på utviklingen av en norsk nasjonal identitet på 1800-tallet* (Oslo, 1998).

8. See Julius Clausen, *Skandinavismen historisk fremstillet* (Copenhagen, 1900), 1–20; H. Arnold Barton, "The Swedish Succession Crises of 1809 and 1810, and the Question of Scandinavian Union," *Scandinavian Studies* 42 (1970): 311–13.

9. For the indigenous Scandinavian background of reactions to the American and French Revolutions, see Barton, *Scandinavia.*

10. See esp. Olof Jägerskiöld, "Tyrannmord och motståndsrätt," *Scandia* 25 (1962): 113–66; Lolo Krusius-Ahrenberg, *Tyrannmördaren C. F. Ehrensvärd* (Helsinki, 1947); Barton, *Scandinavia,* 200–203.

11. See Mary Wollstonecraft, *Letters Written During a Short Residence in Sweden, Norway, and Denmark,* ed. Carol Postan (Lincoln, NE, 1976), 116; *The Travel Diaries of Thomas Robert Malthus,* ed. Patricia James (Cambridge, 1966), 92; Erik Vea, *Likhetsidéen i Norge i 1790-aarene* (Oslo, 1956); J. A. Seip, "Teorien om det opinionsbestemte enevelde," *Historisk tidsskrift* (Nor.) 38 (1958): 397–463; Barton, *Scandinavia,* chaps. 8–10, esp. 181–83.

12. For a detailed account of the Nordic lands during the Napoleonic Wars, see Barton, *Scandinavia*, chaps. 10–13.

13. See esp. Barton, "Swedish Succession"; Birger Sjövall, *Georg Adlersparrre och tronfrågan 1809* (Lund, 1917); Leland B. Sather, "The Prince of Scandinavia: A Biography of Prince Christian August of Schleswig-Holstein-Sonderburg-Augustenburg, 1768–1810" (Ph.D. diss., University of California at Santa Barbara, 1975).

14. See esp. H. Arnold Barton, *Count Hans Axel von Fersen: Aristocrat in an Age of Revolution* (Boston, 1975), chaps. 15 and 16.

15. A good deal of controversy surrounds the origins of Carl Johan's "Policy of 1812." See Barton, *Scandinavia*, 316–20.

16. Oscar Alin, *Den svensk-norska unionen. Uppsatser och aktstycken*, 2 vols. (Stockholm, 1889–91), 1:1:12–33, esp. 13.

17. Barton, *Scandinavia*, 295–97, 336–38; Yngvar Nielsen, *Lensgreve Johan Caspar Herman Wedel-Jarlsberg*, 3 vols. (Christiania, 1901–2), 1:257–60; Sam Clason and Carl af Petersens, eds., *För hundra år sedan. Skildringar och bref från revolutionsåren 1809–1810*, 2 vols. (Stockholm, 1909–10), 2:37.

18. Barton, *Scandinavia*, 337–38. Cf. esp. Jörgen Weibull, *Carl Johan och Norge 1810–1814* (Göteborg, 1957).

19. [Christian VIII,] *Kong Christian VIII.s Dagbøger og Optegnelser*, vol. 1, *1799–1814*, ed. Axel Lindvald (Copenhagen, 1943), 337; Barton, *Scandinavia*, 341–42.

20. Christian Magnus Falsen, *Hvad har Norge at haabe?* (Christiania, 1814); Terje Leiren, "1814 and British Opinion," *Scandinavian Studies* 47 (1975): 364–82; Lars Tangeraas, "Castlereagh, Bernadotte and Norway," *Scandinavian Journal of History* 8 (1983): 193–223.

21. Alin, *Svensk-norska unionen*, 2:2:127–36, esp. 131.

22. Ibid., 2:2:305–6. Cf. Torvald Höjer, *1810–1844*, vol. 3, part 2, of *Den svenska utrikespolikens historia*, ed. Nils Ahnlund (Stockholm, 1954), 215. For the Act of Union, see Bernhard Dunker, *Om Revision af Foreningsakten mellom Sverige og Norge*, 2 vols. (Copenhagen, 1866–68), 2:196–205.

23. Carl von Bonsdorff, *Opinioner och stämningar i Finland 1804–1814* (Helsingfors, 1918), 171; *Hedvig Elisabeth Charlottas dagbok*, ed. Carl Carlsson Bonde and Cecilia af Klercker, 9 vols. (Stockholm, 1902–42), 9:269, 351n., 353; Weibull, *Carl Johan*, 290–93.

2. The Civic Vision

1. See H. Arnold Barton, *Scandinavia in the Revolutionary Era, 1760–1815* (Minneapolis, 1986), 306.

2. See Peter Englund, *Det hotade huset* (Stockholm, 1989); Michael Roberts, "The Swedish Aristocracy in the Eighteenth Century," in *Essays in Swedish History* (Minneapolis, 1967), 269–85.

3. See Tom Söderberg, *Den namnlösa medelklassen* (Stockholm, 1956) and *Två sekel svensk medelklass från gustaviansk tid till nutid* (Stockholm, 1972).

4. See Sten Carlsson, *Ståndssamhälle och ståndspersoner 1700–1815. Studier rörande det svenska ståndssamhällets upplösning*, 2d ed. (Lund, 1973); E. Ingers and Sten Carlsson, *Bonden i svensk historia*, 3 vols. (Stockholm, 1949–56).

5. Sverre Steen, *Tidsrummet 1770 til omkring 1814*, vol. 7 of *Norske folks liv og histo-rie gjennem tidene*, ed. Edvard Bull et al. (Oslo, 1933), 386.

6. Stein Kuhnle, "Stemmeretten i 1814," *Historisk tidsskrift* (Nor.) 51 (1972): 373–90.

7. On the Norwegian constitution of 1814, see T. Andenæs, ed., *The Constitution of Norway and Other Documents of National Importance*, 2d ed. (Oslo, 1960); Barton, *Scandinavia*, 343–48, 352; Oscar Alin, *Den svensk-norska unionen. Uppsatser och aktstycken*, 2 vols. (Stockholm, 1889–91), 2:13–45; Sverre Steen, *Det frie Norge*, vol. 1, *1814* (Oslo, 1951), 140–41, 156–75.

8. Cf. Alf Kaartvedt, "Unionen som politisk energikilde," in *Fra arvefiende til samboer*, ed. Grete Værnø (Stockholm and Oslo, 1990), 76.

9. For details on these disturbances, see Barton, *Scandinavia*.

10. See, e.g., Jens Arup Seip, *Utsikt over Norges historie*, 2 vols. (Oslo, 1974, 1981), 1:61–70; Carl Schnitler, *Slægten fra 1814. Studier over norsk embedsmandskultur i klassicismens tidsalder 1814–1840* (Kristiania, 1911).

11. Jens Arup Seip, "Teorien om det opinionsbestemte enevelde," *Historisk tidsskrift* (Nor.) 38 (1958): 397–463; Halvdan Koht, *Norsk bondereising. Fyrebuing til bondepoli-tikken* (Oslo, 1926).

12. Knut Mykland, *Kampen om Norge 1784–1814*, vol. 9 of *Norges historie*, ed. Knut Mykland (Oslo, 1978), 380; Halvdan Koht, "Trongen til demokrati i 1814," *Historisk tidsskrift* (Nor.) 34 (1947): 143, 149–51; J. Seip, "Teorien," 397–98, 443; Barton, *Scandi-navia*, 345–47.

13. See, e.g., Oscar Albert Johnsen, *Norges bønder. Utsyn over den norske bondestands historie*, 2d ed. (Oslo, 1936).

14. *Hedvig Elisabeth Charlottas dagbok*, ed. Carl Carlsson Bonde and Cecilia af Klercker, 9 vols. (Stockholm, 1902–42), 9:538–39.

15. Francis Sejersted, *Den vanskelige frihet: 1814–1851*, vol 10 of *Norges historie*, ed. Knut Mykland (Oslo, 1978), 42–50, 344; J. Seip, *Utsikt*, 1:75–76; Halvdan Koht, "Bonde-politikken," *Samtiden* 19 (1908): 441.

16. Torvald Höjer, *Carl XIV Johan*, 3 vols. (Stockholm, 1939–60), 3:186–87.

17. Samuel Laing, *Journal of a Residence in Norway During the Years 1834, 1835, and 1836; Made with a View to Enquire into the Moral and Political Economy of that Coun-try, and the Condition of Its Inhabitants* (London, 1837), 126.

18. There is a large literature regarding Carl Johan's relations with the Storting. See esp. Sejersted, *Den vanskelige frihet*; Höjer, *Carl XIV Johan*, vol. 3; Alf Kaartvedt, "Karl Johan i Norge. Författningskamp och utrikespolitik," in *Karl XIV Johan — en europeisk karriär*, Skrifter från Kungl, Husgerådskammaren 9 (Stockholm, 1998), 115–39.

19. Jacob Wallenberg, *Min son på galejan* (1770; Prisma ed., Stockholm, 1960), 37. Cf. Arne Lidén, *Den norska strömningen i svensk litteratur under 1800-talet*, vol. 1 (Upp-sala, 1926) [no vol. 2 followed], chap. 1, on which the following section on the period up to 1814 is largely based.

20. Pehr Kalm, *Resa till Norra America*, 3 vols. (Stockholm, 1753–61), 1:137.

21. See H. Arnold Barton, *Northern Arcadia: Foreign Travelers in Scandinavia, 1765–1815* (Carbondale, IL, 1998), esp. chap. 6.

22. C. A. Adlersparre, *1809 års revolution och dess män*, 2 vols. (Stockholm, 1849), 2:141.

23. Lidén, *Den norska strömningen*, 7; *Excellensen Grefve A. F. Skjöldebrands memoarer*, ed. Henrik Schück, 5 vols. (Stockholm, 1903–4), 5:188–224.

24. *Hedvig Elisabeth Charlottas dagbok*, 9:306–7, 384, 408–9; Esaias Tegnér, *Samlade skrifter* (Stockholm, 1884), 5:96; Lidén, *Den norska stromningen*, 10.

25. Sven Nilsson, *Dagboksanteckningar under en resa från Södra Sverige till Nordlanden i Norge 1816* (Lund, 1879), 74.

26. Jörgen Weibull, *Carl Johan och Norge* (Göteborg, 1957), 296–301, 309–10, 314, 317–18, 329–30, 335–36, 338–40.

27. Sam Clason, *Karl XIII och Karl XIV Johan*, vol. 11 of *Sveriges historia till våra dagar*, ed. Emil Hildebrand and Ludvig Stavenow (Stockholm, 1923), 282.

28. Berit Borell, *De svenska liberalerna och representationsfrågan på 1840-talet* (Uppsala, 1948), 11, 18, 24–25; Johan Norberg, *Den svenska liberalismens historia* (Stockholm, 1998), 67–93; C. H. Anckarsvärd, *En svensk mans sysselsättning den 17 maj* (Stockholm, 1828). On the whole question of representation reform during the nineteenth century, see Wilhelm Erik Svedelius, *Representationsreformens historia* (Stockholm, 1889). Berit Borell's work remains basic for the period here under consideration. For a more theoretical discussion of the representation question at the crucial Riksdag of 1840–41, see Gunnar Rexius, "Det svenska tvåkammarsystemets tillkomst och karaktär. Med särskild hänsyn till principernas grundläggning 1840–41," *Skrifter utgivna av Humanistiska Vetenskaps-Samfundet i Uppsala* 17:2 (Uppsala, 1915), which places greater emphasis upon international, as opposed to Norwegian, influences, which receive only passing mention.

29. J. G. Richert and C. H. Anckarsvärd, *Förslag till National-Representation* (Stockholm, 1830), esp. iii–xv, 22–25, 35, 52–75; Cf. Jan Christensen, *Bönder och herrar. Bondeståndet i 1840-talets liberala representationsdebatt. Exemplen Gustaf Hierta och J P Theorell* (Göteborg, 1997), 144; Borell, *De svenska liberalerna*, 18–27.

30. C. H. Anckarsvärd, *Politisk trosbekännelse* (Stockholm, 1833), esp. 136–37, 158–61, 172–73, 176.

31. C. P. Agrelius, *Swenska Folkets Återställelse till ett enklare och bättre, med Norrska Folkets mera öfwerensstämmande Samhällstillstånd* (Vadstena, 1833), esp. 2–5. Cf. Christensen, *Bönder och herrar*, 31–32.

32. J. Seip, *Utsikt*, 1:148–58; Sejersted, *Den vanskelige frihet*, 338.

33. Sejersted, *Den vanskelige frihet*, 342–56

34. See esp. Theodore C. Blegen, *Norwegian Migration to America, 1825–1860* (Northfield, MN, 1931), and *Land of Their Choice: The Immigrants Write Home* (Minneapolis, 1955); Ingrid Semmingsen, *Veien mot vest*, vol. 1 (Oslo, 1941).

35. [C. A. von Scheele,] *Några korta Underrättelser om Amerika, till Upplysning och Nytta till dem som ämna dit utvandra* (Stockholm, 1841). Cf. Ole Rynning, *Sandfærdig Beretning om Amerika til Oplysning og Nytte for Bonde og Menigmand* (Christiania, 1838), English trans. Theodore C. Blegen, *Ole Rynning's True Account of America* (Minneapolis, 1926). Rynning's booklet is largely credited with having started the "America Fever" in Norway.

36. Blegen, *Norwegian Migration*, 65–70, and *Land of Their Choice*, 21–27.

37. Axel Friman, George M. Stephenson, and H. Arnold Barton, eds., *America: Reality and Dream: The Freeman Letters from Sweden and America* (Rock Island, IL, 1996), 14, 54.

38. H. Arnold Barton, *Letters from the Promised Land: Swedes in America, 1840–1914* (Minneapolis, 1975), 32. On the relationship between America, emigration, and the Swedish liberals, see Nils Runeby, *Den nya världen och den gamla. Amerikabild och emigrationsuppfattning i Sverige, 1820–1860* (Uppsala, 1969), and H. Arnold Barton, *A Folk Divided: Homeland Swedes and Swedish Americans, 1840–1940* (Carbondale, IL, 1994), chaps. 1, 2.

39. *Hederwärda Bonde-Ståndets Protocoller wid Lagtima Riksdagen i Stockholm år 1834 och 1835* (Stockholm, 1835), 7:271–84, 301; Erik Fahlbeck, *Ståndsriksdagens sista skede 1809–1866*, vol. 8 of *Sveriges Riksdag*, ed. Nils Edén et al., 18 vols. (Stockholm, 1931–36), 324–26; Borell, *De svenska liberalerna*, 30–31; Christensen, *Bönder och herrar*, 31–38, 88–96, 146–48; Norberg, *Den svenska liberalismens historia*, 74–76.

40. *Bonde-Ståndets Protocoller 1834–35*, 7:284–296.

41. *Höglofliga Riddarskapet och Adeln vid Lagtima Riksdagen i Stockholm, År 1834* (Stockholm, 1835) 14:301, 347, 365–65. Cf. Borell, *De svenska liberalerna*.

42. Borell, *De svenska liberalerna*, 21–30. Cf. esp. Anckarsvärd, *Politisk trosbekännelse*, 158–60.

43. Sten Carlsson, "Ståndsriksdagens slutskede (1809–1866)," in *Riksdagen genom tiderna*, ed. Herman Schück et al. (Stockholm, 1985), 205–6. Cf. S. Carlsson, *Ståndssamhälle*, 279–324; Norberg, *Den svenska liberalismens historia*, 105–7, 109–12, 119.

44. "Memorial [Nr. 38] angående National-representationens ombildning" (1840), 70 pp., esp. 17, in *Bihang till Samtlige Riks-Ståndens Protocoll vid Lagtima Riksdagen i Stockholm, Åren 1840 och 1841*, vol. 3, *Constitutions-Utskottets Memorial, Utlåtanden och Betänkanden* (Stockholm, 1840–41). Cf. Christensen, *Bönder och herrar*, 168–80.

45. *Hederwärda Bonde-Ståndets Protocoller wid Lagtima Riksdagen i Stockholm år 1840* (Stockholm, 1840), 8:224, 227–28. Cf. Christensen, *Bönder och herrar*, 165.

46. *Bonde-Ståndets Protocoller 1840*, 8:174, 342–43.

47. Ibid., 8:364–66.

48. Ibid., 8:359–59. For other examples of support, see also 8:280–81, 365.

49. Ibid., 8:192–3, 240–41, 378–79; Christensen, *Bönder och herrar*, 153–59.

50. *Hederwärda Borgar-Ståndets Riksdagsprotocoller 1840* (Stockholm, 1840), 8:352–55, 358–59; Norberg, *Den svenska liberalismens historia*, 95, 103, 120–21.

51. *Borgar-Ståndets Riksdagsprotocoller 1840*, 8:370–71.

52. Ibid., 8:459.

53. *Höglofliga Riddarskapet och Adeln vid Lagtima Riksdagen i Stockholm, År 1840* (Stockholm, 1841), 15:54–55, 62–63.

54. Ibid., 26–27, 46–47, 55–59. Cf. Fahlbeck, *Ståndsriksdagens sista skede*, 346.

55. *Minerva* (Stockholm), 10 Oct. 1836, quoted in Lidén, *Den norska strömningen*, 8–9, 17, 21–22.

56. Ibid., 20.

57. Fahlbeck, *Ståndsriksdagens sista skede*, 343–46; Christensen, *Bönder och herrar*, 178, 180; *Bonde-Ståndets Protocoller 1840*, 8:403

58. *Bonde-Ståndets Protocoller 1840*, 8:342, 357–59. *Riddarskapet och Adeln 1840*, 15:59. Cf. Borell, *De svenska liberalerna*, 65–66. On *Aftonbladet*, other liberal and conservative newspapers, and America, see esp. Runeby, *Den nya världen*; Barton, *A Folk Divided*, chaps. 1–2.

59. Cf. Rexius, "Det svenska tvåkammarsystemets tillkomst."

60. Lidén, *Den norska strömningen*, 180–81; Sejersted, *Den vanskelige frihet*, 355–56, 358–59.

61. Lidén, *Den norska strömningen*, 20; Borell, *De svenska liberalerna*, 26–27, 30, 61–62, 179–85.

62. Carl Hallendorff, *Oskar I och Karl XV*, vol. 12 of *Sveriges historia till våra dagar*, ed. Emil Hildebrand and Ludvig Stavenow (Stockholm, 1923), 12–16, 49–51; Borell, *De svenska liberalerna*, 180–85, 237–39, 243–34, 257, 261–64, 269, 272–76, 281, 291–92; Christensen, *Bönder och herrar*, 318–19. Cf. J. Seip, *Utsikt*, 1:176–206; Oddvar Bjørklund, *Marcus Thrane — Sosialistleder i et u-land* (Oslo, 1970); Terje I. Leiren, *Marcus Thrane: A Norwegian Radical in America* (Northfield, MN, 1987).

63. Borell, *De svenska liberalerna*, 237–39, 242, 245, 257, 274–76, 284; Fahlbeck, *Ståndsriksdagens sista skede*, 357–71, 378–83; Hallendorff, *Oskar I och Karl XV*, 59–69.

64. Halvdan Koht, "Norsk hjelp til svensk demokrati," *Scandia* 18 (1947): 252–64 (quotations in English).

65. Samuel Laing, *Journal of Norway* and *A Tour of Sweden in 1838; Comprising Observations on the Moral, Political, and Economical State of the Swedish Nation* (London, 1839). Cf. Bernard Porter, "Virtue or Vice in the North: The Scandinavian Writings of Samuel Laing," *Scandinavian Journal of History* 23 (1998): 153–72; Mark Davies, *A Perambulating Paradox: British Travel Literature and the Image of Sweden, c. 1770–1870* (Lund, 1999), 291–94, 354.

66. Laing, *Journal of Norway*, iii–iv, 120–22, 331, 333, 479–80.

67. Ibid., 321–22, 455.

68. Ibid., 133–36.

69. Ibid., 122, 125, 458–59.

70. Laing, *Tour of Sweden*, 32–34, 42–43, 149–51, 337.

71. Ibid., 35–36, 77–91, 116–19, 275–96.

72. Ibid., 108–49.

73. Ibid., 219–20, 276–77, 323.

74. Ibid., 102–7, 351–55. Cf. Leif Kihlberg, *Lars Hierta i helfigur* (Stockholm, 1968).

75. Laing, *Tour of Sweden*, 379–424; Laing, *Journal of Norway*, 121, 131–32, 196.

76. See Samuel Bring, *Itineraria Suecana. Bibliografisk förteckning över resor i Sverige fram till 1950* (Stockholm, 1954), 191, 204, for references to British press commentary on Laing's accounts; [Magnus Björnstjerna,] *On the Moral State and Political Union of Sweden and Norway, in Answer to Mr. Laing's Statement* (London, 1840). In *Northern Arcadia*, 176, I maintain that British interest in Norway was largely attributable to the sympathetic travel accounts of such British travelers as Mary Wollstonecraft, Thomas Malthus, and E. D. Clarke at the end of the eighteenth century.

77. Björnstjerna, *On the Moral State*, 1–2.

78. Ibid., 6–7.

79. Ibid., 14–19.

80. Ibid., 25–32, 49–51.

81. Ibid., 36–43.

82. Ibid., 47–48, 53–54.

83. Ibid., 63.

84. Samuel Laing, "Sweden and Norway: Mr. Laing's Reply to a Pamphlet," *Monthly Chronicle* 6 (1840): 385–97. Cf. Davies, *Perambulating Paradox*, 395–97.

85. Charles Loring Brace, *The Norse-Folk; or, a Visit to the Homes of Norway and Sweden* (New York, 1857), 24–25, 133. Cf. L. Andersson, "Två amerikaner i Oscar I:s Sverige," in *Festskrift till Alma Söderhjelm* (Stockholm, 1945), 115–21.

86. Brace, *Norse-Folk*, iii–iv, 54, 57–58, 142, 146–49, 188–89.

87. Ibid., 76, 148–49, 245, 302–3, 335, 386–87, 455, 461–64.

88. Bayard Taylor, *Northern Travel: Summer and Winter Pictures: Sweden, Denmark and Lapland* (New York, 1887), 239–40, 327–29, 346, 360, 379–81, 402–3, 405–6, 413, 417, 434. This book was first published with the more accurate subtitle, *Winter Pictures of Sweden, Lapland and Norway* (New York, 1857).

89. For a good description of the reform, see Franklin D. Scott, *Sweden: The Nation's History*, 2d ed. (Carbondale, IL, 1988), 389–90. Cf. Ingers and Carlsson, *Bonden i svensk historia*, 3:301; Christensen, *Bönder och herrar*, 152–53, 304–7, 324; Kuhnle, "Stemmeretten i 1814."

90. Lorenz Dietrichson, *En norrmans minnen från Sverige*, trans. Klara Johansson (Stockholm, 1901–2), 2:36. This useful work includes the sections dealing with Sweden in Dietrichson's extensive memoirs, *Svundne Tider. Af en Forfatteres Ungdoms-Erindringer*, 4 vols. (Kristiania, 1896–1917).

91. Cf. Koht, "Norsk hjelp," 263–64.

92. See Kaartvedt, "Karl Johan i Norge," 138–39.

93. Göran B. Nilsson, "Unionen som inte blev någon union," *Nyt norsk tidsskrift* 2 (1985): 14–20. Cf. the chapters on specific liberal reforms in B. J. Hovde, *The Scandinavian Countries, 1720–1865: The Rise of the Middle Classes*, vol. 2 (Boston, 1943).

94. Norberg, *Den svenska liberalismens historia*, 167.

95. Nilsson, "Unionen," 16, 18.

3. High Noon and Decline of the Union

1. Sam Clason, *Karl XIII och Karl XIV Johan*, vol. 11 of *Sveriges historia till våra dagar*, ed. Emil Hildebrand and Ludvig Stavenow (Stockholm, 1923), 402–5; Francis Sejersted, *Den vanskelige frihet: 1814–1851*, vol. 10 of *Norges historie*, ed. Knut Mykland (Oslo, 1978), 384–86.

2. Carl Hallendorff, *Oskar I och Karl XV*, vol. 12 of *Sveriges historia till våra dagar*, ed. Emil Hildebrand and Ludvig Stavenow (Stockholm, 1923), 401–3; Hans Try, *To kulturer — en stat 1851–1884*, vol. 11 of *Norges historie*, ed. Knut Mykland (Oslo, 1979), 45–57; Raymond E. Lindgren, *Norway-Sweden: Union, Disunion, and Scandinavian Integration* (Princeton, 1959), 51–52, 56–57; T. K. Derry, *A Short History of Norway* (London, 1957), 174; Harold Larson, *Björnstjerne Björnson: A Study in Norwegian Nationalism* (New York, 1944), 98. For the Union Committee's proposal, see Bernhard Dunker, *Om Revision af Foreningsakten mellom Sverige og Norge*, 2 vols (Copenhagen, 1866–68), 2:206–32.

3. See esp. Julius Clausen, *Skandinavismen historisk fremstillet* (Copenhagen, 1900); Hallendorff, *Oskar I och Karl XV*, 73–91; Åke Holmberg, *Skandinavismen i Sverige vid 1800-talets mitt (1843–1863)* (Göteborg, 1946).

4. Cf. H. Arnold Barton, "The Swedish Succession Crises of 1809 and 1810, and the Question of Scandinavian Union," *Scandinavian Studies* 42 (1970): 309–33.

5. Cf. Lawrence Steefel, *The Schleswig-Holstein Question* (Cambridge, MA, 1932).

6. See esp. Hallendorff, *Oskar I och Karl XV*, 73–91, 115–35; Allan Jansson, *1844–1872*, vol. 3, part 3, of *Svenska utrikespolitikens historia* (Stockholm, 1961), 106–7; T. K. Derry, *A History of Modern Norway, 1814–1972* (Oxford, 1973), 89–91; *Sveriges och Norges traktater med främmande makter*, 15 vols. (Stockholm, 1877–1954), 11:307–10.

7. See esp. Theodore Jorgensen, *Norway's Relation to Scandinavian Unionism, 1815–1871* (Northfield, MN, 1935); John Sanness, *Patrioter, intelligens og skandinaver. Norske reaksjoner på skandinavismen før 1848* (Oslo, 1959). Cf. Jens Arup Seip, *Utsikt over Norges historie*, 2 vols. (Oslo, 1974, 1981), 2:39–42; Fritz von Dardel, *Minnen*, 4 vols. (Stockholm, 1911–13), 2:87; Francis Bull, *Bjørnstjerne Bjørnson* (Kristiania, 1923; originally published in *Norsk biografisk leksikon*, ed. Edvard Bull et al., vol. 1, Kristiania, 1923), 28–29.

8. Hallendorff, *Oskar I och Karl XV*, 100, 305–46; A. Jansson, *1844–1872*, 180–234; Try, *To kulturer*, 451; Derry, *History of Modern Norway*, 90–91; Göran B. Nilsson, "Den verkningslösa unionen?" in *Fra arvefiende til samboer*, ed. Grete Værnø (Stockholm and Oslo, 1990), 54–55, and "Unionen som inte blev någon union," *Nyt norsk tidsskrift* 2 (1985): 18.

9. Wilhelm Keilhau, *Tidsrummet fra omkring 1875 til omkring 1920*, vol. 10 of *Norske folks liv og historie gjennem tidene*, ed. Edvard Bull et al. (Oslo, 1935), 93; Gurli Linder, *På den tiden. Några bilder från 1870-talets Stockholm* (Stockholm, 1924), 322–25.

10. Clason, *Karl XIII och Karl XIV Johan*, 398–99.

11. *Protocoll hållna hos höglofiige Ridderskapet och Adeln vid Lagtima Riksdagen i Stockholm, År 1859–1860* (Stockholm, 1859), 1:62–100, 385–87; Hallendorff, *Oskar I och Karl XV*, 58, 261–78; Lindgren, *Norway-Sweden*, 50; Arne Lidén, *Den norska strömningen i svensk litteratur under 1800-talet* (Uppsala, 1926), 28–30; Henrik Hedlund, *S. A. Hedlund. Hans liv och gärning*, 2 vols. (Göteborg, 1929–30), 1:323; Nils Elvander, "Från liberal skandinavism till konservativ nationalism i Sverige," *Scandia* 27 (1961): 366–86, esp. 370–74.

12. J. Seip, *Utsikt*, 2:31–33; Derry, *Short History of Norway*, 175. Cf. Rolf Danielsen, "Den norske oppfatning av unionen," in Værnø, *Fra arvefiende*, 44–45, 48.

13. Alf Kaartvedt, "Karl Johan i Norge. Författningskamp och utrikespolitik," in *Karl XIV Johan — en europeisk karriär*, Skrifter från Kungl, Husgerådskammaren 9 (Stockholm, 1998), 128–29.

14. J. Seip, *Utsikt*, 1:106–11; Sejersted, *Den vanskelige frihet*, 359, 366–72, 387–91.

15. Alf Kaartvedt, "Carl Johan-statuen. En politisk manifestasjon," *Carl Johans Förbundets handlingar 1994–1998* (Uppsala, 1999), 17–22. Cf. Hallendorff, *Oskar I och Karl XV*, 137–41.

16. Bjørnstjerne Bjørnson, *Brevveksling med svenske 1858–1909*, ed. Øyvind Anker, Francis Bull, and Örjan Lindberger, 3 vols. (Oslo, 1960–61), 2:69.

17. On the ideological *Kulturkampf* in Norway, see esp. J. Seip, *Utsikt*, vol. 2. Cf. Jörgen Fredrik Ording, Einar Östvedt, and Odd Hölaas, *Norges historia. Från äldsta tid till våra dagar* (Malmö, 1949), 295–300; Try, *To kulturer*, 506–18. The fullest account of the political struggle is Alf Kaartvedt, *Kampen mot parlamentarismen 1880–1885* (Oslo, 1956).

18. Alf Kaartvedt, *Kampen*, and "Unionen som politisk energikilde," in Værnø, *Fra arvefiende*, 80; Folke Lindberg, *1872–1914*, vol. 3, part 4, of *Svenska utrikespolitikens historia*, ed. Nils Ahnlund (Stockholm, 1958), 62–71, and *Kunglig utrikespolitik. Studier och essayer från Oskar II:s tid*, 2d ed. (Stockholm, 1966), 80–94.

19. See, e.g., Try, *To kulturer*, 525–27.

20. Cf. Kaartvedt, "Unionen," 78.

21. On Bjørnson's role, see esp. Francis Bull, "Bjørnson og Sverige," in *Bjørnson-Studier*, ed. Gerhard Gran (Kristiania, 1911), 171–281 (quote, p. 206), and *Bjørnstjerne Bjørnson*; Bjørnson, *Brevveksling med svenske*, 1:xi–xxxviii; cf. ibid., 2:71; Øystein Sørensen, *Bjørnstjerne Bjørnson og nasjonalismen* (Oslo, 1997); Larson, *Björnson*.

22. Try, *To kulturer*, 496; Bjørnson, *Brevveksling med svenske*, 2:19–21; Bjørnstjerne Bjørnson, *Artikler og Taler*, ed. C. Collin and H. Eitrem, 2 vols. (Kristiania, 1912–13), 1:482–87, 2:221; Per Amdam and Aldo Keel, *Bjørnstjerne Bjørnson*, 2 vols. (Oslo, 1993, 1999), esp. 2:35–46, 59–66, 279–81; Sørensen, *Bjørnstjerne Bjørnson*, 88, 93–94, 98, 131; Ernst Sars, *Historisk Inledning til Grundloven* (Kristiania, 1882); Hedlund, *Hedlund*, 2:106–22, 418–30; Olle Gellerman, *S. A. Hedlund — legendarisk tidningsman och liberal politiker* (Stockholm, 1998), esp. 153–63.

23. Bjørnson, *Artikler og Taler*, 1:487, 538; 2:46; and *Brevveksling med svenske*, 2:19–21; Larson, *Björnson*, 84–91.

24. See esp. Larson, *Björnson*, 78–86.

25. See, e.g., Per Fuglum, *Norge i støpeskjeen 1884–1920*, vol. 12 of *Norges historie*, ed. Knut Mykland (Oslo, 1978), 22–23; Hallendorff, *Oskar I och Karl XV*, 382–86. On the Swedish *Lantmannaparti*, see Edvard Thermænius, *Lantmannapartiet. Dess uppkomst, organisation och tidigare utveckling* (Uppsala, 1928); E. Ingers and Sten Carlsson, *Bonden i svensk historia*, 3 vols. (Stockholm, 1949–56), 3:389–496 (Carlsson).

26. See esp. Thermænius, *Lantmannapartiet*, chap. 10.

27. Bjørnson, *Brevveksling med svenske*, 1:71, 97–102, 130. Cf. F. Bull, "Bjørnson og Sverige," 194.

28. S. J. Boëthius, *Oskar II*, vol. 13 of *Sveriges historia till våra dagar*, ed. Emil Hildebrand and Ludvig Stavenow (Stockholm, 1925), 109, 111; Thermænius, *Lantmannapartiet*, 391–423; Kaartvedt, *Kampen*, 200–218, 374, 553, 556; Hedlund, *Hedlund*, 2:268–84; Gellerman, *Hedlund*, 158–60; Ingers and Carlsson, *Bonden i svensk historia*, 3:440–41; G. Nilsson, "Den verkningslösa unionen?" 53; Bjørnson, *Brevveksling med svenske*, 2:179, 3:93; Stig Hadenius and Torgny Nevéus, eds., *Majestät i närbild. Oscar II i brev och dagböcker* (Uppsala, 1960), 81, 109; Kaartvedt, "Unionen," 80; Lindberg, *1872–1914*, 70–71. Cf. F. Bull, "Bjørnson og Sverige," 211–12.

29. Lindgren, *Norway-Sweden*, 61; Stig Boberg, "Realitet och politisk argumentering i konsulatfrågan 1890–1891," *Scandia* 34 (1968): 24–65; G. Nilsson, "Unionen," 15.

30. Bjørnson, *Artikler og Taler*, 2:135–38, 197–99, 233–34, 501; Bjørnson, *Brevveksling med svenske*, 1:108–9; 2:74, 87, 104; 3:5–6; 37–38; F. Bull, *Bjørnstjerne Bjørnson*, 57–58, and "Bjørnson og Sverige," 225, 229, 262; Amdam and Keel, *Bjørnson*, 2:281–83.

31. See, e.g., Derry, *History of Modern Norway*, 86, 90–91, 139–40; Hallendorff, *Oskar I och Karl XV*, 137; Nils Elvander, *Harald Hjärne och konservatismen. Konservativ idédebatt i Sverige 1865–1922* (Uppsala, 1961), 187–96.

32. Bjørnson, *Brevveksling med svenske*, 2:82, 104; 3:6–7, 98, 110, 123–26, 131, 144, 227, 232; Bjørnson, *Artikler og Taler*, 2:400–1; Sørensen, *Bjørnstjerne Bjørnson*, 160. Cf. Andr. M. Hansen, "Tidens tankar," *Samtiden* 16 (1905): 121–22, and 17 (1906): 567–68; Sigurd Ibsen, "Da unionen løsnede," *Samtiden* 17 (1906): 197–236, esp. 231–36.

33. Sten Carlsson, "Norrmän i Sverige 1814–1905," in *Grupper och gestalter. Historiska studier* (Stockholm, 1964), 80–81.

34. Oscar Alin, *Unionens betydelse för Sverige* (Stockholm, 1896), esp. 9–13. Cf. his *Den svensk-norska unionen. Uppsatser och aktstycken*, 2 vols. (Stockholm, 1889–91), and *Fjärde artikeln i fredstraktaten i Kiel d. 4 jan. 1814* (Stockholm, 1899). See also [Rudolf Kjellén,] *Hvad har Sverige vunnit genom unionen med Norge? Ett väktarrop till svenska folket* (Stockholm, 1892); Rudolf Kjellén, "Nationalitetsidén," in *Svenska krusbär. En historiebok om Sverige och svenskarna*, ed. Björn Linnell and Mikael Löfgren (Stockholm, 1996), 276–96, esp. 294, and "Fosterlandet. Ett begreppsanalys" (1899), in *Nationell samling. Politiska och etiska fragment* (Stockholm, 1906), 162–71; Elvander, *Harald Hjärne*, 197–247, esp. 207, 211–20, 234–45.

35. Lindberg, *Kunglig utrikespolitik*, 94–133, esp. 113, 118–21, and 1872–1914, 95–100.

36. Paul Knaplund, ed., *British Views on Norwegian-Swedish Problems, 1880–1895: Selections from the Diplomatic Correspondence* (Oslo, 1952), esp. 173–74, 176; Adolf Hedin, *De ministeriella målen och unionen* (Stockholm, 1892); Elvander, *Harald Hjärne*, 220–21; Leif Kihlberg, *Ständigt i opposition 1888*, part 1 of *Dagens nyheter och demokratins genombrott*, 2 vols. (Stockholm, 1960), 82–88. Cf. Karl Staaf, "Tal för de norska gästerna hållet vid föreningen Verdandis 10-årsfest i Uppsala den 27 maj 1892," in *Berättare och förkunnare i svensk litteratur*, ed. Johannes Edfelt and Axel Strindberg (Stockholm, 1942), 250–56.

37. Knaplund, *British Views*, 253. Cf. Lindberg, *Kunglig utrikespolitik*, 98–99, 106–8, 114–16, 118–21, 231. On pro-unionist views in Norway at this time, see, e.g., Helge Danielsen, "Nasjonalisme i Høyre før 1905," in Øystein Sørensen, ed., *Jakten på det norske. Perspektiver på utviklingen av en norsk nasjonal identitet på 1800-tallet* (Oslo, 1998), 372–82.

38. Zeth Höglund, *Hjalmar Branting och hans livsgärning*, 2 vols. (Stockholm, 1928–29), 1:285–91.

39. Birgitta Rapp, *Richard Bergh — konstnär och kulturpolitiker 1890–1915* (Stockholm, 1978), chap. 2, esp. 62; Bjørnson, *Brevveksling med svenske*, 3:114, 121; Ellen Key, *Svensk eller storsvensk patriotism?* (Stockholm, 1899).

40. Knaplund, *British Views*, 264; Lindgren, *Norway-Sweden*, 75; Sten Carlsson, "Tvåkammarriksdagens första skede (1867–1921)," in *Riksdagen genom tiderna*, ed. Herman Schück et al. (Stockholm, 1985), 228.

41. Kjellén, *Hvad har Sverige vunnit?* Cf. Lindberg, 1872–1914, 119–24; Evert Vedung, "Norvegomani och fosterländskhet," in Værnø, *Fra arvefiende*, 85–86.

42. Bjørnstjerne Bjørnson, "Forhandling, bare forhandling, eller det, som kan føre til krig," *Samtiden* 15 (1904): 329–30. Sørensen, *Bjørnstjerne Bjørnson*, 135.

43. See Vedung, "Norvegomani," 92; Kaartvedt, "Unionen," 82–83; Halvdan Koht, "Tillit i Norden," *Samtiden* 17 (1906): 580–90, esp. 584–86; Erik Rudeng, "Forord. Tilbakeblikk på den svensk-norske unionen," in *Union & secession. Perspektiv på statsbildningsprocesser och riksupplösningar*, ed. Sven Eliæson and Ragnar Bjørk (Stockholm, 2000), 9–13. On the position of *Høyre* during the crisis years, see esp. Alf Kaartvedt, *Drømmen om borgerlig samling 1884–1918*, vol. 1 of *Høyres historie*, ed. Francis Sejersted, 4 vols. (Oslo, 1984); H. Danielsen, "Nasjonalisme"; Rolf Danielsen, "Samlingspartiet og unionen," *Historisk tidsskrift* (Nor.) 41 (1962): 303–20.

44. Lindgren, *Norway-Sweden*, 131; Fuglum, *Norge i støpeskjeen*, 116–18. The most detailed account of the dissolution crisis is Jörgen Weibull, *Inför unionsupplösningen 1905. Konsulatfrågan* (Stockholm, 1962).

45. Hadenius and Nevéus, *Majestät i närbild*, 140–46; Inga Zachau, *Prins Eugen, nationalromantikern* (Stockholm, 1989), 315–22. Cf. Larson, *Björnson*, 117; Terje I. Leiren, "Sigurd Ibsen and the Origins of National Monarchy in Norway," *Scandinavian Studies* 51 (1979): 392–412. Remarkably, only Zachau mentions the possible candidature of Prince Eugen; none of the works on Bjørnson do so. In a private letter dated 23 Nov. 1893, Knut Hamsun had suggested Prince Eugen as a suitable candidate for the throne of an independent Norway. Cited in Bjørn Fontander, *Käraste Pontus. Kronprins Gustafs brev under unionskrisen* (Stockholm, 1999), 113–14.

46. This account of the final years and dissolution of the union is based primarily on Lindgren's sober and even-handed treatment in *Norway-Sweden*. Cf. Boëthius, *Oskar II*, 226–27; Lindberg, *Kunglig utrikespolitik*, 148–58; Elvander, *Harald Hjärne*, 250–51.

47. F. Bull, *Bjørnstjerne Bjørnson*, 63, and "Bjørnson og Sverige," 259–63, 266; Bjørnson, *Artikler og Taler*, 2:259–64, 266, 397–99; Lindgren, *Sweden-Norway*, 113–14; Fuglum, *Norge i støpeskjeen*, 118–21. Cf. *Times* (London), 26 March, 1, 12, 18 April 1905; Fridtjof Nansen, *Norway and the Union with Sweden* (New York, 1905); Terje I. Leiren, "American Press Opinion and Norwegian Independence in 1905," in *Norwegian-American Studies*, vol. 27 (Northfield, MN, 1977), 224–42.

48. Prins Eugen, *Breven berätta. Upplevelser och iakttagelser. Åren 1886–1913* (Stockholm, 1942), 178; Rapp, *Richard Bergh*, 64–70; August Strindberg's articles in *Samlade skrifter*, ed. John Landquist, 55 vols. (Stockholm, 1912–19), 54:429–42. Cf. Leif Kihlberg, *Folktribunen Adolf Hedin* (Stockholm, 1972), and *Karl Staaf*, 2 vols. (Stockholm, 1962–63); Nils Edén, *Sweden for Peace* (Uppsala, 1905).

49. *Brand. Illustrerad socialistisk tidning* (1905), 1:1; 6:5, 7; 7:5–6; 9:1–2; Adolf Hedin, *Tal och skrifter*, ed. Valfrid Spångberg, 2 vols. (Stockholm, 1904, 1915), 2:313; Höglund, *Hjalmar Branting*, 1:365–71; Rapp, *Richard Bergh*, 65; Zeth Höglund, *Ned med vapnen. En vidräkning med militarismen* (Malmö, 1906); Koht, "Tillit i Norden," 588–90.

50. Vedung, "Norvegomani," 84–93.

51. Elvander, *Harald Hjärne*, 218; Lindberg, *Kunglig utrikespolitik*, 150–51, 153.

52. Boëthius, *Oskar II*, 163, 223; Elvander, *Harald Hjärne*, 185–256, esp. 187–220, 234–35, 241–42; Kjellén, *Nationell samling*, 1–18, 130–61, esp. 157–58; Knaplund, *British Views*, 180–81; Harald Hjärne in *Svenska Dagbladet* (Stockholm), 14 Feb., 9 March 1905; Lindgren, *Norway-Sweden*, 98–99.

53. "Det fria Norge," *Brand*, 7:5–6.

54. Evert Vedung,, "Varför ledde Norges secession 1905 inte till krig? *Scandia* 66 (2000): 251–68; Verner von Heidenstam, "Ett nytt 1809," in *Verner von Heidenstams samlade verk*, ed. Kate Bang and Fredrik Böök (Stockholm, 1944), 17:76; Weibull, *Inför unionsupplösningen*, 280–81; Hadenius and Nevéus, *Majestät i närbild*, 142–44; Prins Eugen, *Breven berätta*, 323–30.

55. Yngvar Nielsen, *Norge i 1905* (Kristiania, 1906), preface (n.p.), 12.

56. See Bjørnstjerne Bjørnson, "Vor synd og vor ydmygelse," *Samtiden* 17 (1906): 569–76, esp. 574–75; Koht, "Tillit i Norden," 587–88.

57. F. Bull, "Bjørnson og Sverige," 274; Strindberg, "Norge i Norden," *Samlade skrifter*, 54:432; Höglund, *Hjalmar Branting*, 1:370.

58. This ultimate conciliation is a basic theme of Lindgren's *Norway-Sweden*.

4. The Cultural Vision

1. Sven Nilsson, *Dagboksanteckningar under en resa från Södra Sverige till Nordlanden i Norge 1816* (Lund, 1879), 55, 67, 130. Copenhagen is still sometimes referred in Norway to as *Kongens By*— "the King's Town"—in common speech.

2. Arne Lidén, *Den norska strömningen i svensk litteratur under 1800-talet* (Uppsala, 1926), 13. Cf. *Jacob Aalls stockholmsreise 1823*, ed. Wilhelm Munthe (Oslo, 1944).

3. *Karl XIV Johan — en europeisk karriär*, Skrifter från Kungl, Husgerådskammaren 9 (Stockholm, 1998), 244–48. Also *Aschehougs og Gyldendals store norske leksikon* (Oslo, 1988), 10:68, 569; *Nationalencyklopedin* (Stockholm, 1994), 14:529.

4. *Hedvig Elisabeth Charlottas dagbok*, ed. Carl Carlsson Bonde and Cecilia af Klercker, 9 vols. (Stockholm, 1902–42), 9:366–67, 384, 409; *Excellensen Grefve A. F. Skjöldebrands memoarer*, ed. Henrik Schück, 5 vols. (Stockholm, 1903–4), 5:198–99, 223–24; Lidén, *Den norska strömningen*, 1–2, 7, 10, 12. For foreign visitors' views of Norway and Sweden during the preceding period, see. H. Arnold Barton, *Northern Arcadia: Foreign Travelers in Scandinavia, 1765–1815* (Carbondale, IL, 1998).

5. On foreign inspiration for the nineteenth-century rediscovery of the Nordic heritage in the Scandinavian lands, see Anton Blanck, *Den nordiska renässansen i 1700-talets litteratur* (Stockholm, 1911); Barton, *Northern Arcadia*, 176–77.

6. S. Nilsson, *Dagboksanteckningar*, 111–12; cf. ibid., 73, 116–17, 153, 174; *Hedvig Elisabeth Charlottas dagbok*, 9:409.

7. Anders Fredrik Skjöldebrand, *Picturesque Journey to the North Cape* (London, 1813); C. J. Fahlcrantz, August Anckarsvärd, and Michael Gustaf Anckarsvärd, *Samling af Svenska och Norrska Utsigter*, 2 vols. (Stockholm, 1830). Cf. Eva-Lena Bengtsson et al., *Konsten 1845–1890*, Signums svenska konsthistoria, vol. 10 (Lund, 2000), 419–20.

8. Nils Runeby, *Den nya världen och den gamla. Amerikabild och emigrationsuppfattning i Sverige, 1820–1860* (Uppsala, 1969); H. Arnold Barton, *A Folk Divided: Homeland Swedes and Swedish Americans, 1840–1940* (Carbondale, IL, 1994), chap. 1.

9. See Anne-Lise Seip, "Nation-Building Within the Union: Class and Culture in the Norwegian Nation-State in the Nineteenth Century," *Scandinavian Journal of History* 20 (1995): 35–50; Øystein Sørensen, *Bjørnstjerne Bjørnson og nasjonalismen* (Oslo, 1997), esp. 24–39; Øystein Sørensen, ed., *Jakten på det norske. Perspektiver på utviklingen av en norsk nasjonal indentitet på 1800-tallet* (Oslo, 1998); Oscar J. Falnes, *National Romanticism in Norway* (New York, 1933). Cf. E. J. Hobsbawm and Terrence Ranger, eds., *The Invention of Tradition* (Cambridge, 1983).

10. Cf. Knut Nygaard, *Nordmenns syn på Danmark og danskene i 1814 og de første selvstendighetsår* (Oslo, 1960).

11. For Swedish literature during the nineteenth century, see esp. E. N. Tigerstedt, ed., *Ny illustrerad svensk litteraturhistoria*, 2d ed., 6 vols. (Stockholm, 1965–67), vols. 3 and 4; Lars Lönnroth and Sven Delblanc, eds., *Den svenska litteraturen*, 7 vols. (Stockholm, 1987–90), vols. 2–4; E. N. Tigerstedt, *Svensk litteraturhistoria*, 4th ed. (Stockholm, 1971); Alrik Gustafson, *History of Swedish Literature* (Minneapolis, 1961); Lars Warme, *A History of Swedish Literature*, vol. 3 of *A History of the Scandinavian Literatures*, ed. Sven Rossel (Lincoln, NE, 1996).

12. Kristian Magnus Kommandantvold, *Nabo i speilet. Sverige i norsk litterært perspektiv* (Oslo, 1958), esp. 67–68, 73, 91, 96; Örjan Lindberger, *Wergeland och Sverige*

(Stockholm, 1947), esp. 180–81; Francis Bull, "Bjørnson og Sverige," in *Bjørnson-Studier,* ed. Gerhard Gran (Kristiania, 1911), 174–75, 262; Bjørnstjerne Bjørnson's poem "Under en reise i Sverige" (1866), in *Brevveksling med svenske 1858–1909,* ed. Øyvind Anker, Francis Bull, and Örjan Lindberger, 3 vols. (Oslo, 1960–61), 1:xi.

13. See, e.g., Knut Berg, ed., *Norges kunsthistorie,* 7 vols. (Oslo, 1981–83), vols. 2 and 3, and *Norges malerkunst,* 2 vols. (Oslo, 1993), vol. 1; Andreas Aubert, *Det nye Norges Malerkunst 1814–1900,* 2d ed. (Kristiania, 1908); Carl G. Laurin, Emil Hannover, and Jens Thiis, *Scandinavian Art* (New York, 1922); Niel Kent, *The Triumph of Light and Nature: Nordic Art, 1740–1940* (London, 1987); Torsten Gunnarsson, *Nordic Landscape Painting in the Nineteenth Century,* trans. Nancy Adler (New Haven, 1998).

14. Peter Christen Asbjørnsen and Jørgen Moe, *Norske Huldreeventyr og Folkesagn,* 2 vols (Christiania, 1845–48), and *Norske Folkeeventyr,* 2d ed. (Christiania, 1852). Cf. Falnes, *National Romanticism,* part 3, chaps. 12–15.

15. Finn Benestad and Dag Schjelderup-Ebbe, *Edvard Grieg: The Man and the Artist,* trans. William H. Halvorson and Leland B. Satheren (Lincoln, NE, 1988), esp. 43–44; Einar Haugen and Camilla Cai, *Ole Bull: Romantic Musician and Cosmopolitan Patriot* (Madison, WI, 1993), esp. chap. 11; A.-L. Seip, "Nation-Building," 42, 44; Hans Try, *To kulturer — en stat 1851–1884,* vol. 11 of *Norges historie,* ed. Knut Mykland (Oslo, 1979), 360, 364–65.

16. Kommandantvold, *Nabo i speilet,* 60–66; A.-L. Seip, "Nation-Building," 41; cf. Lindberger, *Wergeland och Sverige.* On Norwegian literature in the nineteenth century, see esp. Francis Bull et al., *Norsk litteraturhistorie,* 2d ed., 6 vols. (Olso, 1957–63), vols. 3 and 4; Edvard Beyer, ed., *Norges litteraturhistorie,* 8 vols. (Oslo, 1995–98), vols. 2–4; Harald Næss, "Norwegian Literature, 1800–1860," and James W. McFarlane, "Norwegian Literature, 1860–1910," in *A History of Norwegian Literature,* ed. Harald Næss (Lincoln, NE, 1993), 82–106, 107–99; Gudleiv Bø, "'Land og lynne' — norske digtere om nasjonal identitet," in Sørensen, *Jakten på det norske,* 112–24.

17. Rudolf Keyser, "Om Nordmændenes Herrkomst og Folke-Slægtskab," *Samlinger til det norske Folks Sprog og Historie* 4 (1839): 263–462; Peter Andreas Munch, *Forn-Swenskans (Swaensku ok Gözku) och Forn-Norskans (Norroenu) Språkbyggnad, jemte ett Bihang om den äldsta Runeskriften* (Stockholm, 1849), and *Det norske Folks Historie,* 8 vols. (Christiania, 1851–63). See also Sverre Steen, "Munch, Peter Andreas," *Norsk biografisk leksikon,* ed. Edvard Bull et al., vol. 9 (Oslo, 1940), 456–62; Ottar Dahl, *Norsk historieforskning i 19. og 20. århundre* (Oslo, 1970), 5, 36–80; Odd Arvid Storsveen, "Henrik Wergeland, P. A. Munch og historiens nasjonale funksjon," in Sørensen, *Jakten på det norske,* 229–42; Bo Grandien, *Rönndruvans glöd. Nygöticistiskt i tanke, konst och miljö under 1800-talet* (Stockholm, 1987), 82–83; Lidén, *Den norska strömningen,* 55–56; Jöran Mjöberg, *Drömmen om sagatiden,* 2 vols. (Stockholm, 1967–68), 1:9–11, 224–25, 18–20; Falnes, *National Romanticism,* chaps. 6 and 7, esp. 123–42.

18. Rudolf Keyser, *Efterladte Skrifter,* 3 vols. (Christiania, 1866–67), 1:12, 21; Peter Andreas Munch, *Samlede Afhandlinger,* 4 vols. (Christiania, 1873–76), 1:122.

19. Snorri Sturlason's *Heimskringla* has appeared in many Scandinavian and eventually other translations since the sixteenth century. Cf. Snorri Sturlason, *Heimskringla: History of the Kings of Norway,* trans. and ed. Lee Hollander (Austin, TX, 1964), 6–13. Cf. Barton, *Northern Arcadia,* 154–55.

20. Lidén, *Den norska strömningen,* 179. The work reviewed was the first part of Ernst

Sars's *Udsigt over den norske Historie,* 4 vols. (Christiania, 1879). On Sars, see Dahl, *Norsk historieforskning,* 93–101, 154–95

21. Alf Kaartvedt, "Karl Johan i Norge. Författningskamp och utrikespolitik," in *Karl XIV Johan — en europeisk karriär,* 136–38. On the conservative school of Norwegian historians, see Dahl, *Norsk historieforskning,* 115–53.

22. Eilert Sundt, *Om Bygnings-Skikken paa Landet i Norge* (Christiania, 1862), and *Husfliden i Norge* (Christiania, 1867). Cf. Grandien, *Rönndruvans glöd,* 222.

23. Ivar Aasen, *Det norske Folkesprogs Grammatik* (Christiania, 1848), and *Ordbog over det norske Folkesprog* (Christiania, 1850); Knud Knudsen, *Om Lydene, Lydtegnene og Retskrivningen i det norske Sprog* (Christiania, 1845), *Haandbog i dansk-norsk Sproglære* (Christiania, 1856), and *Det norske Maalstræv* (Christiania, 1867). Cf. Falnes, *National Romanticism,* part 4 (chaps. 16–20); Per Amdam and Aldo Keel, *Bjørnstjerne Bjørnson,* 2 vols. (Oslo, 1993, 1999), 2:169–73; Per Fuglum, *Norge i støpesjkeen 1884–1920,* vol. 12 of *Norges historie,* ed. Knut Mykland (Oslo, 1978), 413–16.

24. Kommandantvold, *Nabo i speilet,* 91–93; Lorenz Dietrichson, *En norrmans minnen från Sverige,* trans. Klara Johansson, 2 vols. (Stockholm, 1901–02), 1:9–11, 67. Cf. Theodore Jorgensen, *Norway's Relation to Scandinavian Unionism, 1815–1871* (Northfield, MN, 1935); John Sanness, *Patrioter, intelligens og skandinaver. Norske reaksjoner på skandinavismen før 1848* (Oslo, 1959).

25. Dietrichson, *En norrmans minnen,* 1:8–20, 32; Bjørnstjerne Bjørnson, "Hvorledes jeg blev Digter," in *Artikler og Taler,* ed. C. Collin and H. Eitrem (Kristiania, 1912–13), 2:137–42.

26. McFarlane, "Norwegian Literature," 130–31; Åsmund Svendsen, "Konfliktlinjer i historiefaget 1860–1905," in Sørensen, *Jakten på det norske,* 255.

27. On Bjørnson, his nationalism, and his Scandinavianism, see esp. F. Bull, "Bjørnson og Sverige"; Francis Bull, *Bjørnstjerne Bjørnson* (Kristiania, 1923); Harold Larson, *Björnstjerne Björnson: A Study in Norwegian Nationalism* (New York, 1944); Amdam and Keel, *Bjørnstjerne Bjørnson;* Sørensen, *Bjørnstjerne Bjørnson,* esp. 29–31, 93–94 (for his views on history); Ellen Key, "Björnson och Sverige," in *Bjørnstjerne Bjørnson. Festskrift i Anledning af hans 70 Aars Fødelsedag* (Copenhagen, 1902), 41–69.

28. Dietrichson, *En norrmans minnen,* 1:29, 33.

29. Haugen and Cai, *Ole Bull,* 52, 73–74, 145, 152; *Aftonbladet,* 9 Jan. 1843, cited in Lidén, *Den norska strömningen,* 52.

30. Lidén, *Den norska strömningen,* 141–42. Cf. Leif Jonsson and Martin Tegen, *Musiken i Sverige,* 4 vols. (Stockholm, 1992–94), vol. 3; Gregor Andersson, ed., *Musik i Norden* (Stockholm, 1997); G. Jeanson, *August Söderman. En svensk tonsättares liv och verk* (Stockholm, 1926), esp. 82, 88, 92, 272–75, 337; John Horton, *Scandinavian Music: A Short History* (London, 1963).

31. Andreas Lindblom, *Sveriges konsthistoria* (Stockholm, 1947), 842–45, 848–50, 852–53; Laurin et al., *Scandinavian Art,* 128–50; Lidén, *Den norska strömningen,* 55, 141; Torsten Gunnarsson, "Det svenska akademiska måleriet under 1850–1880-talen," in *1880-tal i nordiskt måleri,* ed. Knut Berg, exhibition catalog (Stockholm, 1986), 313–51, and "Landskapsmåleriet," in Bengtsson et al., *Konsten 1845–1890,* 403–61; Gunnarsson, *Nordic Landscape Painting;* Kent, *Triumph of Light and Nature;* Dietrichson, *En norrmans minnen,* 2:72.

32. A.-L. Seip, "Nation-Building," 43. Cf., e.g., Leonard Fredrik Rääf, *Samlingar och anteckningar till en beskrifning öfver Ydre härad i Östergötland*, 5 vols. (Linköping, 1856–75); Nils Månsson Mandelgren's uncompleted *Atlas till Sveriges odlingshistoria* (Stockholm, 1883–84), several parts of which for different provinces have recently been published; Gunnar Hyltén-Cavallius, *Wärend och wirdarne*, 2 vols. (Stockholm, 1863–68); Nils Gabriel Djurklou, *Ur Nerikes folkspråk och folklif* (Örebro, 1860).

33. Arne Biörnstad, ed., *Skansen under hundra år* (Stockholm, 1991), esp. Bo Grandien, "Grogrunden. Tiden före 1891," 9–31; Fredrik Böök, *Artur Hazelius. En levnadsteckning* (Stockholm, 1923); Harald Hals, "Artur Hazelius og Norge," *Fataburen* 1945, 101–12; Tonte Hegard, *Romantikk og fortidsvern. Historien om de første friluftsmuseene i Norge* (Oslo, 1984), esp. 191–212.

34. Lidén, *Den norska strömningen*, 52–56.

35. Mjöberg, *Drömmen om sagatiden*, 2:20–32, 143–51; Grandien, *Rönndruvans glöd*, 112–15; Erica Simon, *Réveil national et culture populaire en Scandinavie: La genèse de la højskole nordique, 1844–1878* (Paris, 1960), 703. Cf. Tigerstedt, *Svensk litteraturhistoria*, 18–19.

36. August Gödecke, "En resa i Norge," *Land och Folk. Tidskrift utgifven af Sällskapet för Nyttiga Kunskapers Spridande* (1873): 308–9. On the significance attached to the Ramsundsberget and Rök finds, see Grandien, *Rönndruvans glöd*, 139, 292. On Gödecke, see H. Arnold Barton, "Peter August Gödecke, den svenska folkhögskolan och Norge," *Personhistorisk tidskrift* 98 (2002): 5–20.

37. Carl Säve, "Sigurds-ristningarne å Ramsundsberget och Gök-stenen. Tvänne fornsvenska minnesmärken om Sigurd Fafnesbane," *Kungl. Vitterhets, historie och antikvitetsakademiens handlingar*, ny följd, 6 (Stockholm, 1868): 321–64; Mjöberg, *Drömmen om sagatiden*, 2:146; Sven B. F. Jansson, *The Runes of Sweden* (Stockholm, 1962).

38. Lidén, *Den norska strömningen*, 45–51. Cf. Lindberger, *Wergeland och Sverige*, 131–48. Cf. Fredrika Bremer, *Strife and Peace; or, Scenes in Norway* (Boston, 1843).

39. F. Bull, *Bjørnstjerne Bjørnson*, 8–11; Larson, *Björnson*, 32–34; Lidén, *Den norska strömningen*, 68–73; McFarlane, "Norwegian Literature," 132–33.

40. Lidén, *Den norska strömningen*, 59–64, 73–75; Dietrichson, *En norrmans minnen*, 1:61–62.

41. Bjørnson, *Brevveksling med svenske*, 1:1, 124–26, 185–88, 235, 2:23; Lotten Dahlgren, *Lyran. Interiörer från 1870- och 1880-talens konstnärliga och litterära Stockholm* (Stockholm, 1913), 278–92; Key, "Björnson och Sverige," 62; Ulf Wittrock, *Ellen Keys väg från kristendom till livstro* (Uppsala, 1953), chap. 4.

42. Dietrichson, *En norrmans minnen*, 1:19–20, 32, 113, 134–35. Cf. Dahlgren, *Lyran*, 264–68.

43. Dietrichson, *En norrmans minnen*, 1:61–62, 138–42.

44. August Strindberg, *Tjänstekvinnans son*, in *Samlade skrifter*, ed. John Landquist, 55 vols. (Stockholm, 1912–19), 18:350–54. *Tjänstekvinnans son* is the general title for Strindberg's four-volume fictionalized autobiography but also, rather confusingly, for its first volume (1886). The volumes that followed are separately entitled *Jäsningstiden* (1886), *I röda rummet* (1887), and *Författaren* (1909) and are hereafter referred to under their individual volume titles. See also August Strindberg, "Den litterära reaktionen i

Sverige," in *Samlade skrifter*, 17:207–8, 216; Dietrichson, *En norrmans minnen*, 1:145–213, esp. 161–71; Fredrik Böök, "Litteraturen under adertonhundratalets senare hälft (1850–1908)," in Boëthius, *Oskar II*, 355–56; Lars Lönnroth and Sven Delblanc, eds., *De liberala genombrotten 1830–1890*, vol. 3 of *Den svenska litteraturen*, 7 vols. (Stockholm, 1987–90), 147.

45. Dietrichson, *En norrmans minnen*, 1:143–45. Overall, regarding Dietrichson's years in Sweden, see also Lidén, *Den norska strömningen*, 80–99.

46. Dietrichson, *En norrmans minnen*, 1:5–7, 27; 2:8–9, 16, 243; Lidén, *Den norska strömningen*, 143–47.

47. Henrik Ibsen, *Brand* (1866), in *The Oxford Ibsen*, ed. James McFarlane et al., vol. 3 (London, 1972). Michael Meyer, in his *Ibsen: A Biography* (New York, 1971), 175–77, questions whether Ibsen actually had read much Kierkegaard, but the philosopher's influence was pervasive at the time.

48. Lidén, *Den norska strömningen*, 102–34, esp. 132–33, 136; Kommandantvold, *Nabo i speilet*, 108; Gurli Linder, *Sällskapsliv i Stockholm under 1880- och 1890-talen. Några minnesbilder* (Stockholm, 1918); Fredrik Böök, *Sveriges moderna litteratur* (Stockholm, 1921), 72 (a work that is summarized in Böök, "Litteraturen 1850–1908"). Also see Gustafson, *History of Swedish Literature*, 246–47.

49. Lidén, *Den norska strömningen*, 135; Gustafson, *History of Swedish Literature*, 246–48.

50. Lidén, *Den norska strömningen*, 227–56, 276–89; Gustafson, *History of Swedish Literature*, 246–47; Olof Lagercrantz, *August Strindberg* (Stockholm, 1979), 101; Michael Meyer, *Strindberg: A Biography* (London, 1985), 25.

51. Böök, *Sveriges moderna litteratur*, 66–68; Lönnroth and Delblanc, *De liberala genombrotten*, 178; Lars Lönnroth and Sven Delblanc, eds., *Den storsvenska generationen 1890–1920*, vol. 4 of *Den svenska litteraturen* (Stockholm, 1989), 9.

52. Böök, *Sveriges moderna litteratur*, 81–84, 131–32; Gustafson, *History of Swedish Literature*, 151–52; Lönnroth and Delblanc, *De liberala genombrotten*, 210–19; Bjørnson, *Brevveksling med svenske*, 2:268–69. Cf., e.g., Anne Charlotte Leffler, *Ur lifvet*, 5 vols. (Stockholm, 1882–90), and *Kampen för lyckan* (Stockholm, 1887); Ernst Ahlgren [Victoria Benedictsson], *Pengar* (Stockholm, 1885); Alfhild Agrell, *Räddad* (Stockholm, 1883), and *Dömd* (Stockholm, 1884).

53. Dietrichson, *En norrmans minnen*, 2:36–37, 173.

54. Ibid., 2:172–73. Georg Sibbern had served as Norwegian minister of state in Stockholm. The Royal Norwegian Guards Regiment, together with the Swedish Guards Regiment, was stationed in Stockholm. Hans Rasmus Astrup and Niels Georg Sørensen were partners in the Swedish timber trade. Astrup returned to Norway in 1885, where he became a prominent member of the Storting and the *Venstre* party. On Sørensen, who remained in Stockholm, married into the Swedish nobility, and became one of the city's wealthiest citizens, see Anna von Ajkay, *Fersenska palatset. Tradition och förnyelse på Blasieholmen* (Stockholm, 1977), 97–99, 103, 132–37.

55. Key, "Björnson och Sverige," 41–69, esp. 49; Dahlgren, *Lyran*, 278–92; Annie Åkerhielm et al., *Anna Hierta-Retzius. En minnesanteckning med stöd av efterlämnade papper* (Stockholm, 1928), 84; F. Bull, "Bjørnson og Sverige," 188–96, 206; Lidén, *Den norska strömningen*, 149–50, 154–56; Grandien, *Rönndruvans glöd*, 134–35, 332.

56. Henrik Ibsen, *Peer Gynt*, act 4; Meyer, *Ibsen*, 213–15, 226, 291–94, 584–89; Dahlgren, *Lyran*, 269–77; Kommandantvold, *Nabo i speilet*, 24; Lidén, *Den norska strömningen*, 169.

57. Meyer, *Ibsen*, 329–30, 333–35, 426–28. On Oscar II's literary interests, cf. Germund Michanek, *Skaldernas konung*. *Oscar II, litteraturen och litteratören* (Stockholm, 1979), esp. 121–28.

58. Gödecke, "Resa i Norge," 195; [August Gödecke], *Turistbref från en resa i Norge sommaren 1875 af Finn* (Stockholm, 1876). Cf. Gurli Linder, *På den tiden. Några bilder från 1870-talets Stockholm* (Stockholm, 1924), 328–29; Grandien, *Rönndruvans glöd*, 136–40. Cf. Barton, "Gödecke"; Bo Grandien, "Landskap och människa," in *Historiens vingeslag. Konst, historia & ornitologi* (Stockholm, 1988), 33–51.

59. Gödecke, "Resa i Norge," 6, 8–9, 12, 26–30, 198–99, 202, 301, 321–22, 314–16, and *Turistbref*, 21, 25–29, 41, 83, 102–3, 110–18, 138–39, 202–6.

60. Gödecke, "Resa i Norge," 15–19, 22–26. Although the modern spelling is *seter*, I use the older form, *sæter* (pl., *sætre*), as it should be more recognizable to English-speaking readers.

61. Ibid., 222–28; cf. Gödecke, *Turistbref*, 36–68.

62. Gödecke, "Resa i Norge," 308–9, 319–21.

63. Ibid., 322–26; Gödecke, *Turistbref*, 147–48.

64. Gödecke, "Resa i Norge," 323; E. K., "Här och der i Thelemarken," *Ny illustrerad Tidning* 13 (1877): 274.

65. Gunnel Weidel, *På fotvandring i Norge med Ellen Key* (Linköping, 1974), esp. 3, 5–7; Bjørnson, *Brevveksling med svenske*, 1:335–36. Cf. Wittrock, *Ellen Keys väg*, 118–24.

66. See esp. Grandien, *Rönndruvans glöd*, part 4. Cf. Dietrichson, *En norrmans minnen*, 228–29; Åkerhielm et al., *Anna Hierta-Retzius*, 103; Eilert Sundt, "Om Bygnings-Skikken paa Landet i Norge," *Tidskrift för byggnadskonst och ingeniörsvetenskap* 5 (1863): 26–32, 48–52, 68–74, 102–5, 129–31, 163–71, and "Bygnings-Skikken paa Landet i Norge," *Tidskrift för byggnadskonst och ingeniörsvetenskap* 7 (1865): 1–4, 78–81, 125–28.

67. Bjørnson, *Brevveksling med svenske*, 1:xii–xiii, 219.

68. Strindberg, *Tjänstekvinnans son*, 396, 450.

69. Dag Thorkildsen, "En nasjonal og moderne utdanning," in Sørensen, *Jakten på det norske*, 265–84; F. Bull, *Bjørnstjerne Bjørnson*, 29–31; Dietrichson, *En norrmans minnen*, 2:57; Grandien, *Rönndruvans glöd*, 100, 105–6, 108–9, 134–35; Lidén, *Den norska strömningen*, 154–60; Mjöberg, *Drömmen om sagatiden*, 2:45–46, 128. Cf. Simon's classic study, *Réveil national*; Barton, "Gödecke," 7–11.

70. Lidén, *Den norska strömningen*, 58–59, 136; Grandien, *Rönndruvans glöd*, 79, 88, 93–100, 131, 233–37; Gustafson, *History of Swedish Literature*, 248–51; Dietrichson, *En norrmans minnen*, 2:53; Strindberg, *Tjänstekvinnans son*, 347–50; *Brand. Illustrerad socialistisk tidning* (1905), 1:1.

71. Lidén, *Den norska strömningen*, 136–38; Simon, *Réveil national*, 706–7; Gunnar Broberg, ed., *Gyllene äpplen. Svensk idéhistorisk läsebok*, 2 vols. (Stockholm, 1991), 1:652–53; Grandien, *Rönndruvans glöd*, 88–91, 100–104, 219–20.

5. Norway and the Swedish Self-Image

1. Arne Lidén, *Den norska strömningen i svensk litteratur under 1800-talet* (Uppsala, 1926), 85–86.
2. Ibid., chap. 6.
3. [Torsten Eklund, ed.,] *Före Röda rummet. Strindbergs ungdomsjournalistik i urval av Torsten Eklund*, Strindbergssällskapets skrifter, vol. 1 (Stockholm, 1946), 127; August Strindberg, *Samlade skrifter*, ed. John Landquist, 55 vols. (Stockholm, 1912–19), 13:132–36. Cf. Lidén, *Den norska strömningen*, 258.
4. August Strindberg, "Nationalitet och svenskhet," in *Samlade skrifter*, 16:143–71, esp. 149, 152–53. Cf. *Svenska krusbär. En historiebok om Sverige och svenskarna*, ed. Björn Linnell and Mikael Löfgren (Stockholm, 1996), 200–201.
5. August Strindberg, *Jäsningstiden*, in *Samlade skrifter*, 18:354–55, 358.
6. Ibid., 358. Cf. George Drysdale, *The Elements of Social Science or Physical, Sexual, and Natural, Religion* (London, 1883; Swedish trans., 1884); Max Nordau, *Die conventionelle Lügen der Kulturmenschheit* (Leipzig, 1883; Swedish trans. 1884); Olof Lagercrantz, *August Strindberg*, trans. Anselm Hollo (London, 1984), 166–67; Lars Lönnroth and Sven Delblanc, eds., *De liberala genombrotten 1830–1890*, vol. 3 of *Den svenska litteraturen*, 7 vols. (Stockholm, 1987–90), 186–87.
7. August Strindberg, *Giftas. Äktenskapshistorier*, part 1, vol. 14 of *Samlade skrifter*, esp. 7–36, 37–77, 188–210; Michael Meyer, *Strindberg: A Biography* (London, 1985), 130–34; *Strindberg's Letters*, trans. and ed. Michael Robinson, 2 vols. (Chicago, 1992), 1:160. Cf. Lönnroth and Delblanc, *De liberala genombrotten*, 227–29.
8. August Strindberg, *Giftas. Äktenskapshistorier*, part 2, vol. 15 of *Samlade skrifter*, esp. 226–40. Cf. Strindberg, *Jäsningstiden*, 265.
9. Michael Meyer, *Ibsen: A Biography* (New York, 1971), 465–66, 591, 732.
10. August Strindberg, *Författaren*, in *Samlade skrifter*, 19:197–98.
11. Bjørnstjerne Bjørnson, *Brevveksling med svenske 1858–1909*, ed. Øyvind Anker, Francis Bull, and Örjan Lindberger, 3 vols. (Oslo, 1960–61), 2:124, 176–78. Volume 2 of that work includes for the first time the entire correspondence between Bjørnson and Strindberg.
12. Strindberg, *Författaren*, 198–201; August Strindberg, "Björnstjerne Björnson," in *Samlade skrifter*, 17:234–45; Meyer, *Strindberg*, 121–22; Henrik Schück and Karl Warburg, *Illustrerad svensk litteraturhistoria*, 2d ed., 4 vols. (Stockholm, 1911–16), 4:2:475n.
13. Per Amdam and Aldo Keel, *Bjørnstjerne Bjørnson*, 2 vols. (Oslo, 1993, 1999), 2:135–41; Bjørnson, *Brevveksling med svenske*, 2:207–21; Strindberg, *Författaren*, 201–3; *Strindberg's Letters*, 1:157–59, 162–63, 165, 167.
14. Strindberg, *Samlade skrifter*, 23:508. Cf. Meyer, *Ibsen*, 591.
15. Ellen Key, "Björnson och Sverige," in *Bjørnstjerne Bjørnson. Festskrift i Anledning af hans 70 Aars Fødelsedag* (Copenhagen, 1902).
16. "Under en reise i Sverige," quoted in Bjørnson, *Brevveksling med svenske*, 1:1:xi. See also 3:190.
17. See, e.g., Bjørnson, *Brevveksling med svenske*, 3:170. Cf. Olle Gellerman, *S. A. Hedlund — legendarisk tidningsman och liberal politiker* (Stockholm, 1998), 153–54.
18. Staffan Björck, *Heidenstam och sekelskiftets Sverige* (Stockholm, 1946), 71–72, 168.

19. Verner von Heidenstam, *Renässans. Några ord om en annalkande ny brytningstid inom litteraturen*, in *Uppsatser och tal* (Stockholm, 1930), 7–37, reprinted in *Verner von Heidenstams samlade verk*, ed. Kate Bang and Fredrik Böök, 23 vols. (Stockholm, 1943–44), vol. 18. Cf. Oscar Levertin and Verner von Heidenstam, *Pepitas bröllop. En litteraturanmälan* (Stockholm, 1890). See also Björck, *Heidenstam*, 74, 181–84; Fredrik Böök, *Verner von Heidenstam*, 2 vols. (Stockholm, 1945–46), 1:184–85; Alrik Gustafson, *A History of Swedish Literature* (Minneapolis, 1961), 253.

20. Verner von Heidenstam, *Dikter*, in *Samlade verk*, 6:178–80. Cf. Björck, *Heidenstam*, 76–77.

21. Björck, *Heidenstam*, 30–31, 74, 78, 93; Bjørnson, *Brevveksling med svenske*, 3:10–11.

22. Kristian Magnus Kommandantvold, *Nabo i speilet. Sverige i norsk litterært perspektiv* (Oslo, 1958), 148; Gustaf Fröding, "Om humor" and "Björnstjerne Björnson" [1], in *Prosa* (Stockholm, 1935), 31–37, 110–13. Cf. Gustafson, *History of Swedish Literature*, 318–19; Fredrik Böök, *Sveriges moderna litteratur* (Stockholm, 1921), 181.

23. Böök, *Sveriges moderna litteratur*, 181; Gustafson, *History of Swedish Literature*, 252–53; Lars Lönnroth and Sven Delblanc, eds., *Den storsvenska generationen 1890–1920*, vol. 4 of *Den svenska litteraturen* (Stockholm, 1989), 16, 73. Cf. August Strindberg, *Ordalek och småkonst* (Stockholm, 1905).

24. Kommandantvold, *Nabo i speilet*, 148–49; James W. McFarlane, "Norwegian Literature, 1860–1910," in *A History of Norwegian Literature*, ed. Harald Næss (Lincoln, NE, 1993), 184–94; Meyer, *Ibsen*, 276–77.

25. At the very time I was beginning to see Swedish national romanticism in terms of a reaction against Norwegian influences, the American art historian Michelle Facos was independently reaching the same conclusion, most specifically in the area of art; see her "Norway and the Definition of Swedish National Identity," in *The Dividing Line: Borders and National Peripheries*, ed. Lars-Folke Lindgren and Maunu Häyrynen (Helsinki, 1997), 87–101, esp. 87, 90, and *Nationalism and the Nordic Imagination: Swedish Art of the 1890s* (Berkeley, 1998). It should, however, be noted that the term *Nasjonalromantikk* has sometimes been used to describe a particular trend *within* Norwegian neoromantic art during the late nineteenth century toward fable and decorative symbolism. See, e.g., Leif Østby, *Fra naturalisme til nyromantikk. En studie i norsk malerkunst* (Oslo, 1934), chap. 4.

26. The literature on aspects of Swedish national romanticism is immense. For a thought-provoking overview of the time, see Gunnar Broberg, "När svenskarna uppfann Sverige. Anteckningar till ett hundraårsjubileum," in *Tänka, tycka, tro. Sveriges historia underifrån*, ed. Gunnar Broberg, Ulla Wikander, and Klas Åmark (Stockholm, 1993), 171–96.

27. Böök, *Sveriges moderna litteratur*, 173–74.

28. For general characterizations of Swedish literary national romanticism, see, e.g., Böök, *Sveriges moderna litteratur*; E. N. Tigerstedt, *Svensk litteraturhistoria*, 4th ed. (Stockholm, 1971); E. N. Tigerstedt, ed., *Ny illustrerad svensk litteraturhistoria*, 2d ed., 6 vols. (Stockholm, 1965–67), vol. 4; Lönnroth and Delblanc, *Den storsvenska generationen*; Gustafson, *History of Swedish Literature*; Lars Warme, *A History of Swedish Literature*, vol. 3 of *A History of the Scandinavian Literatures*, ed. Sven Rossel (Lincoln, NE, 1996); Selma Lagerlöf, *Gösta Berlings saga* (1891; Stockholm, 1971), 265.

29. Verner von Heidenstam, *Dikter* (Stockholm, 1895), *Ett folk* (Stockholm, 1902), *Karolinerna*, 2 vols. (Stockholm, 1897–98), *Folkungaträdet*, 2 vols. (Stockholm, 1905–7), *Svenskarne och deras hövdingar*, 2 vols. (Stockholm, 1908–10).

30. Oscar Levertin, *Från Gustaf III:s dagar* (Stockholm, 1896), *Rococonoveller* (Stockholm, 1899). Cf. Henrik Schück and Oscar Levertin, eds., *Svenska memoarer och bref*, 11 vols. (Stockholm, 1900–1918), containing letters and memoirs from the Gustavian era; Georg Landberg, *Gustaf III inför eftervärlden* (Stockholm, 1968), 63–73; Lagerlöf, *Gösta Berlings saga*, and *Drottningar i Kungahälla* (Stockholm, 1899), *En herrgårdssägen* (Stockholm, 1899).

31. Gustaf Fröding, *Gitarr och dragharmonika* (Stockholm, 1891), *Nya dikter* (Stockholm, 1894), *Räggler å pasascher*, 2 vols. (Stockholm, 1895–97). See also Ebbe Schön, "Folkets sångmö. Nittiotlisterna och folkkulturen," *Fataburen 1991.90 tal* (Stockholm, 1991), 19–43.

32. Erik Axel Karlfeldt, *Vildmarks- och kärleksvisor* (Stockholm, 1895), *Fridolins visor och andra dikter* (Stockholm, 1898), *Fridolins lustgård och Dalmålningar på rim* (Stockholm, 1901).

33. Selma Lagerlöf, *Jerusalem*, 2 vols. (Stockholm, 1901–2).

34. See, e.g., Richard Bergström, "En ny vetenskap," in *Litteratur och natur* (Stockholm, 1889), reprinted in *Svenska krusbär*, 213–16; Sigfrid Svensson, *Från gammalt till nytt på 1800-talets svenska landsbygd* (Stockholm, 1977), and *Bygd och yttervärld. Studier över förhållandet mellan nyheter och tradition* (Stockholm, 1979).

35. See esp. Fredrik Böök, *Artur Hazelius. En levnadsteckning* (Stockholm, 1923); Arne Biörnstad, ed., *Skansen under hundra år* (Stockholm, 1991); *Skansen: Traditional Swedish Style* (Stockholm and London, 1995). Also see H. Arnold Barton, "Skansen and the Swedish Americans," *Swedish-American Historical Quarterly* 48 (1997): 164–80.

36. Gustaf af Geijerstam, "Hur tankarna komma och gå. Intryck från Skansen," *Ord och Bild* 1 (1892): 18–27; Karl-Erik Forsslund, *Storgården. En bok om ett hem* (Stockholm, 1900), and *Hembygdsvård*, 2 vols. (Stockholm, 1914), esp. 2:133–34; Göran Rosander, *Karl-Erik Forsslund: Författaren, folkbildaren, hembygdsvårdaren* (Hedemora, 1991); Gustaf Näsström, *Dalarna som svenskt ideal* (Stockholm, 1937).

37. On the national romantic revival and the creation of folk tradition, see, e.g., Nils-Arvid Bringæus, *Årets festseder* (Stockholm, 1976); Barbro Klein and Mats Widbom, eds., *Swedish Folk Art: All Tradition Is Change* (New York, 1994); H. Arnold Barton, "Cultural Interplay Between Sweden and Swedish America," *Swedish-American Historical Quarterly* 43 (1992): 5–18. Cf. E. J. Hobsbawm and Terrence Ranger, eds., *The Invention of Tradition* (Cambridge, 1983), esp. Hobsbawm's introductory essay.

38. Alex. Olsson, *På turistfärd genom Amerika och Europa* (San Francisco, 1909), 57.

39. See, e.g., Barton, "Cultural Interplay."

40. See, e.g., Per Fuglum, *Norge i støpeskjeen 1884–1920*, vol. 12 of *Norges historie*, ed. Knut Mykland (Oslo, 1978), 409–16; Tonte Hegard, *Romantikk og fortidsvern. Historien om de første friluftsmuseene i Norge* (Oslo, 1984), 150, 153, 185–87.

41. Facos, "Norway," 87. On Swedish art, including its wider Scandinavian context, see Andreas Lindblom, *Sveriges konsthistoria* (Stockholm, 1947); Carl G. Laurin, Emil Hannover, and Jens Thiis, *Scandinavian Art* (New York, 1922); Carl G. Laurin, *Sverige genom konstnärsögon* (Stockholm, 1911); Kirk Varnedoe, [ed.,] *Northern Light: Realism*

and *Symbolism in Scandinavian Painting, 1880–1910* (Brooklyn, 1982); Kirk Varnedoe, [ed.,] *Northern Light: Nordic Art at the Turn of the Century* (New Haven, 1988); Niel Kent, *The Triumph of Light and Nature: Nordic Art, 1740–1940* (London, 1987); Facos, *Nationalism*; Torsten Gunnarsson, *Nordic Landscape Painting in the Nineteenth Century*, trans. Nancy Adler (New Haven, 1998); Eva-Lena Bengtsson et al., *Konsten 1845–1890*, Signums svenska konsthistoria, vol. 10 (Lund, 2000); Jan Torsten Ahlstrand et al., *Konsten 1890–1915*, Signums svenska konsthistoria, vol. 11 (Lund, 2001).

42. Bo Lindwall, "Konstnärsrevolterna," and Torsten Gunnarsson, "Det svenska akademiska måleriet under 1850–1880-talen," in *1880-tal i nordiskt måleri*, ed. Knut Berg, exhibition catalog (Stockholm, 1986), 17–24, 313–26.

43. Lindwall, "Konstnärsrevolterna"; Facos, *Nationalism*, 7–26; Bo Lindwall, "Artistic Revolution in the Nordic Countries," and Salme Savajas-Korte, "The Scandinavian Artists' Colony in France," in Varnedoe, *Northern Light: Realism*, 35–42, 60–66; Georg Pauli, *Pariserpojkarne* (Stockholm, 1926), and *Opponenterna* (Stockholm, 1927). On the close comradeship between Norwegian and Swedish artists in Paris, see Christian Skredsvig's nostalgic reminiscences, *Dage og nætter bland kunstnere* (Christiania, 1908).

44. Gunnarsson, *Nordic Landscape Painting*, 165–66.

45. Ibid., chap. 4; Sixten Ringbom, "Nordiskt 80-tal: luft och ljus," in Berg, *1880-tal i nordiskt måleri*, 7–16; Knut Berg, ed., *Norges kunsthistorie*, 7 vols. (Oslo, 1981–83), 5:109–210.

46. Cf. Bo Lindwall, ed., *Konstnärskolonin i Grèz* (Viken, 1993).

47. Knut Berg and Oscar Thue, "Sosial tendens-kunst," in Berg, *1880-tal i nordiskt måleri*, 25–32, esp. 29–32.

48. See Knud Voss, *Skagensmalerne* (Copenhagen, 1986).

49. Richard Bergh, "Svenskt konstnärskynne," in *Om konst och annat* (Stockholm, 1908), 146–64, esp. 148. Cf. *Svenska krusbär*, 314–31; Lindblom, *Sveriges konsthistoria*, 878; Inga Zachau, *Prins Eugen, nationalromantikern* (Stockholm, 1989), 88–90.

50. Bergh, "Svenskt konstnärskynne," 152–53, 164; Georg Pauli, *Konstnärsbrev*, 2 vols. (Stockholm, 1928), 1:32–33.

51. Prins Eugen, *Breven berätta. Upplevelser och iakttagelser. Åren 1886–1913* (Stockholm, 1942), 83. Cf. Zachau, *Prins Eugen*, 88–90.

52. Richard Bergh, "Målaren Ernst Josephson," in *Om konst och annat*, 72–74; Facos, *Nationalism*, 97.

53. Østby, *Fra naturalisme til nyromantikk*; Berg, *Norges kunsthistorie*, 5:109–210; Gunnarsson, *Nordic Landscape Painting*, 206–12; Marit Ingeborg Lange, "Fra den hellige lund til Fleskum. Kitty L. Kielland og den nordiske sommernatt," *Kunst og Kultur* 60 (1977): 69–92; Meret Werenskiold, "Fleskum-kolonien 1886 og den norske sommernatt. Naturalisme eller nyromantikk?" *Kunst og Kultur* 71 (1988): 2–30.

54. Prins Eugen, *Breven berätta*, 85–87, 113; Prins Eugen, *Vidare berätta breven* (Stockholm, 1945), 25–26. Cf. Tone Skedsmo, "Prins Eugen og Norge," in *Prins Eugen (1865–1947)*, [ed. Knut Berg] (Oslo, 1988), 15–33. The 1889 Paris Exposition produced yet another minor political crisis within the Swedish-Norwegian union. The Storting supported official Norwegian participation, which Oscar II refused for Sweden, since the Exposition celebrated the hundredth anniversary of the French Revolution. The Swedish Artists' Union, with support from Pontus Fürstenberg and others, thereupon

organized an unofficial exhibit of its own in the general arts pavillion. See Folke Lindberg, *Kunglig utrikespolitik. Studier och essayer från Oskar II:s tid.* 2d ed. (Stockholm,
1966), 62–79; Zachau, *Prins Eugen,* 70–75; Facos, "Norway," 89–90.

55. Prins Eugen, *Breven berätta,* 95, 99–101; cf. Richard Bergh, "Om Werenskiold
och Thaulow," in *Om konst och annat,* 46–63; Facos, *Nationalism,* 31, 93–94, 96, and
"Norway," 96–98.

56. Prins Eugen, *Breven berätta,* 154, 157, 302, and *Vidare berätta breven,* 21–24,
63–63, 71, 78; Skedsmo, "Prins Eugen," 15, 19.

57. *Tradisjon og fornyelse. Norge rundt århundreskiftet,* [ed. Tone Skedsmo,] exhibition catalog (Oslo, 1994), 400.

58. Richard Bergh, "Karl Nordström och det moderna stämningsmåleriet," in *Om
konst och annat,* 120.

59. Bergh, "Svenskt konstnärskynne," 156–57; Allan Ellenius, "Aspekter på bildkonsten och den nationella romantiken vid sekelskiftet," in *Att vara svensk,* [ed. Gunnar
Broberg, Ulla Wikander, and Klas Åmark] (Stockholm, 1985), 67–69; Facos, *Nationalism,* 23–24.

60. See esp. Berg, *Norges kunsthistorie,* vol. 5; Åse Moe Torvanger, "Tradisjon og
fornyelse. Norsk arkitektur rundt århundreskiftet," in *Tradisjon og fornyelse,* 348–82;
Stephan Tschudi-Madsen, "Dragestilen — Honnør til en hånet stil," *Vestlandske kun-
stindustrimuseum, Årbok 1949–1950* (Bergen, 1952), 19–62; Jens Christian Eldal, *His-
torisme i tre* (Oslo, 1998), chap. 6; Albert Steen, "Tradition and Revival: The Past in
Norway's National Consciousness," in *Norwegian Folk Art: The Migration of a Tradition,* ed. Marion Nelson (New York and Oslo, 1995), 249–58. Cf. Lorenz Dietrichson,
Den Norske Treskærerkunst (Christiania, 1878), and *Norges Stavkirker* (Christiania,
1892); Lorenz Dietrichson and Holm Munthe, *Die Holzbau Norwegens in Vergangen-
heit und Gegenwart* (Berlin, 1893). Cf. Oscar Montelius, *Sveriges fortid,* 3 vols.
(Stockholm, 1872–74).

61. Bo Grandien, *Rönndruvans glöd. Nygöticistiskt i tanke, konst och miljö under
1800-talet* (Stockholm, 1987), 204.

62. Lindblom, *Sveriges konsthistoria,* chap. 72; Eva Eriksson, *Den moderna stadens
födelse. Svensk arkitektur 1890–1920* (Stockholm, 1994), esp. 16, 20, 198–219; Barbara
Miller Lane, *National Romanticism and Modern Architecture in Germany and the
Scandinavian Lands* (Cambridge, 2000); Torben Grut, "Strödda reflexioner och fakta
angående Stockholms posthus," *Arkitektur och dekorativ konst* 33 (1903): 98; Bengt O. H.
Johansson, "Svensk arkitekturpolitik under 1900-talets första decennium," *Ars suetica* 2
(1970): 53–54.

63. Elisabet Stavenow-Hidemark, *Villabebyggelse i Sverige 1900–1925* (Stockholm,
1971), esp. 69–89; Lane, *National Romanticism,* chap. 2; *Stockholms förstäder och vil-
lasamhällen* (Stockholm, 1911); Näsström, *Dalarna som svenskt ideal;* Gustaf Carlsson,
ed., *Svenska allmogehem* (Stockholm, 1909), 16.

64. See, e.g., Carl Larsson, *Ett hem* (Stockholm, 1899); Ellen Key, *Skönhet för alla*
(Stockholm, 1899), and *Hemmets århundrade,* ed. Ronny Ambjörnsson (Stockholm,
1976), including Ambjörnsson's introduction; Stavenow-Hidemark, *Villabebyggelse,*
90–104; Tone Skedsmo, "Hos kunstnere, polarforskere og mesener," *Kunst og Kultur* 65
(1982): 131–51.

65. *August Bondesons visbok. Folkets visor sådana de lefva och sjungas ännu i vår tid*, 2 vol. (Stockholm, 1903); Gregor Andersson, ed., *Musik i Norden* (Stockholm, 1997); Leif Jonsson and Martin Tegen, *Musiken i Sverige*, 4 vols. (Stockholm, 1992–94), vol. 3; John Horton, *Scandinavian Music: A Short History* (London, 1963); John H. Yoell, *The Nordic Sound: Explorations into the Music of Denmark, Norway, Sweden* (Boston, 1974).

66. See Arthur Lindhagen, "Högtidstal vid Svenska turistföreningens 50-årsjubileum I Uppsalas universitets aula den 27 febr. 1935," *Svenska turistföreningens årskrift 1935*, 9–32; Hugo Selin, "Hur det började," Stig Synnergren, "Då och nu," Margareta Biörnstad, "Fosterland och hembygd," and Gunnar Broberg and Karin Johannisson, "Styr som örnen din färd till fjällen. Några linjer I den tidiga turismens idéhistoria," in *Svenska turistföreningen 100 år. Svenska turistföreningens årskrift 1986*, 7–18, 19–29, 29–55, 56–79.

67. C. J. L. Almqvist, "Svenska fattigdomens betydelse," in *Samlade verk*, ed. Bertil Romberg et al., 51 vols. (Stockholm, 1993–), 8:298–99. Cf. *Svenska krusbär*, 156–57. The title of Linnell and Löfgren's book comes from Almqvist's oft-quoted lines, "Blott Sverige svenska krusbär har" (only Sweden has Swedish gooseberries)—the meaning of which, and of the cited article, is that however humble it may be, Swedes may be proud of it because it is *Swedish*. Their book is an anthology of writings from the mid-nineteenth century to the present on the Swedish national character. For an earlier collection of such writings, see Josua Mjöberg, *Svenskt lynne* (Lund, 1917).

68. August Gödecke, "En resa i Norge," *Land och Folk. Tidskrift utgifven af Sällskapet för Nyttiga Kunskapers Spridande* (1873): 4–5, 194–95; Verner von Heidenstam, "Om svenskarnes lynne," in *Samlade verk*, 9:28 (first published in *Ord och Bild* 1 [1896]).

69. Bergh, "Svenskt konstnärskynne," 146–47, 153–54, and "Karl Nordström," 117–18. Cf. M. Biörnstad, "Fosterland och hembygd," 33; Laurin, *Sverige genom konstnärsögon*, esp. 23–24, 27, 56–58.

70. Prins Eugen, *Breven berätta*, 180–81. Cf. Prins Eugen, *Vidare berätta breven*, 62–63, 67–68, 70–71. See also Laurin, *Sverige genom konstnärsögon*, 23–24.

71. Carl Malmsten, "Om svensk karaktär inom konstkulturen," in *Om svensk karaktär inom konstkulturen* (Stockholm, 1916), 19–20, 40. Cf. *Svenska krusbär*, 387–407.

72. Erik Axel Karlfeldt, "I Dalarne," *Svenska turistföreningens årskrift 1926*, 1–2. Cf. Mark Davies, *A Perambulating Paradox: British Travel Literature and the Image of Sweden, c. 1770–1870* (Lund, 1999), 134–36, for British travelers' reactions to the Swedish, as compared with the Norwegian, landscape.

73. See H. Arnold Barton, *Northern Arcadia: Foreign Travelers in Scandinavia, 1765–1815* (Carbondale, IL, 1998), chap. 6.

74. *Excellensen Grefve A. F. Skjöldebrands memoarer*, ed. Henrik Schück, 5 vols. (Stockholm, 1903–4), 5:198–99; *Höglofliga Riddarskapet och Adeln vid Lagtima Riksdagen i Stockholm, År 1840* (Stockholm, 1841), 15:26; K. A. Lindström in *Nya Dagligt Allehanda*, 14 July 1860, quoted in Lidén, *Den norska strömningen*, 28.

75. Strindberg, *Jäsningstiden*, 356–58.

76. Meyer, *Ibsen*, 430; Strindberg, "Björnstjerne Björnson," 234.

77. Böök, *Sveriges moderna litteratur*, 77–78.

78. Paul Knaplund, ed., *British Views on Norwegian-Swedish Problems, 1880–1895: Selections from the Diplomatic Correspondence* (Oslo, 1952), 243.

79. Almqvist, "Svenska fattigdomens betydelse," 297–312, esp. 290–93, 311–12. Cf. *Svenska krusbär*, 139–70, esp. 149–52, 165–70.

80. Strindberg, "Nationalitet och svenskhet," 153–54, 167. Cf. *Svenska krusbär*, 194–212, esp. 195, 201–3, 209–10.

81. Oscar Levertin, "Gustaf III," and "Bellmans hemlighet," in *Från Gustaf III:s dagar* (1896), 3d ed. (Stockholm, 1908), 4–42, esp. 6–9, and 43–88, esp. 74–81. Cf. *Svenska krusbär*, 217–33. See also Landberg, *Gustaf III*, 63–68.

82. Verner von Heidenstam, "Hagdahls kokbok," in *Samlade verk*, 22:192–200, esp. 192–93; Heidenstam, "Om svenskarnes lynne," 10–30, esp. 10–11, 14–18, 25, 29–30. Cf. *Svenska krusbär*, 224–38. See also Böök, *Heidenstam*, 2:42–52.

83. Verner von Heidenstam, "Om patriotismen," *Dagens Nyheter*, 27 Sept. 1897. Cf. Böök, *Heidenstam*, 2:141–42; Björck, *Heidenstam*, 95.

84. Ellen Key, "Om patriotism. Öppet bref till min vän Verner von Heidenstam," in *Tankebilder*, 2 vols. (Stockholm, 1898), 2:2–46, esp. 3–6, 11, 18–19, 27–36. This letter was first published in *Vintergatan* in 1897. Cf. *Svenska krusbär*, 239–65.

85. Verner von Heidenstam, "Om det nationella som teori och känsla," *Dagens Nyheter*, 2 Jan. 1898, reprinted in *Samlade verk*, 9:102–11, and "Inbillningens logik," in *Samlade verk*, 9:177.

86. See Lönnroth and Delblanc, *Den storsvenska generationen*, 15–16, 73–74, 113; Böök, *Heidenstam*, 2:50–51, 119. Cf. *Stockholm med omgifningar samt 1897 års Industri-Utställning i ord och bild* (Stockholm, 1896).

87. See Helena Nyblom, "Fosterlandskärlek," Rudolf Kjellén, "Nationalitetsidén," Harald Hjärne, "Folkraser och politik," Rudolf Kjellén, "Fosterlandet. Ett begreppsanalys," and Harald Hjärne, "Nationalismens århundrade," in *Svenska krusbär*, 266–75, 276–96, 297–302, 303–8, 309–13; cf. Björck, *Heidenstam*, chap. 1, esp. 17–19.

88. Gustav Sundbärg, *Det svenska folklynnet* (Stockholm, 1911), 4, 6, 17–18, 29–33, 37, 56, 73–74, 77, 81–83, 86, 116, 135–37. Note Sundbärg's earlier section on "folk character" in *Sveriges land och folk. Historisk-statistisk handbok*, ed. Gustav Sundbärg (Stockholm, 1901), 126–31, which presented essentially the same national traits in a more positive light, and his essays "Emigrationen," *Föreningen Heimdals föreläsningar läsåret 1905–1906*, 8 (Uppsala, 1906), and "Emigrationen II," *Heimdals politiska småskrifter*, 2:1 (Uppsala 1907), which prefigure the negative view of these characteristics in *Det svenska folklynnet*. Cf. Francis Bull, "Bjørnson og Sverige," in *Bjørnson-Studier*, ed. Gerhard Gran (Kristiania, 1911), 263.

89. Carl G. Laurin, *Svensk självpröfning* (Stockholm, 1912). Cf. Åke Daun and Ingrid Forsman, "Gustav Sundbärg och det svenska folklynnet," in *Att vara svensk*, 33–46; H. Arnold Barton, *A Folk Divided: Homeland Swedes and Swedish Americans, 1840–1940* (Carbondale, IL, 1994), 135–37, 159–61.

Epilogue and Conclusions

1. Prins Eugen, *Vidare berätta breven* (Stockholm, 1946), 89–90; Bo Grandien, *Rönndruvans glöd. Nygöticistiskt i tanke, konst och miljö under 1800-talet* (Stockholm, 1987), 288; Bjørnstjerne Bjørnson, *Brevveksling med svenske 1858–1909*, ed. Øyvind Anker, Francis Bull, and Örjan Lindberger, 3 vols. (Oslo, 1960–61), 3:260.

2. Lorenz Dietrichson, *Svundne Tider. Af en Forfatteres Ungdoms-Erindringer*, 4 vols. (Kristiania, 1896–1917), and the Swedish edition, *En norrmans minnen från Sverige*, trans. Klara Johansson, 2 vols. (Stockholm, 1901–2), esp. 1:29–30, 2:9–17; Yngvar Nielsen, *Norge i 1905* (Kristiania, 1906), and *Under Oscar II's regjering. Oplevelser og Optegninger 1872–1884* (Kristiania, 1912), esp. 11–13. Cf. Ottar Dahl, *Norsk historieforskning i 19. og 20. århundre* (Oslo, 1970), 145–46.

3. Bjørnson, *Brevveksling med svenske*, 3:238–39, 248; Fredrik Böök, *Verner von Heidenstam*, 2 vols. (Stockholm, 1945–46), 2:270. Cf. Bjørnstjerne Bjørnson, "Vor synd og vor ydmygelse," *Samtiden* 17 (1906): 569–76.

4. Ernst Günther, *Minnen från ministertiden i Kristiania åren 1905–1908* (Stockholm, 1928), 32, 101–4; Raymond E. Lindgren, *Norway-Sweden: Union, Disunion, and Scandinavian Integration* (Princeton, 1959), 211. It may also be recalled that one of Norway's best-known exports to this day is King Oscar Sardines from Stavanger, with the king's imposing portrait on every can!

5. Carl G. Laurin, *Svensk själfpröfning* (Stockholm, 1912), 112–13; Birgitta Rapp, *Richard Bergh — konstnär och kulturpolitiker 1890–1915* (Stockholm, 1978), 68; Verner von Heidenstam, "Ett nytt 1809," in *Verner von Heidenstams samlade verk*, ed. Kate Bang and Fredrik Böök, vol. 17 (Stockholm, 1944), 73–77; Böök, *Heidenstam*, 2:270; Bjørnson, *Brevveksling med svenske*, 3:257. Cf. Conny Mithander, "1905 — genombrottet för en ny konservativ nationalism," in *Union & secession. Perspektiv på statsbildningsprocesser och riksupplösningar*, ed. Sven Eliæson and Ragnar Bjørk (Stockholm, 2000), 205–15.

6. Staffan Björck, *Heidenstam och sekelskiftets Sverige* (Stockholm, 1946), 78, 95, 238–39, 244; Örjan Lindberger, "Verner von Heidenstam och Bjørnstjerne Bjørnson," *Edda* (1960): 215–27; Bjørnson, *Brevveksling med svenske*, esp. 3: 257, 264–65; Francis Bull, *Bjørnstjerne Bjørnson* (Kristiania, 1923), 66; Verner von Heidenstam, "Till Björnstjerne Björnson vid hans sjuttioårsfest i Kristiania 1902," in *Samlade verk*, 17:25–26; Böök, *Heidenstam*, 2:141, 159. Cf. Lars Lönnroth and Sven Delblanc, eds., *Den storsvenska generationen 1890–1920*, vol. 4 of *Den svenska litteraturen* (Stockholm, 1989), 17, 19.

7. Gustaf Näsström, *Dalarna som svenskt ideal* (Stockholm, 1937), 197–258, esp. 137, 159, 199–200, 203–7. On the earlier Norwegian Youth Movement, organized in 1896 into the national *Norigs Ungdomslag*, see Per Fuglum, *Norge i støpeskjeen 1884–1920*, vol. 12 of *Norges historie*, ed. Knut Mykland (Oslo, 1978), 416–17; Mona Klippenberg, "Ut or unionane? Den frilynte ungdomsrørsla i framvekstårene," in *Jakten på det norske. Perspektiver på utviklingen av en norsk nasjonal identitet på 1800-tallet*, ed. Øystein Sørensen (Oslo, 1998), 357–70, esp. 365.

8. Björck, *Heidenstam*, 267–69; Böök, *Heidenstam*, 2:279–81; Heidenstam, *Samlade verk*, 17:5–7, 73–77.

9. Björck, *Heidenstam*, 292, 314; Böök, *Heidenstam*, 2:280–81.

10. Verner von Heidenstam, "Vid Björnsons bår i Kristiania den 3 maj 1910," in *Samlade verk*, 17:68–69; Bjørnson, *Brevveksling med svenske*, 1:xxxviii, 3:266; F. Bull, *Bjørnstjerne Bjørnson*, 69.

11. [J. E. Ekström,] *Reseminnen från Norge 1855. Samlade af E . . . m* (Eskilstuna, 1856), 44; Bjørnson, *Brevveksling med svenske*, 3:162; Gustaf Sundbärg, *Det svenska folklynnet* (Stockholm, 1911), 74. Cf. Laurin, *Svensk själfpröfning*, 99.

12. Calla Curman, "Bref till en norsk dam från hennes svenska vännina," in *Minnen* (Stockholm, 1926), 213–20, esp. 215, 217.

13. Second verse of *Du gamla, du fria.*

14. Bjørnstjerne Bjørnson, *Artikler og Taler,* ed. C. Collin and H. Eitrem, 2 vols. (Kristiania, 1912–13), 2:459. Also Øystein Sørensen, *Bjørnstjerne Bjørnson og nasjonalismen* (Oslo, 1997), 131, 160; Francis Bull, "Bjørnson og Sverige," in *Bjørnson-Studier,* ed. Gerhard Gran (Kristiania, 1911), 266.

15. Lindgren, *Norway-Sweden.*

16. See, e.g., Stanley V. Anderson, *The Nordic Council: A Study of Scandinavian Regionalism* (Seattle, 1967); Erik Solem, *The Nordic Council and Scandinavian Integration* (New York, 1977). Cf. Ellen Key, *Några tankar om skandinavismens framtid* (Stockholm, 1906); Rapp, *Richard Bergh,* 73.

17. Gurli Linder, *På den tiden. Några bilder från 1870-talets Stockholm* (Stockholm, 1924), 29.

18. See esp. Lindgren, *Norway-Sweden;* Göran B. Nilsson, "Unionen som inte blev någon union," *Nyt norsk tidsskrift* 2 (1985): 14–20, "Den verkningslösa unionen?" in *Fra arvefiende til samboer,* ed. Grete Værnø (Stockholm and Oslo, 1990), 49–56, and "Edvard Grieg och den svensk-norska unionens underliga historia," *Nyt norsk tidsskrift* 11 (1994): 131–39; Evert Vedung, "Norvegomani och fosterländskhet," in Værnø, *Fra arvefiende,* 84–93; Fuglum, *Norge i støpeskjeen,* 94, 104; Prins Eugen, *Breven berätta. Upplevelser och iakttagelser. Åren 1886–1913* (Stockholm, 1942), 330.

19. Prins Eugen, *Breven berätta,* 223–24.

20. See G. Nilsson, "Unionen," 15, 19, "Den verkningslösa unionen?" 49–50, and "Edvard Grieg," 131–32, 137, 139; Bjørnson, *Brevveksling med svenske,* 2:141. Cf. H. Arnold Barton, *Scandinavia in the Revolutionary Era, 1760–1815* (Minneapolis, 1986), 362–64.

21. Henrik Schück and Karl Warburg, *Illustrerad svensk litteraturhistoria,* 2d ed., 4 vols. (Stockholm, 1911–16), 4:1:46–47, 4:2:289–99; Fredrik Böök, *Sveriges moderna litteratur* (Stockholm, 1921), esp. 66–85; Arne Lidén, *Den norska strömningen i svensk litteratur under 1800-talet* (Uppsala, 1926); Björck, *Heidenstam;* Alrik Gustafson, *A History of Swedish Literature* (Minneapolis, 1961). Cf. Lars Lönnroth and Sven Delblanc, eds., *De liberala genombrotten 1830–1890* and *Den storsvenska generationen 1890–1920,* vols. 3 and 4 of *Den svenska litteraturen,* 7 vols. (1987–90); Lars G. Warme, *A History of Swedish Literature,* vol. 3 of *A History of the Scandinavian Literatures,* ed. Sven Rossel (Lincoln, NE, 1996).

22. Grandien, *Rönndruvans glöd;* Michelle Facos, "Norway and the Definition of Swedish National Identity," in *The Dividing Line: Borders and National Peripheries,* ed. Lars-Folke Lindgren and Maunu Häyrynen (Helsinki, 1997), 87–101, and *Nationalism and the Nordic Imagination: Swedish Art of the 1890s* (Berkeley, 1998).

23. Gunnar Rexius, "Det svenska tvåkammarsystemets tillkomst och karaktär. Med särskild hänsyn till principernas grundläggning 1840–41," *Skrifter utgivna av Humanistiska Vetenskaps-Samfundet i Uppsala* 17:2 (Uppsala, 1915), 358 pp.; Lidén, *Den norska strömningen,* esp. chap. 1; Halvdan Koht, "Norsk hjelp til svensk demokrati," *Scandia* 18 (1947): 252–64; Berit Borell, *De svenska liberalerna och representationsfrågan på 1840-talet* (Uppsala, 1948); Jan Christensen, *Bönder och herrar. Bondeståndet i 1840-talets liberala representationsdebatt. Exemplen Gustaf Hierta och J P Theorell* (Göteborg, 1997); Johan Norberg, *Den svenska liberalismens historia* (Stockholm, 1998).

24. Værnø, *Fra arvefiende.*

25. Based on correspondence and oral information to the author since 1998 from Øystein Sørensen (Oslo), Stig Ekman (Stockholm), Göran B. Nilsson (Linköping), and Alf Kaartvedt (Bergen).

26. G. Nilsson, "Den verkningslösa unionen?" Both Edvard Thermænius, *Lantmannapartiet. Dess uppkomst, organisation och tidigare utveckling* (Uppsala, 1928), and Alf Kaartvedt, *Kampen mot parlamentarismen 1880–1885* (Oslo, 1956), nonetheless remain valuable concerning the relations between the Norwegian *Venstre* and the Swedish *Lantmannaparti.*

27. Nils Elvander, *Harald Hjärne och konservatismen. Konservativ idédebatt i Sverige 1863–1922,* Skrifter utgivna av Statsvetenskapliga föreningen i Uppsala, vol. 42 (Uppsala, 1961), 241–46; Rudolf Kjellén, *Nationell samling. Politiska och etiska fragment* (Stockholm, 1906); Adrian Molin, *Svenska spörsmål och kraf* (Stockholm, 1905), and *Vanhäfd* (Stockholm, 1911); H. Arnold Barton, *A Folk Divided: Homeland Swedes and Swedish Americans, 1840–1940* (Carbondale, IL, 1994), 166–68.

28. Halvdan Koht, "Trongen til demokrati i 1814," *Historisk tidsskrift* (Nor.) 34 (1947): 133–51; Alf Kaartvedt, "Karl Johan i Norge. Författningskamp och utrikespolitik," in *Karl XIV Johan — en europeisk karriär,* Skrifter från Kungl. Husgerådskammaren 9 (Stockholm, 1998), 138–39, and "Unionen som politisk energikilde," in Værnø, *Fra arvefiende,* 78–83; G. Nilsson, "Den verkningslösa unionen?" 51.

29. G. Nilsson, "Den verkningslösa unionen?" 51–52; Elvander, *Harald Hjärne,* 253–54; Kaartvedt, "Unionen," 82.

30. Kaartvedt, "Unionen," 83; Prins Eugen, *Vidare berätta breven,* 91–92. Cf. Tone Skedsmo, "Prins Eugen og Norge," in *Prins Eugen (1865–1947),* [ed. Knut Berg] (Oslo, 1988), 26.

31. Prins Eugen, *Breven berätta,* 282; August Strindberg, "Nationalitet och svenskhet," in *Samlade skrifter,* ed. John Landquist, 55 vols. (Stockholm, 1912–19), 16:149; Verner von Heidenstam, "Om svenskarnes lynne," in *Samlade verk,* 9:21.

32. Michael Meyer, *Ibsen: A Biography* (New York, 1971), 770–74; Per Amdam and Aldo Keel, *Bjørnstjerne Bjørnson,* 2 vols. (Oslo, 1993, 1999), 1:456–63; Bjørnson, *Brevveksling med svenske,* vol. 3. Cf. Ellen Key, "Björnson och Sverige," in *Bjørnstjerne Bjørnson. Festskrift i anledning af hans 70 Aars Fødelsedag* (Copenhagen, 1902), 41–69; Heidenstam, "Till Björnstjerne Björnson," 25–26; "Bjørnsons Tale ved Nobelbanketten 10 December 1903," in Bjørnson, *Artikler og Taler,* 2:482–85.

33. G. Nilsson, "Edvard Grieg," esp. 131, 138–39; Finn Benestad and Dag Schjelderup-Ebbe, *Edvard Grieg: The Man and the Artist,* trans. William H. Halvorson and Leland B. Satheren (Lincoln, NE, 1988), 347–48, 352, 360. Cf. Rapp, *Richard Bergh,* 53; Prins Eugen, *Vidare berätta breven,* 78.

34. Benestad and Schjelderup-Ebbe, *Edvard Grieg,* 375–76; Lidén, *Den norska strömningen,* 292–93. See also, e.g., Selma Lagerlöf's warm tributes to Bjørnson's influence on her writings in 1902 and 1906 in Bjørnson, *Brevveksling med svenske,* 3:172, 253. Cf. Arne Lidén, "Selma Lagerlöf och Bjørnstjerne Bjørnson," in *Studier tillägnade Anton Blanck den 29 december 1946* (Uppsala, 1946), 322–31.

35. Horace, *Epodes,* 2:1; Strindberg, *Jäsningstiden,* in *Samlade skrifter,* 18:354.

36. Samuel Laing, *A Tour of Sweden; Comprising Observations on the Moral, Political, and Economical State of the Swedish Nation* (London, 1839), iv–v.

37. Lidén, *Den norska strömningen,* 292.

38. Laurin, *Svensk själfpröfning*, 53, 55–56; Fredrika Bremer, *Brev*, ed. K. Johansson and E. Kleman, 4 vols (Stockholm, 1915–29), 3:79; Erica Simon, *Réveil national et culture populaire en Scandinavie. La genèse de la højskole nordique, 1844–1878* (Paris, 1960), 688–89; Facos, "Norway," 87.

39. Anne-Lise Seip, "Det norske 'vi' — Kulturnasjonalisme i Norge," in Sørensen, *Jakten på det norske*, 107; Harold Larson, *Björnstjerne Björnson: A Study in Norwegian Nationalism* (New York, 1944), 55, 62; August Strindberg, "Svenska folkvisor — som ikke äro svenska" (1877), in *Före Röda rummet. Strindbergs ungdomsjournalistik i urval av Torsten Eklund*, [ed. Torsten Eklund] (Stockholm, 1946), 263–67, and "Nationalitet och svenskhet" (1883), in *Samlade skrifter*, 16:143–71; Oscar Levertin, "Carl Michael Bellman," in *Från Gustaf III:s dagar*, 3d ed. (Stockholm, 1908), 77, 79; Heidenstam, "Om svenskarnes lynne," 29–30.

40. Sten Carlsson, "Norrmän i Sverige 1814–1905," in *Grupper och gestalter. Studier om individ och kollektiv i nordisk och europeisk historia* (Stockholm, 1964), 75–90; Günther, *Minnen från ministertiden*, 22; Anders Norberg, "In- och utvandrare i Sveriges riksdag," in *Utvandrare och invandrare i Sveriges historia*, ed. Olov Isaksson (Stockholm, 1997), 305, 306, 308.

41. Sundbärg, *Det svenska folklynnet*, 77.

42. Kristian Magnus Kommandantvold, *Nabo i speilet. Sverige i norsk litterært perspektiv* (Oslo, 1958), 243; F. Bull, "Bjørnson og Sverige," 242.

43. Kommandantvold, *Nabo i speilet*, esp. 138, 179, 210–11.

44. Verner von Heidenstam, "Om patriotismen," *Dagens Nyheter*, 27 Sept. 1897. Cf. Björck, *Heidenstam*, 95; Heidenstam, "Om svenskarnes lynne," 25. Cf., e.g., Nils Collett Vogt, "Svenskerne og vi," in *Levende og døde. Smaa portrætter og skildringer* (Kristiania, 1922), 183–92.

45. Vogt, "Svenskerne og vi," 188, 191–92.

46. See my forthcoming article, "Swedish Americans and the Viking Discovery of America", in *Interpreting the Promise of America: Essays in Honor of Odd Sverre Lovoll*, ed. Todd W. Nichol (Northfield, MN, 2002), 61–78.

47. See, e.g., Lloyd Hustvedt, *Rasmus Bjørn Anderson, Pioneer Scholar* (Northfield, MN, 1966); Joh. A. Enander, *Förenta Staternas Historia, utarbetad för den Svenska Befolkningen i Amerika*, 2d ed., 2 vols. (Chicago, 1882), 1:1:59–51: Barton, *A Folk Divided*, 65; C. F. Peterson, *Sverige i Amerika* (Chicago, 1898), 289–94; P. P. Waldenström, *Nya färder i Amerikas Förenta Stater* (Stockholm, 1902), 50, 316; Carl Sundbeck, *Svenskarne i Amerika. Deras land, antal och kolonier. En kort öfversikt till tjänst för emigranter och för våra svensk-amerikanska kolonier intresserade* (Stockholm, 1900), esp. 5, 91–92; James M. Kaplan, "Coming from America: Birger Sandzén's Travel Narrative of 1905," *Swedish-American Historical Quarterly* 50 (1999): 28, 30–31, 37; Sverre Arrestad, "What War Snus Hill?" in *Makers of an American Immigrant Legacy: Essays in Honor of Kenneth O. Bjorck*, ed. Odd S. Lovoll (Northfield, MN, 1980), 159–72.

48. Bjørnson, *Brevveksling med svenske*, 2:71; Sørensen, *Bjørnstjerne Bjørnson*, 32–35; Kenneth Clark, *Civilisation: A Personal View* (New York, 1969), 258.

Select Bibliography

This listing does not include all the works cited in the notes, only the most important ones. Full bibliographic information is provided meanwhile for every title in the first reference to it in the notes for each chapter.

Agrelius, C. P. *Swenska Folkets Återställelse till ett enklare och bättre, med Norrska Folkets mera öfwerensstämmande Samhällstillstånd.* Vadstena, 1833.

Ahlstrand, Jan Torsten, et al. *Konsten 1890–1915,* Signums svenska konsthistoria, vol. 11. Lund, 2001.

Alin, Oscar. *Den svensk-norska unionen. Uppsatser och aktstycken.* 2 vols. Stockholm, 1889–91.

Almqvist, C. J. L. *Samlade verk.* Ed. Bertil Romberg et al. Vol. 8. Stockholm, 1993.

Amdam, Per, and Aldo Keel. *Bjørnstjerne Bjørnson.* 2 vols. Oslo, 1993, 1999.

Andersson, Gregor, ed. *Musik i Norden.* Stockholm, 1997.

Barton, H. Arnold. *A Folk Divided: Homeland Swedes and Swedish Americans, 1840–1940.* Carbondale, IL, 1994.

———. *Northern Arcadia: Foreign Travelers in Scandinavia, 1765–1815.* Carbondale, IL, 1998.

———. "Peter August Gödecke, den svenska folkhögskolan och Norge." *Personhistorisk tidskrift* 98 (2002): 5–20.

———. *Scandinavia in the Revolutionary Era, 1760–1815.* Minneapolis, 1986.

———. "The Swedish Succession Crises of 1809 and 1810, and the Question of Scandinavian Union." *Scandinavian Studies* 42 (1970): 309–33.

Benestad, Finn, and Dag Schjelderup-Ebbe. *Edvard Grieg: The Man and the Artist.* Trans. William H. Halvorson and Leland B. Satheren. Lincoln, NE, 1988.

Bengtsson, Eva-Lena, et al. *Konsten 1845–1890.* Signums svenska konsthistoria, vol. 10. Lund, 2000.

Berg, Knut, ed. *1880-tal i nordiskt måleri.* Exhibition catalog. Stockholm, 1986.

———. *Norges kunsthistorie.* 7 vols. Oslo, 1981–83.

———. *Norges malerkunst.* 2 vols. Oslo, 1993.

Bergh, Richard. *Om konst och annat.* Stockholm, 1908.

Biörnstad, Arne, ed. *Skansen under hundra år.* Stockholm, 1991.

Björck, Staffan. _Heidenstam och sekelskiftets Sverige._ Stockholm, 1946.

Bjørnson, Bjørnstjerne. _Artikler og Taler._ Ed. C. Collin and H. Eitrem. 2 vols. Kristiania, 1912–13.

———. _Brevveksling med svenske 1858–1909._ Ed. Øyvind Anker, Francis Bull, and Örjan Lindberger. 3 vols. Oslo, 1960–61.

[Björnstjerna, Magnus.] _On the Moral State and Political Union of Sweden and Norway, in Answer to Mr. Laing's Statement._ London, 1840.

Boëthius, S. J. _Oskar II._ Vol. 13 of _Sveriges historia till våra dagar,_ ed. Emil Hildebrand and Ludvig Stavenow. Stockholm, 1925.

[Bondeståndet.] _Hederwärda Bonde-Ståndets Protocoller wid Lagtima Riksdagen i Stockholm år 1840._ Vol. 8. Stockholm, 1840.

———. _Hederwärda Bonde-Ståndets Protocoller wid Lagtima Riksdagen i Stockholm år 1834 och 1835._ Vols. 7 and 8. Stockholm, 1834–35.

Böök, Fredrik. _Artur Hazelius. En levnadsteckning._ Stockholm, 1923.

———. _Sveriges moderna litteratur._ Stockholm, 1921.

———. _Verner von Heidenstam._ 2 vols. Stockholm, 1945–46.

Borell, Berit. _De svenska liberalerna och representationsfrågan på 1840-talet._ Uppsala, 1948.

[Borgarståndet.] _Protocoll, hållna hos Välloflige Borgare-Ståndet wid Lagtima Riksdagen i Stockholm år 1840 och 1841._ Vol. 8. Stockholm, 1840–41.

Brace, Charles Loring. _The Norse-Folk; or, a Visit to the Homes of Norway and Sweden._ New York, 1857.

Bring, Samuel. _Itineraria Suecana. Bibliografisk förteckning över resor i Sverige fram till 1950._ Stockholm, 1954.

Broberg, Gunnar. "När svenskarna uppfann Sverige. Anteckningar till ett hundraårsjubileum." In _Tänka, tycka, tro. Sveriges historia underifrån,_ ed. Gunnar Broberg, Ulla Wikander, and Klas Åmark, 171–96. Stockholm, 1993.

Bull, Francis. "Bjørnson og Sverige." In _Bjørnson-Studier,_ ed. Gerhard Gran, 171–281. Kristiania, 1911.

———. _Bjørnstjerne Bjørnson._ Kristiania, 1923. Originally published in _Norsk biografisk leksikon,_ ed. Edvard Bull, Anders Krogvig, and Gerhard Gran. Vol. 1. Kristiania, 1923.

Carlsson, Sten. "Norrmän i Sverige 1814–1905." In _Grupper och gestalter. Studier om individ och kollektiv i nordisk och europeisk historia,_ 75–90. Stockholm, 1964.

———. _Ståndssamhälle och ståndspersoner 1700–1815. Studier rörande det svenska ståndssamhällets upplösning._ 2d ed. Lund, 1973.

Christensen, Jan. _Bönder och herrar. Bondeståndet i 1840-talets liberala representationsdebatt. Exemplen Gustaf Hierta och J P Theorell._ Göteborg, 1997.

Clason, Sam. _Karl XIII och Karl XIV Johan._ Vol. 11 of _Sveriges historia till våra dagar,_ ed. Emil Hildebrand and Ludvig Stavenow. Stockholm, 1923.

Clausen, Julius. _Skandinavismen historisk fremstillet._ Copenhagen, 1900.

Dahl, Ottar. _Norsk historieforskning i 19. og 20. århundre._ Oslo, 1970.

Dahl, Willy. _Norges litteratur 1814–1980._ 3 vols. Oslo, 1981–89.

Derry, T. K. *A History of Modern Norway, 1814–1972*. Oxford, 1973.

————. *A Short History of Norway*. London, 1957.

Dietrichson, Lorenz. *En norrmans minnen från Sverige*. 2 vols. Trans. Klara Johansson. Stockholm, 1901–2.

————. *Svundne Tider. Af en Forfatteres Ungdoms-Erindringer*. 4 vols. Kristiania, 1896–1917.

[Eklund, Torsten, ed.] *Före Röda rummet. Strindbergs ungdomsjournalistik i urval av Torsten Eklund*. Strindbergssällskapets skrifter, vol. 1. Stockholm, 1946.

Eliæson, Sven, and Ragnar Bjørk. *Union & secession. Perspektiv på statsbildningsprocesser och riksupplösningar*. Stockholm, 2000.

Ellenius, Allan. "Aspekter på bildkonsten och den nationella romantiken vid sekelskiftet." In *Att vara svensk*, [ed. Gunnar Broberg, Ulla Wikander, and Klas Åmark,] 65–72. Stockholm, 1984.

Elvander, Nils. "Från liberal skandinavism till konservativ nationalism i Sverige." *Scandia* 27 (1961): 366–86.

————. *Harald Hjärne och konservatismen. Konservativ idédebatt i Sverige 1865–1922*. Skrifter utgivna av Statsvetenskapliga föreningen i Uppsala, vol. 42. Uppsala, 1961.

Elviken, Andreas. "The Genesis of Norwegian Nationalism." *Journal of Modern History* 3 (1931): 365–91.

Eriksson, Eva. *Den moderna stadens födelse. Svensk arkitektur 1890–1920*. Stockholm, 1994.

Eugen, Prins. *Breven berätta. Upplevelser och iakttagelser. Åren 1886–1913*. Stockholm, 1942.

————. *Vidare berätta breven*. Stockholm, 1945.

Facos, Michelle. *Nationalism and the Nordic Imagination: Swedish Art of the 1890s*. Berkeley, 1998.

————. "Norway and the Definition of Swedish National Identity." In *The Dividing Line: Borders and National Peripheries*, ed. Lars-Folke Lindgren and Maunu Häyrynen, 87–101. Helsinki, 1997.

Fahlbeck, Erik. *Ståndsriksdagens sista skede 1809–1866*. Vol. 8 of *Sveriges Riksdag*, ed. Nils Edén et al. 18 vols. Stockholm, 1931–36.

Falnes, Oscar J. *National Romanticism in Norway*. New York, 1933.

Fröding, Gustaf. *Prosa*. Stockholm, 1935.

Fuglum, Per. *Norge i støpeskjeen 1884–1920*. Vol. 12 of *Norges historie*, ed. Knut Mykland. Oslo, 1978.

Gödecke, August. "En resa i Norge." *Land och Folk. Tidskrift utgifven af Sällskapet för Nyttiga Kunskapers Spridande* (1873): 1–32, 193–231, 289–328.

[————]. *Turistbref från en resa i Norge sommaren 1875 af Finn*. Stockholm, 1876.

Grandien, Bo. *Rönndruvans glöd. Nygöticistiskt i tanke, konst och miljö under 1800-talet*. Stockholm, 1987.

Gunnarsson, Torsten. *Nordic Landscape Painting in the Nineteenth Century*. Trans. Nancy Adler. New Haven, 1998.

Gustafson, Alrik. *History of Swedish Literature*. Minneapolis, 1961.

Hadenius, Stig, and Torgny Nevéus, eds. *Majestät i närbild. Oscar II i brev och dagböcker*. Uppsala, 1960.

Hallendorff, Carl. *Oskar I och Karl XV*. Vol. 12 of *Sveriges historia till våra dagar*, ed. Emil Hildebrand and Ludvig Stavenow. Stockholm, 1923.

Haugen, Einar, and Camilla Cai. *Ole Bull: Norway's Romantic Musician and Cosmopolitan Patriot*. Madison, 1993.

Hedin, Adolf. *Tal och skrifter*. Ed. Valfrid Spångberg. 2 vols. Stockholm, 1904–15.

[Hedvig Elisabeth Charlotta, queen of Sweden and Norway.] *Hedvig Elisabeth Charlottas dagbok*. Ed. Carl Carlsson Bonde and Cecilia af Klercker. 9 vols. Stockholm, 1902–42.

Hegard, Tonte. *Romantikk og fortidsvern. Historien om de første friluftsmuseene i Norge*. Oslo, 1984.

[Heidenstam, Verner von.] *Verner von Heidenstams samlade verk*. Ed. Kate Bang and Fredrik Böök. 23 vols. Stockholm, 1943–44.

Höglund, Zeth. *Hjalmar Branting och hans livsgärning*. 2 vols. Stockholm, 1928–29.

Höjer, Torvald. *Carl XIV Johan*. 3 vols. Stockholm, 1939–60.

———. *1810–1844*. Vol. 3, part 2 of *Svenska utrikespolitikens historia*, ed. Nils Ahnlund. Stockholm, 1954.

Horton, John. *Scandinavian Music: A Short History*. London, 1963.

Hovde, B. J. *The Scandinavian Countries, 1720–1865: The Rise of the Middle Classes*. 2 vols. Boston, 1943.

Ibsen, Henrik. *The Oxford Ibsen*. Trans. and ed. James W. McFarlane et al. 8 vols. New York, 1960–77.

———. *Samlede verker*. Ed. Halvdan Koht, Francis Bull, and Diedrik Arup Seip. 21 vols. Oslo, 1928–57.

Ingers, E., and Sten Carlsson. *Bonden i svensk historia*. 3 vols. Stockholm, 1949–56.

Jansson, Allan. *1844–1872*. Vol. 3, part 3 of *Svenska utrikespolitikens historia*, ed. Nils Ahnlund. Stockholm, 1961.

Johnsen, Oscar Albert. *Norges bønder. Utsyn over den norske bondestands historie*. Kristiania, 1919.

Jonsson, Leif, and Martin Tegen. *Musiken i Sverige*. 4 vols. Stockholm, 1992–94.

Jorgensen, Theodore. *Norway's Relation to Scandinavian Unionism, 1815–1871*. Northfield, MN, 1935.

Kaartvedt, Alf. "Carl Johan-statuen. En politisk manifestasjon." In *Carl Johans Förbundets handlingar 1994–1998*, 17–22. Uppsala, 1999.

———. *Kampen mot parlamentarismen 1880–1885*. Oslo, 1956.

———. "Karl Johan i Norge. Författningskamp och utrikespolitik." In *Karl XIV Johan — en europeisk karriär*, 115–39. Skrifter från Kungl. Husgerådskammaren 9. Stockholm, 1998.

Karl XIV Johan — en europeisk karriär. Skrifter från Kungl. Husgerådskammaren 9. Stockholm, 1998.

Keilhau, Wilhelm. *Tidsrummet fra omkring 1875 til omkring 1920*. Vol. 10 of *Norske folks liv og historie gjennem tidene*, ed. Edvard Bull et al. Oslo, 1935.

Kent, Niel. *The Triumph of Light and Nature: Nordic Art, 1740–1940*. London, 1987.

Key, Ellen. "Björnson och Sverige." In *Bjørnstjerne Bjørnson. Festskrift i Anledning af hans 70 Aars Fødelsedag, 41–69*. Copenhagen, 1902.

Knaplund, Paul, ed. *British Views on Norwegian-Swedish Problems, 1880–1895: Selections from the Diplomatic Correspondence*. Oslo, 1952.

Koht, Halvdan. "Norsk hjelp til svensk demokrati." *Scandia* 18 (1947): 252–64.

———. "Trongen til demokrati i 1814." *Historisk tidsskrift* (Norwegian) 34 (1947): 133–51.

Kommandantvold, Kristian Magnus. *Nabo i speilet. Sverige i norsk litterært perspektiv*. Oslo, 1958.

Lagercrantz, Olof. *August Strindberg*. Trans. Anselm Hollo. London, 1984. (Swedish original, Stockholm, 1979.)

Laine, Barbara Miller. *National Romanticism and Modern Architecture in Germany and the Scandinavian Countries*. Cambridge, 2000.

Laing, Samuel. *Journal of a Residence in Norway During the Years 1834, 1835, and 1836; Made with a View to Enquire into the Moral and Political Economy of that Country, and the Condition of Its Inhabitants*. London, 1837.

———. *A Tour of Sweden in 1838; Comprising Observations on the Moral, Political, and Economical State of the Swedish Nation*. London, 1839.

Lange, Marit Ingeborg. "Fra den hellige lund til Fleskum. Kitty L. Kielland og den nordiske sommernatt." *Kunst og Kultur* 60 (1977): 69–92.

Larson, Harold. *Björnstjerne Björnson: A Study in Norwegian Nationalism*. New York, 1944.

Laurin, Carl G. *Svensk självprövning*. Stockholm, 1912.

———. *Sverige genom konstnärsögon*. Stockholm, 1911.

Laurin, Carl G., Emil Hannover, and Jens Thiis. *Scandinavian Art*. New York, 1922.

Levertin, Oscar. *Från Gustaf III:s dagar*. 3d ed. Stockholm, 1908.

Lidén, Arne. *Den norska strömningen i svensk litteratur under 1800-talet*. Vol. 1. Uppsala, 1926. [No vol. 2 followed.]

Lindberg, Folke. *1872–1914*. Vol. 3, part 4 of *Svenska utrikespolitikens historia*, ed. Nils Ahnlund. Stockholm, 1958.

———. *Kunglig utrikespolitik. Studier och essayer från Oskar II:s tid*. 2d ed. Stockholm, 1966.

Lindblom, Andreas. *Sveriges konsthistoria*. Stockholm, 1947.

Lindgren, Raymond E. *Norway-Sweden: Union, Disunion, and Scandinavian Integration*. Princeton, 1959.

Lönnroth, Lars, and Sven Delblanc, eds. *Den svenska litteraturen*. 7 vols. Stockholm, 1987–90.

Malmsten, Carl. *Om svensk karaktär inom konstkulturen*. Stockholm, 1916.

McFarlane, James W. "Norwegian Literature, 1860–1910." In *A History of Norwegian Literature*, ed. Harald Næss, 107–99. A History of Scandinavian Literatures, ed. Sven Rossel, vol. 2. Lincoln, NE, 1993.

"Memorial [Nr. 38] angående National-representationens ombildning" [1840]. In *Bihang till Samtlige Riks-Ståndens Protocoll vid Lagtima Riksdagen i Stockholm, Åren 1840 och 1841*. Vol. 3, *Constitutions-Utskottets Memorial, Utlåtanden och Betänkanden*. Stockholm, 1840–41.

Meyer, Michael. *Ibsen: A Biography*. New York, 1971.

——. *Strindberg: A Biography*. London, 1985.

Michanek, Germund. *Skaldernas konung. Oscar II, litteraturen och litteratören*. Stockholm, 1979.

Mjöberg, Jöran. *Drömmen om sagatiden*. 2 vols. Stockholm, 1967–68.

Mykland, Knut, ed. *Norges historie*. 13 vols. Oslo, 1976–79.

Næss, Harald. "Norwegian Literature, 1800–1860." In *A History of Norwegian Literature*, ed. Harald Næss, 82–106. A History of Scandinavian Literatures, ed. Sven Rossel, vol. 2. Lincoln, NE, 1993.

——, ed. *A History of Norwegian Literature*. A History of Scandinavian Literatures, ed. Sven Rossel, vol. 2. Lincoln, NE, 1993.

Näsström, Gustaf. *Dalarna som svenskt ideal*. Stockholm, 1937.

Nilsson, Göran B. "Edvard Grieg och den svensk-norska unionens underliga historia." *Nyt norsk tidsskrift* 11 (1994): 131–39.

——. "Unionen som inte blev någon union." *Nyt norsk tidsskrift* 2 (1985): 14–20.

Nilsson, Sven. *Dagboksanteckningar under en resa från Södra Sverige till Nordlanden i Norge 1816*. Lund, 1879.

Norberg, Johan. *Den svenska liberalismens historia*. Stockholm, 1998.

Norsk biografisk leksikon. Ed. Edvard Bull, Anders Krogvig, and Gerhard Gran. 19 vols. Kristiania/Oslo, 1921–67.

Norske folks liv og historie gjennem tidene. Ed. Edvard Bull et al. 10 vols. Oslo, 1929–38.

Nygaard, Knut. *Nordmenns syn på Danmark og danskene i 1814 og de første selvstendighetsår*. Oslo, 1960.

Ording, Jörgen Fredrik, Einar Östvedt, and Odd Hölaas. *Norges historia. Från äldsta tid till våra dagar*. Malmö, 1949.

Rapp, Birgitta. *Richard Bergh — konstnär och kulturpolitiker 1890–1915*. Stockholm, 1978.

Rexius, Gunnar. "Det svenska tvåkammarsystemets tillkomst och karaktär. Med särskild hänsyn till principernas grundläggning 1840–41." *Skrifter utgivna av Humanistiska Vetenskaps-Samfundet i Uppsala* 17:2. Uppsala, 1915.

Richert, J. G., and C. H. Anckarsvärd. *Förslag till National-Representation*. Stockholm, 1830.

[Riddarskapet och Adeln.] *Höglofliga Riddarskapet och Adeln vid Lagtima Riksdagen i Stockholm, År 1840*. Vol. 15. Stockholm, 1841.

——. *Höglofliga Riddarskapet och Adeln vid Lagtima Riksdagen i Stockholm, År 1834*. Vol. 14. Stockholm, 1835.

——. *Protocoll hållna hos högloflige Ridderskapet och Adeln vid Lagtima Riksdagen i Stockholm, År 1859–1860*. Vol. 1. Stockholm, 1859–60.

Schnitler, Carl. *Slægten fra 1814. Studier over norsk embedsmandskultur i klassicismens tidsalder 1814–1840*. Kristiania, 1911.

Schück, Henrik, and Karl Warburg. *Illustrerad svensk litteraturhistoria*. 2d ed. 4 vols. Stockholm, 1911–16. Vol. 4, parts 1 and 2.

Scott, Franklin D. *Sweden: The Nation's History*. 2d ed., Carbondale, IL, 1988.

Seip, Anne-Lise. "Nation-Building within the Union: Class and Culture in the Norwegian Nation-State in the Nineteenth Century." *Scandinavian Journal of History* 20 (1995): 35–50.

Seip, Jens Arup. *Utsikt over Norges historie.* 2 vols. Oslo, 1974, 1981.

Sejersted, Francis. *Den vanskelige frihet: 1814–1851.* Vol. 10 of *Norges historie,* ed. Knut Mykland. Oslo, 1978.

Simon, Erica. *Réveil national et culture populaire en Scandinavie: La genèse de la højskole nordique, 1844–1878.* Paris, 1960.

Skedsmo, Tone. "Prins Eugen og Norge." In *Prins Eugen (1865–1947),* [ed. Knut Berg,] 15–33. Oslo, 1988.

[Skjöldebrand, A. F.] *Excellensen Grefve A. F. Skjöldebrands memoarer.* Ed. Henrik Schück. 5 vols. Stockholm, 1903–4).

Sørensen, Øystein. *Bjørnstjerne Bjørnson og nasjonalismen.* Oslo, 1997.

———, ed. *Jakten på det norske. Perspektiver på utviklingen av en norsk nasjonal identitet på 1800-tallet.* Oslo, 1998.

Stavenow-Hidemark, Elisabet. *Villabebyggelse i Sverige 1900–1925.* Stockholm, 1971.

Steen, Sverre. *Det frie Norge.* Vol. 1, *1814.* Oslo, 1951.

Strindberg, August. *Samlade skrifter.* Ed. John Landquist. 55 vols. Stockholm, 1912–19.

Sundbärg, Gustav. *Det svenska folklynnet.* Stockholm, 1911.

Svenska krusbär. En historiebok om Sverige och svenskarna. [Ed. Björn Linnell and Mikael Löfgren.] Stockholm, 1996.

Svenska turistföreningen 100 år. Svenska turistföreningens årskrift 1986. Stockholm, 1986.

Svenska utrikespolitikens historia. Ed. Nils Ahnlund. 5 vols. Stockholm, 1951–61.

Svenskt biografiskt lexikon. Ed. Göran Nilzén et al. 149 parts [to 1999]. Stockholm, 1918–.

Svensson, Sigfrid. *Från gammalt till nytt på 1800-talets svenska landsbygd.* Stockholm, 1977.

Sveriges historia till våra dagar. Ed. Emil Hildebrand and Ludvig Stavenow. 15 vols. Stockholm, 1919–26.

Taylor, Bayard. *Northern Travel: Summer and Winter Pictures: Sweden, Denmark and Lapland.* 1857. New York, 1887.

Thermænius, Edvard. *Lantmannapartiet. Dess uppkomst, organisation och tidigare utveckling.* Uppsala, 1928.

Tigerstedt, E. N. *Svensk litteraturhistoria.* 4th ed. Stockholm, 1971.

Tradisjon og fornyelse. Norge rundt århundreskiftet. [Ed. Tone Skedsmo.] Exhibition catalog. Oslo, 1994.

Try, Hans. *To kulturer — en stat 1851–1884.* Vol. 11 of *Norges historie,* ed. Knut Mykland. Oslo, 1979.

Værnø, Grete, ed. *Fra arvefiende til samboer.* Stockholm and Oslo, 1990.

Varnedoe, Kirk, [ed.] *Northern Light: Nordic Art at the Turn of the Century.* New Haven, 1988.

———, [ed.] *Northern Light: Realism and Symbolism in Scandinavian Painting, 1880–1910.* Brooklyn, 1982.

Weibull, Jörgen. *Carl Johan och Norge 1810–1814.* Göteborg, 1957.

————. *Inför unionsupplösningen 1905. Konsulatfrågan.* Stockholm, 1962.

Werenskiold, Meret. "Fleskum-kolonien 1886 og den norske sommernatt. Naturalisme eller nyromantikk?" *Kunst og Kultur* 71 (1988): 2–30.

Wittrock, Ulf. *Ellen Keys väg från kristendom till livstro.* Uppsala, 1953.

Zachau, Inga. *Prins Eugen, nationalromantikern.* Stockholm, 1989.

Index

Aasen, Ivar, 96, 100–101
academies and learned societies, 8, 9, 38–39, 134, 141
Adelborg, Ottilia, 132
Adlersparre, Georg, 11, 12, 14, 28
Aftonbladet (Stockholm), 33, 35–38, 45–46, 51, 95, 99, 104, 116
Agrelius, C. P., 30–31
Agrell, Alfhild, 109
Ahlgren, Ernst. *See* Benedictsson, Victoria
Åkerhjelm, Gustaf, 74
Alexander I (emperor of Russia), 10, 12, 17, 18
Alfvén, Hugo, 132, 134, 137, 143
Alin, Oscar, 74–75
Almqvist, Carl Jonas Love, 145, 150–51, 207n67
America and Americans, 9, 16, 22, 28, 29, 32–34, 44–45, 46, 47–48, 49, 53, 89–90, 93, 99, 131, 133, 136, 143, 148, 155, 165, 168, 174, 177, 181
Anckarsvärd, August, 89
Anckarsvärd, Carl Henrik, 29–31, 34, 37–38, 39, 63, 177
Anckarsvärd, Michael Gustaf, 89
Andersen, Hans Christian, 152
Ankarcrona, Gustaf, 132, 133
antiquity: classical, 116; Nordic, 4, 28, 53, 89–91, 94–104, 106, 111–13, 114, 116–17, 118, 141–43, 146, 164, 168, 172, 174, 180–81

Appleton, John, 47
applied arts: Norwegian, 141–42; Swedish, 114, 132–33
archaeology, 101–2
architecture: Norwegian, 101, 141–42, 168, 172; Swedish, 114, 132–33
Armfelt, Gustaf Mauritz, Baron, 18
art: Norwegian, 88, 91–92, 100, 120, 134–41, 165, 167–68, 171–72, 175, 178, 203n25, 205n54; Swedish, 89, 100, 106–7, 114, 120, 134–41, 146, 157, 168, 171, 178, 200n25, 205n54
Asbjørnsen, Peter Christen, 92, 96, 100, 104
Aschehoug, Torkel Halvor, 62
Astrup, H. R., 70, 110, 200n54
Aulestad, 113, 114, 162

Backer, Harriet, 135, 138
Balke, Peder, 92
Bastien-Lepage, Jules, 136
Bauer, John, 133
Bellman, Carl Michael, 127, 130–31, 151–52, 177, 179
Benedictsson, Victoria (*pseud.* Ernst Ahlgren), 108–9, 128
Bergen, 7–8, 24, 27, 28, 87, 93
Bergh, Gerda, 161
Bergh, Richard, 76, 134–38, 139, 140–41, 146
Bernadotte, Jean-Baptiste. *See* Carl XIV Johan

Bernadotte dynasty, 51, 69, 82
Berwald, Franz, 143
Beskow, Elsa, 133
Birger, Hugo, 135
Bismarck, Otto von, 61, 68, 71
Björck, Oscar, 135, 137
Björck, Staffan, 168
Bjørnson, Bjørnstjerne, 67, 68–74, 76–79,
    83, 91, 97–100, 103–10, 113–15, 117, 119–
    24, 126–28, 140–41, 149–50, 153, 157, 159,
    160–65, 167, 171, 172, 175, 177, 179, 181,
    182, 195n45
Björnstjerna, Magnus, Count, 51–53
Blanche, August, 116
Blommér, Nils Jakob, 92
Bodø, 26, 64
Bohuslän, 6, 103, 140
Bondesson, August, 133
Böök, Fredrik, 107, 129, 149–50, 168
Borell, Berit, 168
Bosse, Harriet, 121
Boström, Erik Gustaf, 78
Brace, Charles Loring, 53–54
Brand (Social Democratic newspaper,
    Stockholm), 79–81, 116
Brandes, Georg, 108, 128, 181
Branting, Hjalmar, 76, 141
Bremer, Fredrika, 103–4, 109, 176
Broberg, Gunnar, 117
Bull, Francis, 162
Bull, Ole, 92–93, 99, 104, 109, 171

Cabet, Étienne, 46
Cappelen, August, 92
Carl X Gustaf (king of Sweden), 6
Carl XII (king of Sweden), 6–7, 130, 157
Carl XIII (king of Sweden and Norway),
    11, 13, 15–18, 25
Carl XIV Johan (king of Sweden and
    Norway), 13–17, 18, 20, 23, 25–27, 29, 31,
    32, 35, 36, 46, 48, 51, 55, 56, 58, 61–62,
    64, 65, 67, 92, 93, 95–96, 170
Carl XV (king of Sweden and Norway),
    55, 58, 60–61, 63, 100, 106

Carl August (crown prince of Sweden), 11,
    12, 14, 28
Carl Johan (crown prince of Sweden and
    Norway). *See* Carl XIV Johan
Carlsson, Sten, 55, 177
Cassel, Peter, 33–34
Christensen, Jan, 168
Christian II (king of Denmark), 5
Christian III (king of Denmark), 5
Christian August, Prince. *See* Carl August
Christian Frederik, Prince (king of Nor-
    way, 1814), 15–16, 17
Christiania (Kristiania, now Oslo), 7, 8,
    15, 17, 18, 25, 26, 27, 28, 36, 38, 45, 58,
    62, 65, 66, 67, 79, 87–89, 93, 99, 103,
    111, 119, 120, 133, 134, 136, 138, 140, 142,
    159, 160, 163, 177, 178
Clark, Kenneth, 182
Clason, Sam, 63
climate, 3, 147, 149, 150
Collett, Camilla, 94, 109
constitution: Norwegian (Eidsvoll), 14–17,
    19, 22–24, 28–31, 34–38, 39, 45–46,
    48–49, 51, 53, 54–55, 56, 62–63, 64–66,
    68–69, 73, 87, 93, 96, 104, 111, 161, 169,
    170, 172, 180; Swedish, 11, 16, 18, 19–23,
    25–27, 34, 37, 41, 50, 53, 54, 64
Continental Blockade, 10, 11, 12, 13
Copenhagen, 7–11, 88, 91, 134, 136, 181,
    196n1
Curman, Calla, 159, 163–64
Curman, Carl, 116, 159

Dagens nyheter (Stockholm), 75, 118, 156,
    162
Dahl, Johan Christian, 91–92
Dahllöf, J. F., 39, 44
Dalarna, 54, 129, 131–32, 140, 143, 162
Dalman, L. J., 29
Dalman, Wilhelm Fredric, 35, 46, 63
Danielsson, Anders, 34–35
Denmark and Danes, 4–7, 9–11, 12, 14, 15,
    17, 19, 24, 25, 26, 42, 52, 59, 61, 64–65,
    70, 79, 82, 90–98, 100, 102, 107, 115, 128,

129, 136–37, 139, 143, 152, 153, 157, 165, 167, 172, 176, 179, 180–81
Derry, T. K., 59, 64
Dietrichson, Lorenz, 55, 97–99, 104, 109–10, 114, 115, 120, 141–42, 159, 160, 177
Disraeli, Benjamin, 55
Djurklou, Nils Gabriel, 101
Drysdale, George, 121
D'Uncker, Carl Henrik, 100
Dunker, Bernhard, 46
Düsseldorf, 92, 100, 103, 104, 134, 135, 171

Eckersberg, Christoffer Wilhelm, 92
economy: Norwegian, 3–4, 7, 10, 11, 15, 25, 31, 39–40, 43, 48, 50, 52, 54, 65, 77, 88, 111–12, 150, 165, 171; Swedish, 4, 7, 10, 48, 50, 77, 150, 156, 158, 165
Edelfeldt, Albert, 135
Egedius, Halfdan, 141
Ehrenhoff, Herman, 43
Eidsvoll. *See under* constitution
Ekström, J. E., 163
elites, social, political, cultural, 4, 6, 22, 24–25, 30–32, 34, 37–38, 45–46, 49, 51–52, 56–58, 65–68, 70, 72, 76, 81, 88, 96, 103, 112, 114, 116, 129, 132–33, 141, 154–55, 165, 170, 172
Ellenius, Allan, 141
Ellsworth, Henry, 48
Elvander, Nils, 63
emigration, emigrants, 32–34, 38, 47, 54, 131, 133, 155, 156, 157, 170, 177–78, 181–82
Engelbrektsson, Engelbrekt, 5, 117, 129
Engström, Jon, 118
Erik of Pomerania, 4–5
Essen, Siri von, 121, 136
estates (*ständer*), of Swedish Riksdag, 21, 30, 36, 50, 54–55; burghers, 5, 21–22, 39, 41–42, 44; clergy, 5, 21, 38–39, 44; nobility, 5, 21–22, 29, 35–36, 42–44, 55, 63, 70, 148; peasantry, 5, 21, 24, 34–36, 39–41, 44, 45, 47, 53, 168, 169. *See also* Riksdag
Eugen, Prince, 75, 78, 79, 138–40, 146–47, 159, 166–67, 171, 172, 195n45

Facos, Michelle, 134, 168, 176
Fagerlin, Ferdinand, 100
Fahlcrantz, Carl Johan, 89
Fåhræus, O. I., 45–46
Falsen, Christian Magnus, 16
Fearnley, Thomas, 92
feminism, 67, 94, 107–9, 120–21, 129, 150
Fersen, Count Axel von, 12, 13, 20
Finland and Finns, 4–7, 11–15, 17, 28, 50, 60, 75, 77, 135, 161, 165, 167, 170, 176, 180
Fjæstad, Gustaf, 140
flag, controversies over, 62, 69–70
Fleskum, 138–39, 140
Flintoe, Johan, 92
Flygare-Carlén, Emilie, 103
Fogelberg, Bengt Erland, 92
folk culture and folk life: Norwegian, 4, 92–93, 96, 99–104, 111–13, 133–34, 138, 141–42, 172, 175; Swedish, 4, 99–102, 131–33, 138, 143–44, 156, 162
folk high schools: Danish, 115; Norwegian, 56, 115; Swedish, 56, 115–16, 132, 133
foreign affairs, 26, 59, 64–65, 72–75, 77–78, 156. *See also* constitution; government
Forssell, Hans, 76
Forsslund, Karl-Erik, 132
France and the French, 9–10, 12–13, 16, 29, 45, 48, 51, 53, 60, 88, 123, 125, 136–39, 142, 145–47, 151, 168, 172
franchise: in Norway, 16, 23–25, 36, 55, 56, 61, 68, 77, 169–70, 180; in Sweden, 22–23, 30, 34, 40, 55, 61, 169–71
Frederik III (king of Denmark), 5
Frederik VI (king of Denmark), 9, 11–12, 14–15
Frederik, Prince. *See* Frederik VI
Fredrikshamn (Hamina), Peace of, 12
Friman, Carl, 33
Fröding, Gustaf, 127, 131, 157, 179
Fuglum, Per, 166
Fürstenberg, Pontus, 135, 205n54

Gallen-Kallela, Akseli, 135
Gällivare, 144
Gasmann, Hans, 33
Gegerfelt, Victor von, 114
Gegerfelt, Wilhelm von, 137
Geijer, Erik Gustaf, 39, 90–91, 104, 106, 143
Geijerstam, Gustaf af, 107–8, 128
Germany and Germans, 4, 6–7, 10, 13–14, 27, 42, 50, 53, 59–61, 65, 68, 72, 75, 79, 87, 99, 107, 137, 143, 167
Gödecke, Peter August, 102, 106, 111–13, 115, 145–46, 174
Götar (Goths), 94, 101
Göteborg (Gothenburg), 22, 70, 110, 123, 135, 160, 182
Göteborgs Aftonblad (Göteborg), 79–80
Göteborgs Handels- och Sjöfartstidning (Göteborg), 69, 110, 116
Götiska Förbundet, 90, 91, 100, 104
Götrek, Pär, 46–47
government: Norwegian, under Danish rule, 5–9, 24, 27, 69, 87–89; Norwegian, in 1814, 15–16; Norwegian, under Norwegian-Swedish Union, 17–18, 28, 37, 41, 48, 53, 65–67, 169–71, 174; Swedish, 5, 6, 9, 13, 19–22, 29, 37, 51, 72, 167, 168–71. *See also* constitution
Grandien, Bo, 117, 168
Great Britain and the British (English), 10–11, 14, 53–55, 60–61, 69, 75–76, 80, 87–88, 90, 92, 99, 136, 143, 149, 150, 168, 182, 190n76
Grèz-sur-Loing, 136, 137
Grieg, Edvard, 93, 100, 109, 119, 134, 143, 149, 153, 173, 175
Grundtvig, Nicolai Frederik Severin, 90, 115, 181
Grut, Torben, 142
Gude, Hans, 92, 100, 109, 113, 135, 139
Günther, Ernst, 160–61, 177
Gustaf [I] Vasa (king of Sweden), 5, 51, 129
Gustaf II Adolf (king of Sweden), 129–30
Gustaf III (king of Sweden), 6, 9, 18, 88, 130–32, 151

Gustaf IV Adolf (king of Sweden), 6, 10–12, 19, 28, 51
Gustaf, Crown Prince (from 1907, Gustaf V, king of Sweden), 75, 80–81
Gustafson, Alrik, 168

Haakon VII (king of Norway), 82
Hagerup, Nina, 109
Hamilton, Henning, 46
Hamsun, Knut, 128, 195n45
Hansen, Constantin, 92
Hanson, Carl, 109
Hansson, Per, 39
Harald V (king of Norway), 82
Hardanger, 113–14
Hartmansdorff, August von, 87–88
Hartmansdorff, Carl von, 47
Hazelius, Artur, 101, 131–34
Hebbe, Thecla, 104–5
Hedberg, Tor, 108
Hedin, Adolf, 72, 75, 79–80, 110, 115–16, 177
Hedin, Sven, 79
Hedlund, Henrik, 160
Hedlund, Sven Adolf, 69–71, 73–74, 110, 114–16, 167, 182
Hedvig Elisabeth Charlotta (queen of Sweden and Norway), 25, 28, 88–89
Hegel, Frederik, 181
Heidenstam, Verner von, 81, 124–28, 130, 137–38, 141, 146, 152–57, 160–63, 168, 172, 177, 179–180
Helsingius, H. D., 41
hembygdsgårdar, 132
Herder, Johann Gottfried von, 174
Hertervig, Lars, 92
Heurlin, Sven, 40, 44
Hierta, Gustaf, 34
Hierta, Lars Johan, 35–36, 45–46, 51
Hildebrand, Hans, 102
historiography, 94–96, 98, 101, 112, 129–31, 165–66, 168–69, 179, 182
Hjärne, Harald, 81, 157
Holberg, Ludvig, 8
Holmgren, Ann-Margret, 76, 116, 159, 163
Holmgren, Frithiof, 116

Holmström, Pontus Leonard, 102
Horace (Horatius Quintus), 173–74
Hornemann, C. F. E., 100
Hovland, Gjert Gregoriussen, 33
Høyre (Norwegian conservative party), 68,
    78, 80, 170–71
Hyltén-Cavallius, Gunnar, 101

Ibsen, Henrik, 100, 104, 106–11, 113, 119–22,
    127–28, 149–50, 152–53, 156, 171–72, 175,
    177, 179, 181, 200n47
Ibsen, Sigurd, 77, 163
Iceland and Icelanders, 11, 90, 94, 101–2,
    113, 120, 165, 176, 180

Jaabæk, Søren, 66–67, 70
Jæger, Hans, 136
Jämtland, 6, 144, 147, 162
Janson, Kristofer, 109, 178
Jansson, Eugène, 140
Järnefelt, Eero, 135
Järta, Hans, 18
Jernberg, August, 100
Jönsson, Måns, 40–41, 44
Josephson, Ernst, 135, 137, 138

Kaartvedt, Alf, 65, 171
Kalm, Pehr, 28
Kalmar Union, 4–6, 19, 46, 117, 129
Kanzow, Johan Albert, 35–36
Karlfeldt, Erik Axel, 131, 132, 137
Karlstads-Tidningen (Karlstad), 80
Key, Ellen, 76, 105, 110, 113–16, 123, 143,
    154–56
Keyser, Jacob Rudolf, 94–95, 102
Kiel, Treaty of, 14–17, 26, 63, 170
Kielland, Alexander, 128, 178
Kielland, Kitty, 134–35, 138
Kierkegaard, Søren, 107, 181, 200n47
Kjellén, Rudolf, 80–81, 157, 170
Kjerulf, Halfdan, 93, 113, 120, 143
Klingspor, Mauritz, 42–43, 148
Knudsen, Knud, 97
Koht, Halvdan, 168, 169
Kommandantvold, Kristian Magnus, 91,
    178–79

Konstnärsförbundet, 135
Kreuger, Nils, 135, 136, 140
Krohg, Christian, 121, 134–37, 141
Kronberg, Julius, 149
Krouthén, Johan, 137

labor movements, 46–47, 79–80, 141, 163,
    170–71
Lagerlöf, Selma, 129, 131, 179
Laing, Samuel, 26, 49–53, 174
landholding: in Norway, 7, 49, 52; in Swe-
    den, 7, 20–21, 34, 50, 52
language: Danish (Dano-Norwegian), 6,
    93, 96–97, 109, 140, 181; *Landsmål*,
    96–98; Old Norse *(Norrøn)*, 6, 94,
    96–97, 104; *Riksmål*, 97; Swedish, 4, 12
Lantmannaparti, 70–71, 169
Larson, Marcus, 100
Larsson, Carl, 132–37, 140, 143
Larsson, Liss O., 71
Laurin, Carl G., 158, 161, 175–76, 179
Lay, George, 47–48
Leffler, Anne Charlotte, 108–10, 116, 128
Leif Ericson, 181
Leifsson, Torjus, 101
Levertin, Oscar, 108, 128, 130–31, 151–52,
    177, 179
Lidén, Arne, 107, 168, 175
Lie, Jonas, 120, 121, 123, 124, 175
Liljefors, Bruno, 135, 136
Lindberger, Örjan, 91
Lindblad, Adolf Fredrik, 143
Lindeman, Ludvig Mattias, 92
Linder, Gurli, 165
Lindgren, Raymond E., 165
Lindström, K. A., 148
Linné, Carl von (Linnæus), 27, 28, 130
literature: Danish, 90–91, 105, 108; Ice-
    landic, 90, 94–95, 101, 102, 113, 117, 120,
    141, 180; Norwegian, 90–91, 93–94, 103–
    9, 118–22, 124–28, 134–36, 144, 149–50,
    153, 157, 164, 165, 171–72, 175, 178;
    Swedish, 90–91, 103–9, 118–32, 134–35,
    149–50, 152, 157, 167–68, 171, 178–79
Løvenskiold, Severin, 46
Løvland, Jørgen, 160

Lundegård, Axel, 108, 128
Lundgren, Egron, 111

Måås-Fjetterström, Märtha, 132–33
Maihaugen, 133
Malmström, August, 100, 102, 111
Mandelgren, Nils Månsson, 101
Mannerskantz, Carl Axel, 42
Margaret, Queen, 4
Michelsen, Christian, 78
military forces: Norwegian, 17, 23, 26, 32,
    51, 59–60, 65, 73, 76–82, 109, 200n54;
    Swedish, 16, 17, 19–21, 26, 27, 40, 43, 50,
    57, 59–60, 72–75, 77, 79–82, 116–17, 154,
    170, 200n54
Minerva (Stockholm), 43–44
Moe, Jørgen, 92, 96, 99, 104
Molin, Adrian, 143, 170
Molin, Johan Peter, 100
Montelius, Oscar, 102, 142
morality, 50–53, 89, 96, 103, 106, 136
Moss, Convention of, 17, 18, 89
Munch, Edvard, 180
Munch, Jacob, 92
Munch, Peter Andreas, 94–95, 98, 101,
    102, 104, 109
Munck af Rosenschöld, Nils Rudolph, 42
Munthe, Gerhard, 138, 140–42
music: Norwegian, 92–93, 99, 120, 134,
    143–44, 164, 172–73, 175; Swedish,
    99–100, 104, 132, 134, 143–44, 157, 179

"Nameless Society," 106, 111
Nansen, Fridtjof, 79
Napoleon I (emperor of France), 10, 13–16
Näsström, Gustaf, 162
national identity: Norwegian, 8, 87,
    90–99, 141–42, 176; Swedish, 129–34,
    137–38, 141–44, 147–58, 172, 176–80
Nationaltidende (Christiania), 83
nature and landscapes: Norwegian, 3,
    89–90, 93, 95, 99, 104–5, 111, 118, 138–41,
    145–49; in Sweden, 3, 13, 137–41,
    144–59, 153, 157, 177, 179
Neergaard, Jon, 31
Nicolaysen, Nicolay, 102

Nielsen, Yngvar, 82, 160
Nilsson, Göran B., 56, 61, 161, 169
Nilsson, Sven, 28–29, 87, 89
nobility: in Norway, 5, 9, 15, 23–24, 26,
    36–37, 43, 69, 112; in Sweden, 5, 9, 21,
    28, 31, 35–37, 41, 43, 50–52, 110, 117, 130,
    175
Norberg, Johan, 57, 168
Nordau, Max, 121
Nordenberg, Bengt, 100
Nordenskiöld, Gustaf, 43, 44
Nordenskjöld, Adolf Erik, 116
Nordic Museum, 101, 131
Nordiska Nationalföreningen, 116
Nordiske Musikblade (Copenhagen), 100
Nordraak, Richard, 93, 143
Nordström, Karl, 135–36, 140
Norske Folkemuseum, 133–34
Norske Turistforening, 144
Norwegians, characteristics of, 4, 28, 54,
    69, 88–90, 105, 107, 111–12, 119, 122–23,
    126–27, 141, 148–50, 153–57, 178–79
Norwegian Society for the Preservation of
    Historical Monuments, 91–92
Nyblom, Helena, 139, 157
Ny illustrerad Tidning (Stockholm), 113,
    116
Nyström, Jenny, 135

Oehlenschläger, Adam, 90–91, 106, 180
Olof Skötkonung, king of Sweden, 117
Ord och Bild (Stockholm), 131, 151, 152
Oscar I, king of Sweden and Norway,
    45–47, 55, 58, 60, 62
Oscar II, king of Sweden and Norway,
    61–63, 66–69, 71, 75, 78, 80–83, 111, 133,
    156, 159–61, 172, 205n54, 209n4
Osslund, Helmer, 140

Palm, August, 141
Paris, 13, 31, 46, 88, 119, 122, 135, 137, 138,
    139, 149, 162, 205n54
parliamentarianism: in Norway, 66–68,
    71–72, 80, 169, 170; in Sweden, 20, 30,
    61, 63–64, 68, 72, 169. *See also* constitu-
    tion

Pauli, Georg, 134–37
Pauli, Hanna Hirsch, 135
Pavels Larsen, Bolette, 125–26
peasantry: Danish, 7–8, 70, 115; Norwe-
    gian, 6–8, 24–25, 28, 31–33, 35, 38, 39,
    41, 45–46, 49, 54, 58, 65–67, 69–70,
    88–89, 93, 111–13, 119, 139, 169, 174–75;
    Swedish, 6–8, 28–30, 32–34, 39, 44, 52,
    90–91, 100, 115, 117, 131, 155
Peterson-Berger, Vilhelm, 143
Peterssen, Eilif, 137, 138, 141
Petré, Johan Teodor, 39, 41, 42
philology, 101
Posse, Count Carl, 70–71
privileges, corporate, 20, 22, 24, 37, 50, 56,
    117

Qvarnström, Carl Gustaf, 100

Rääf, Leonard Fredrik, 101
Rahbek, Knud, 10
Ramsundsberget inscription, 102
reform, practical and humanitarian,
    56–57, 169
religion: in Norway, 4, 32, 36, 41, 56, 67,
    113, 149; in Sweden, 4, 21, 36, 56, 113,
    117, 123, 130
representation reform, in Sweden, 20–22,
    29–31, 34–47, 54–56, 58, 70, 148, 168,
    171. *See also* constitution; franchise;
    Riksdag
Reuterskiöld, C. A., 79
revolution: American, 9; of 1848–49, 46,
    65; French, 9, 27, 31, 40, 49, 51, 205n54;
    Swedish, of 1809, 11–12
Rexius, Gunnar, 168
Richert, Johan Gabriel, 29–31, 37–39, 47
Rigsret, 24, 32, 67
Riksdag, 5, 8, 11, 13, 18, 20–22, 24, 29–31,
    34–45, 47, 56–57, 59, 63–64, 67, 70–72,
    75, 80–82, 148, 166, 169–70, 178, 181;
    Reform of 1866, 54–57, 61, 70. *See also*
    constitution; estates; representation
    reform
Rök runestone, 102
Roos, Anna Maria, 133

Rubenson, Albert, 99
Rudeng, Erik, 77
Runeberg, Johan Ludvig, 106
Russia and Russians, 6–7, 10–11, 13–14, 44,
    48, 60, 73–75, 77, 79, 166–67, 170
Rydberg, Viktor, 115–16, 127
Rygh, Oluf, 102
Rynning, Ole, 33

Sahlström, Per, 39–40
Salmson, Hugo, 135
Samlingsparti, Norwegian, 77
Sandvig, Anders, 133
Sars, Ernst, 68–69, 98
Scandinavian Ethnographic Collection,
    101, 131, 133
Scandinavianism, 8–9, 12, 16, 59–61, 63,
    71, 74, 97–99, 101, 103–5, 111, 116, 160,
    164–65, 171–72, 174, 180
Schück, Henrik, 168–69
Schwerin, Count Fredrik Boguslaus von,
    29
Scotland and Scots, 49, 52, 53, 69, 182
Scott, Sir Walter, 182
Seip, Anne-Lise, 94, 176
Selmer, Christian, 93, 143
Sibbern, Georg, 109, 200n47
Simon, Erica, 176
Sinding, Christian, 93, 143
Sjögren, Emil, 143
Skagen, 137
Skandinaviska Sällskapet, 46–47
Skansen, 131–32
Skjöldebrand, Anders Fredrik, 28, 89, 148
Skredsvig, Christian, 134–38
Snoilsky, Count Carl, 106, 173
Snorri Sturlason, 95, 117, 141
Social Democratic Party, Swedish, 76, 79,
    171
societies, learned. *See* academies and
    learned societies
Söderman, August, 99–100, 143
Soelvold, Peder, 31
Sohlman, August, 116
Sophia, queen of Sweden and Norway,
    75, 140, 160

Sørensen, Niels Georg, 110, 200n54
Sørensen, Øystein, 182
Staaf, Karl, 79
Stang, Frederik, 65–66
statholder, 23, 26, 27, 58, 88, 89; contro-
    versy, 62–64, 67, 70, 106
Statsborgeren (Christiania), 31
stave churches, 92, 102, 113, 114, 142
Stavenow-Hidemark, Elisabet, 143
Steen, Sverre, 22
Stenberg, Aina, 133
Stenhammar, Per Ulrik, 99
Stenhammar, Vilhelm, 143
St. John, Sir Spencer Buckingham, 150
Stockholm, 7, 16, 20, 22, 46, 50, 63, 71,
    87–88, 92, 99–101, 105, 108–11, 114, 118,
    122, 127, 129–30, 134–35, 140, 142, 148,
    155–56, 159, 160–61, 172–73, 200n54
Stoltenberg, Mattias, 92
storsvensker ("Great-Swedes"), 74, 76, 79,
    110, 164, 179
Storting, 15–18, 22–32, 36–37, 45–46,
    48–49, 52, 59, 61–66, 70, 73, 76–78,
    80–81, 87–88, 119, 159, 162, 168, 200n54,
    205n54
St. Petersburg, Treaty of, 13
Strindberg, August, 79, 83, 106, 108, 115,
    118–25, 127–28, 134, 136, 148–49, 151,
    172–74, 176–77, 179
Strindlund, Nils, 34
suffrage. *See* franchise
Sundbärg, Gustav, 157–58, 178, 179
Sundbeck, Carl, 181
Sundt, Eilert, 96, 101, 103, 114
Svear, 94, 101
Svendsen, Johan, 93, 143
Svendsen, Peder, 162
Svenonius, Fredrik, 144–45
Svenska Dagbladet (Stockholm), 81, 127,
    131, 160, 161
Svenska Turistföreningen, 144–45
Sverdrup, Johan, 66–71, 73, 117, 177
Swedes, characteristics of, 4, 51, 71, 80,
    88–89, 107, 119–20, 124–26, 141, 147–58,
    161, 175–79, 207n67

Taylor, Bayard, 53–54
Tegnér, Alice, 133
Tegnér, Esaias, 28, 90, 91, 102, 104, 106,
    113, 118, 123, 127, 152, 155
theater: Norwegian, 88, 90, 93, 108,
    120–23; Swedish, 8, 87, 118, 123, 129
Thegerström, Robert, 134, 135
Thrane, Marcus, 47, 65
Tidemand, Adolf, 92, 100, 113
Times (London), 79
Torgny Lagman, 117
transportation, communications, 99, 111,
    144
travel: accounts of, 9, 27, 47–54, 111–14,
    163, 174, 190n76; and tourism, 49–50,
    53–54, 99, 111–14, 142, 144–45, 147, 153
Treffenberg, Curry, 80
Troil, Emil von, 36
Trondheim, 6, 8, 25, 28, 61, 87, 144

Ueland, Ole Gabriel, 32, 59, 65
Ullmann, Viggo, 71
union, Norwegian-Swedish: Act of, 18, 28,
    63, 64, 75; attitudes toward, Norwegian,
    14–15, 17–18, 26–27, 58, 62, 66–69,
    73–74, 77–78, 82–83; attitudes toward,
    Swedish, 31, 41, 52, 55, 63–64, 73–82;
    background of, 6, 13–14; dissolution of,
    78–83, 116, 159–61, 165, 169, 173, 179;
    formation of, 14, 17–18, 109, 165, 166;
    projects for revision of, 58–59, 61, 63,
    65, 77–78. *See also* flag; foreign affairs;
    statholder
universities: Christiania, 8, 15, 32, 68, 87,
    88, 98, 107; Copenhagen, 8, 98; Lund,
    87, 98, 108, 129; Uppsala, 74, 81, 87, 98,
    99, 108, 115, 129, 130, 160, 168
Uppsala, 87, 90, 95, 98, 101–3, 105–6, 111,
    116, 118, 122, 129, 144

Værnø, Grete, 168–69
Valdres, 139–40
Vallgren, Ville, 135
Valsgärde, 102
Värmland, 127, 131, 140

Vedung, Evert, 80
Vendel, 102
Venstre (Norwegian Left party), 68, 70–73, 77, 80, 96, 98, 160, 169–71, 173, 200n54
Verdens Gang (Christiania), 74, 77, 157
Viking age. *See under* antiquity
Visby, 130
Vogt, Nils Collett, 180

Wadman, J. A., 28, 88
Wærn, Carl Fredrik, 39, 41–42
Wahlberg, Alfred, 135
Wahlbom, Carl, 92
Waldenström, Paul Peter, 181
Wallenberg, Jacob, 27
war, 6–7, 9; Crimean, 47, 60; Danish-German, 59–61, 73, 107, 116, 180; Great Northern, 6–7, 157; Norwegian-Swedish, of 1814, 17, 28; Revolutionary and Napoleonic, 10–11, 13–15, 90
Warburg, Karl, 168–69

Wedel-Jarlsberg, Count Herman, 14–16, 27, 58, 62
Welhaven, Johan Sebastian, 93–94, 96, 97, 103, 104, 176, 177
Wennerberg, Gunnar Gunnarsson, 139
Werenskiold, Erik, 122, 124, 135, 140–41, 159, 171
Wergeland, Henrik, 31, 91, 93–94, 96–98, 103, 104, 106, 176–77, 182
Wertlesen, Wilhelm, 141
Wieselgren, Harald, 116
Wikner, Pontus, 106
Wilhelm II, German emperor, 75, 78
Winge, Mårten Eskil, 100
Wirsén, Carl David af, 106

youth movements: Norwegian, 162; Swedish, 162–63

Zorn, Anders, 132, 135, 140
Zweibergk, Fredrik von, 39, 40

H. Arnold Barton is a professor emeritus of history at Southern Illinois University Carbondale. His previous publications have dealt mainly with Scandinavian, particularly Swedish, history in the late eighteenth and early nineteenth century and on Swedes and other Scandinavians in America. His books include *Count Hans Axel von Fersen: Aristocrat in an Age of Revolution; Scandinavia in the Revolutionary Era, 1760–1815; Northern Arcadia: Foreign Travelers in Scandinavia, 1765–1815; Letters from the Promised Land: Swedes in America, 1840–1914; The Search for Ancestors: A Swedish-American Family Saga;* and *A Folk Divided: Homeland Swedes and Swedish Americans, 1840–1940.*